The Aesthetics
of
Stéphane Mallarmé
in Relation to His Public

The Aesthetics
of
Stéphane Mallarmé
in Relation to His Public

Paula Gilbert Lewis

Rutherford • Madison • Teaneck
Fairleigh Dickinson University Press
London: Associated University Presses

Associated University Presses, Inc.
Cranbury, New Jersey 08512

Associated University Presses
108 New Bond Street
London W1Y OQX, England

LIBRARY OF CONGRESS CATALOGING IN PUBLICATION DATA

Lewis, Paula Gilbert.
The aesthetics of Stéphane Mallarmé in relation to his public.

    Bibliography: p.
    Includes index.
    1. Mallarmé, Stéphane, 1842-1898—Aesthetics.
I. Title.
PQ2344.Z5L4   841'.8   74-5898
ISBN 0-8386-1615-1

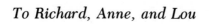

To Richard, Anne, and Lou

Contents

Contents

Preface

The genesis of this book dates from 1966 in Paris when I was first introduced to the poetry of Stéphane Mallarmé. With the constant encouragement of my teacher, M. Raphaël Molho, I decided to continue to study the works of this Symbolist poet and always hoped some day to be able to contribute to the already vast amount of criticism written about him. As my own interests grew, I found it difficult to reconcile my increasingly social orientation toward the study of literature with my admiration for hermetic Mallarméan poetry in its intellectual ivory tower. Luckily, through contact with a former professor at Columbia University, Mr. Richard Raskin, I discovered another aspect of the poet, seen especially in his correspondence, his prose works, and in Le "Livre," the fragments of, perhaps, a last work, left at the time of his death.

In the numerous critiques of Mallarmé's poetry, emphasis has for the most part been placed upon interpretations of the emotional, intellectual, and psychological recesses of the poet's mind, as separated from the exterior world. Critical analyses have stressed his cryptic qualities and his elitism, both as necessary parts of his genius. Only

9

recently has there been a growing awareness of an equally important side of the poet, that of a man deeply attached to or at least deeply desirous of being attached to outside reality. This book is an attempt to offer an objective reevaluation of Mallarmé's attitudes toward social reality, toward the roles of art and the artist in the world, and toward men, as they constitute a future public for this art. Such an approach to a study of Mallarmé may perhaps bring the entire literary movement of Symbolism into closer contact with changing social patterns. A major poet and his work may then seem more relevant than they may appear to some today in light of other more important events.

The material upon which this book is based is increasing. Two additional volumes of Mallarmé's correspondence have already appeared since the inception of this book, and more volumes will soon follow. What these recently published letters show, however, is an even stronger argument for the importance of such a study of Mallarmé. Future volumes will hopefully serve a similar purpose.

This book has been written for the specialist, as well as for the general admirer of Mallarmé's works. It has also been written for those who appreciate French literature, but who may have had no prior knowledge of Mallarmé and his works. All three groups would, perhaps, like to place the seemingly antisocial period of literature known as Symbolism in its proper milieu. It is for this last group of people, however, that all of the quotations from Mallarmé's texts appear in English. Almost all of the material cited in this book has never been previously translated. I have personally translated these passages for the sole purpose of this book. They are, therefore, in no way definitive. I only hope that they can help increase the public of admirers of the works of Stéphane Mallarmé. That was his goal, and that is mine.

Washington, D.C.

Acknowledgments

I would like to thank Editions Gallimard for permission to quote from the following:

Stéphane Mallarmé, *Correspondence 1862-1871*. Recueillie, classée et annotée par Henri Mondor. Paris: NRF © Editions Gallimard, 1959.

Henri Mondor, *Vie de Mallarmé*. édition complète en un volume. 34e édition. Paris: NRF © Editions Gallimard, 1941.

Jacques Scherer, *Le "Livre" de Mallarmé: premières recherches sur des documents inédits*. 6e édition. Paris: NRF © Editions Gallimard, 1957.

The Aesthetics
of
Stéphane Mallarmé
in Relation to His Public

1
An Ambivalent Attitude Toward Social Reality

In a 1928 commentary accompanying the publication of ten letters from Stéphane Mallarmé to Emile Zola, Jean Royère stated that both the poet and the novelist desired to deify the literary work, to glorify the masses of mankind, and ultimately to create a Temple of Art for both.[1] Mallarmé had died in 1898. Except for parts of two recently published critiques of the poet offered by his disciples in the 1890s,[2] one had to wait thirty years before others began to recognize the importance of what can be called a social or even a humanitarian side to his nature. But this attitude did not necessarily concern the society and men that were contemporaries of the poet. Royère, with Mauclair and Morice one

1. Stéphane Mallarmé, *Dix-neuf Lettres de Stéphane Mallarmé à Emile Zola* (Paris: Jacques Bernard, 1929), pp. 73, 74.
2. Barbier, Carl Paul, ed., *Documents Stéphane Mallarmé*. vol. 3. (Paris: Librairie Nizet, 1971). The two disciples are Camille Mauclair, who intended to give a talk on Mallarmé but later published his critique in a Belgian literary journal in 1893 (pp. 205–27), and Charles Morice, who did give such a talk in 1899 (pp. 305–67). See especially pp. 212–19, 322.

of Mallarmé's most fervent disciples, was discussing an ideal, vast, future public, which the poet had included in his theories on art. In a similar vein, Paul Bénichou published an article in 1949 in which he discussed the relationship that ideally would have existed between Mallarmé and this public.[3]

At approximately the time when Mallarmé's awareness of a virtual public was being mentioned, his son-in-law, Dr. Edmond Bonniot, offered the world a new portrait of the poet: that of a man deeply attached to and concerned with the problems of everyday life.[4] But only again in 1948 did another critic, André Lebois, examine this new image of Mallarmé, in relation to the politics of the poet's day. Lebois, however, overstated his case when he argued that the poet was not an ivory tower artist.[5] Using accurate but isolated facts from Mallarmé's life and basing his conclusions solely on texts written during the 1890s, Lebois presented the poet as a man extremely liberal in his attitudes toward society and socially aware of the masses to the point of being *engagé* (involved).

Mallarmé's opinions of mankind in general, contemporary politics, society with its various classes, and the men composing those specific social classes were very complex. Confusing also were his desires for a future society, an ideal public, and a particular function for art and the poet in that perfected world. With regard to both the actual present and the desired future, parallel strains of scornful elitism and humanitarianism persisted in his attitudes. The intellectual and isolationist facets of this poet and his works have been widely studied. What is needed is an objective

---

3. Paul Bénichou, "Mallarmé et le public," *L'Ecrivain et ses travaux* (Paris: Corti, 1967), pp. 69–88.
4. Edmond Bonniot, "Mallarmé et la vie," *Revue de France* 1, no. 10 (1 janvier 1930): 59–71.
5. André Lebois, "Stéphane Mallarmé et la politique," *Mercure de France* 121 (1 septembre 1948): 69–78. See also Pierre Batistini, "Mallarmé, poète de la foule," *La Revue moderne des arts et de la vie* (1 avril 1949), pp. 16–17.

reevaluation of the socially aware or perhaps involved artist, developing from and existing simultaneously with the more traditionally accepted side of the man. Closely related to this social aspect of Mallarmé will be seen his need for and planned methods of communication with a public that he scorned and yet desired.

After carefully studying Mallarmé's creative works and correspondence, one discovers that the poet's first political references do not appear until 1863 when he was twenty-one years old. Although Henri Mondor describes him as having little concern for all exterior political events until 1871, he is also quick to explain that such a detached attitude was partially a problem of life in the isolated provinces of France during the mid-nineteenth century.[6] During a trip to London in 1863, however, Mallarmé expressed to his dearest friend, Henri Cazalis, a political attitude that was not to alter greatly throughout his life: "You know that all of my political illusions have disappeared one by one. . . . All of these vain political disputes pass because they have nothing absolute in them."[7]

The poet did finally move from a stifling life in the French provinces to Paris almost immediately after the conclusion of the Franco-Prussian War in 1871. While in Avignon, however, he could not evade news of the distressing conflict, nor of the subsequent problems in Paris that were due to the Prussian occupation and the action of the Commune. "There is in today's atmosphere an unknown dose of woe and insanity," wrote Mallarmé to Frédéric Mistral in 1870; ". . . modern history . . . subsists on some-

6. Henri Mondor, *Vie de Mallarmé* (Paris: Gallimard, 1941), pp. 304–5; *Mallarmé lycéen* (Paris: Gallimard, 1954), pp. 311–12.
7. Stéphane Mallarmé, *Correspondance 1862–1871,* ed. Henri Mondor (Paris: Gallimard, 1959), pp. 93–94. According to Mondor, these political illusions were the ideological ones of a liberal youth who leaned toward a belief in anarchy. In 1863 a Polish revolt against Russian authority, totally crushed by the latter, prompted sympathy in liberal milieux. Despite his lessening confidence in political expediency, Mallarmé attended a London meeting in favor of Poland.

thing other than these childish old things. I have never so completely hated Foolishness."[8] Like most of his close friends at that time, Mallarmé loathed the idiocy and uselessness of war, was deeply concerned about the siege of Paris, and was pleased about the proclamation of a French Republic in 1870.[9] He impartially witnessed the sad events of his day but was deeply grieved. He felt that political ills were so overpowering that they became troubles that could not concern him.[10] He could be aware of the turbulence around him without desiring any active involvement.

His attitude during the short-lived Paris Commune was one essentially of a concern for the safety of the French capital. Fearful for the future of France, Mallarmé equated both the Prussian occupation and the Communards' attempts with the plague.[11] Underlying his opinion of the Franco-Prussian conflict and of the Commune was a lack of confidence in any direct physical action to achieve peace in the world. The firmness of such an attitude can be substantiated by certain facts known about his convictions during the anarchist bombings in 1894. In 1898 Camille Mauclair wrote a novel entitled *Le Soleil des morts*.[12] The hero of this work, based on the literary and artistic circles at the end of the nineteenth century, is a poet, Calixte Armel. Throughout the novel, Mauclair links Armel to an anarchistic cause because of a common desire, with that of the masses to overthrow the bourgeoisie in power. Armel and his fellow poets were impatient for action and change in the government and society and, like the anarchists, were anx-

---

8. *Ibid.*, p. 333. Despite his decrying the foolishness of war and political men, Mallarmé himself refused to travel in Germany during the rest of his life and always sent his wife and children alone to visit his wife's family in the neighboring country.
9. *Ibid.*, p. 334.
10. *Ibid.*, pp. 336, 346, 350, 351.
11. *Ibid.*, pp. 350–51, 355–56. If one is to judge on the basis of Mallarmé's letters, it seems as though the poet did not react at all to the suppression of the Commune.
12. Camile Mauclair, *Le Soleil des morts: roman contemporain* (Paris: Paul Ollendorff, 1898).

ious to see this change occur. These beliefs attributed to Armel were supposedly based upon Mallarmé's own sympathetic statements about the French anarchists of the 1890s. Mallarmé did, in fact, find some semblance of himself in this fictitious hero; he was even pleased to be regarded by Mauclair as such a man.[13]

But Mauclair went beyond Mallarmé in creating his character. The poet's real attitude toward the anarchists and their method of inducing change was sympathetic but less optimistic. In point of fact,' he felt that some action was necessary, but, although he could commiserate with anarchists such as Ravachol and Vaillant in their despair of effecting this change, to him their means were destructive and futile. Even his support of the anarchist Fénéon was primarily due to a desire to help a personal friend, rather than an involvement with a political cause per se.[14]

Mallarmé vehemently opposed all forms of direct confrontation. As an epigraph to an important 1895 prose article, "L'Action restreinte" (Limited Action), he composed an enlightening poem, "Petit Air (Guerrier)" (Little Tune [Warlike]), which can serve as a brief summation of the poet's feelings on military action:

> It suits me, except for remaining silent about it
> To feel from the hearth
> A soldier's trousers
> Redden against my leg.[15]

According to this first ironic stanza, Mallarmé would wear a soldier's uniform as long as he did not have to be disturbed by leaving the warmth of his home.

As a related aspect of the mediocrity of politics and gov-

13. Stéphane Mallarmé, *Propos sur la poésie*, ed. Henri Mondor (Monaco: Editions du Rocher, 1953), pp. 205–6, 224–25.
14. Mondor, *Vie de Mallarmé*, pp. 681–83, 688–89.
15. Stéphane Mallarmé, *Oeuvres complètes* (Paris: Editions Gallimard, "Bibliothèque de la Pléiade," 1945), p. 66.

ernment, one can trace the poet's attitude toward society in general. Although, once again, he never became actively involved in trying to change society, there is sufficient evidence to demonstrate that he was aware, especially in his later years, of the distressing state of social justice around him and of the lack of action or the inadequacy of government efforts to ameliorate such a situation.

During the late 1880s, Mallarmé began to recognize a paradox between the contemporary structure of social classes and a need to escape from social realities. In contemporary society many men are reduced to leading difficult and unhappy lives. The state has a duty to provide its citizens with some means of escape, most conveniently and successfully in the form of theater, as a compensation for social ills, but governments have failed in this responsibility. Ironically, however, even if such an official form of artistic escape were available to all men, social conditions would not afford them enough leisure time to benefit from these theatrical performances. And if sufficient time were allotted, then many men would be too tired from their daily routines to enjoy such joyous pastimes.[16]

Throughout the prose articles of the 1890s, examples abound that exhibit an increasing concern about social injustice in contemporary society. With a sarcastic recognition of the fiction of justice as a result of the Panama Canal scandal of 1893, Mallarmé seriously deplored a hollow concept of society that exists merely as a false shelter for the gullible masses.[17] But maintaining hope for true justice in a stable, organized society, as in contemporary England and not in France, he believed that the political cities and

16. Mallarmé, "Le Genre ou des modernes," O.c., pp. 313–14; "Crayonné au théâtre," O.c., p. 294; "Solennité," O.c., p. 334; "Notes sur le théâtre," O.c., p. 345.
17. Mallarmé, "Or (Faits-Divers)," O.c., p. 1578; "Sauvegarde," O.c., p. 419.

states of his day would eventually perish in favor of a future ideal society.[18]

Distress about social inequities can imply an awareness of class distinctions. In 1895 Mallarmé wrote five prose articles, published in *La Revue blanche* and grouped into a series of articles called "Variations sur un sujet" (Variations on One Subject), in which he discussed such an awareness.[19] According to him, the existence of a separation among social classes can be regarded as one of the fundamental causes of a lack of communication among men. This was one of his deepest concerns: "Always the case: no place to be together; I fear that contact can never occur among men."[20] Although sadly cognizant of his particularly infrequent contact with other social classes, especially with working people, Mallarmé did not know how to effect a reconciliation. He understood the existing hatred and scorn of intellectuals by manual laborers but naively invited all men to reestablish some form of equality.[21]

In the article "La Cour" (The Court), Mallarmé's attitude toward social classes is somewhat more complex: modern democracy is confusing to everyone because, in its attempt at equality among all, no one can distinguish among any natural groups of men. What is needed is a more subtle return of a noble class in order to rectify these vague egalitarian notions and to abolish a situation that has arisen from a purely erroneous taste for equity.[22] Such an attitude may be viewed as coming from a poet who consistently re-

18. Mallarmé, "Sur l'évolution littéraire," *O.c.*, p. 866; "La Musique et les lettres," *O.c.*, p. 636, 653.
19. Mallarmé, "Conflit," *O.c.*, p. 355–60; "Bucolique," *O.c.*, pp. 401–5; "Solitude," *O.c.*, pp. 405–9; "Confrontation," *O.c.*, pp. 409–12; "La Cour," *O.c.*, pp. 412–16.
20. Mallarmé, "Conflit," *O.c.*, p. 358.
21. Mallarmé, "Confrontation," *O.c.*, p. 409.
22. Mallarmé, *O.c.*, p. 413.

tained a strongly aristocratic disdain toward all except an elite few, but three other interpretations are also possible. In the first place, Mallarmé was vehemently opposed to democracy as he saw it because he felt that it could never achieve any true equality among men. Second, the return of distinct social classes may be an intermediary stage, awaiting a more equitable society in the future. Finally, and, as shall be seen, most important of all, in Mallarmé's ideal future society social classes will no longer be meaningful.

If social injustice causes unhappiness in many of its citizens and creates a need for escape, but hinders the satisfaction of the desire for such, another factor contributing at least to the third problem is organized religion. The influence of a religious upbringing and the constant preoccupation with a need for some religious belief can be more fully studied in Adile Ayda's criticism, although her attempt to categorize Mallarmé solely as a religious being is too limiting.[23] But one can not deny the important effect on the maturing poet of his Catholic childhood in Sens. His earliest poems do exhibit a deep faith in God and man's ability to overcome his earthly state in order to be transformed after death into a heavenly angel.[24] After an abandonment of God and religion in a formalized sense, Mallarmé never ceased his search to rediscover this early belief in salvation for man.

But such a transformation would have to be effected by means other than those confined within the limits of contemporary organized religion. Its replacement would retain the magnificent tradition of powerful rituals and ceremonies, but its vulgarity, mediocrity, and complexity would

23. Adile Ayda, Le Drame intérieur de Mallarmé ou l'origine des symboles mallarméens (Istanbul: Editions "La Turquie Moderne," 1955).
24. Mallarmé, O.c., pp. 3–10.

be eliminated. For Mallarmé, modern religion is a monstrous rather than glorious chimera, whose stagnation, represented by medieval cathedrals, hinders man's natural sentiments and desires for elementary magic.[25]

Recognizing that man possesses certain innate sentiments thwarted by the negative aspects of religion implies an optimistic attitude toward mankind in general. Mallarmé's opinion of man, however, was extremely complex, oscillating from a purely disdainful viewpoint to a naively optimistic one. An arrogant attitude toward all men except a chosen few can first be seen in the 1862 prose article, "Hérésies artistiques: l'art pour tous" (Artistic Heresies: Art for All). Such an opinion of men and an elitist presentation of the poet and poetry were to be modified in later years but never totally negated. In this article Mallarmé displays a disgust for all men as an improper public for poetry. Everyone, except for fellow artists, belongs to the multitude of men who, in their stupidity, believe that they can understand poetic works. Unlike the mysterious written notes of music, poetry is read in the schools, and men, using a common vocabulary, see themselves as experts in interpretation. The young Mallarmé advocates withholding poetry from most men who in modern times have falsely become vain because of their useless titles of citizens of a state.[26]

The attitude that a poet should assume, according to Mallarmé, is one of scorn toward most men, whom he includes in a group called "the crowd," "the multitude," "the throng," "the common," or "the masses," and pride in a superior vocation. An excess of pride will eventually lead to a fear of surpassing mortal limitations while attempting to

25. Mallarmé, "Catholicisme," *O.c.*, p. 392; "De Même," *O.c.*, p. 397; "Magie," *O.c.*, p. 399.
26. Mallarmé, *O.c.*, p. 257–60.

rival God and of falling into the depths of failure as another Lucifer. But in 1862, Mallarmé believed that such pride is warranted because the poet is superior to all men. He is an aristocrat, a member of an elite in a supposedly democratic nation: "Let us remember that the poet . . . is not the level beneath which other men crawl; it is the crowd which is the level, and he soars above."[27]

A belief in the superior genius of poets as human or divine beings chosen to understand, re-create, or even to create the fundamental truths of humanity and of the universe remained in Mallarmé's thoughts throughout his life. Even when this scorn for other men became tempered as he matured, the pride of being a poet persisted. From his earliest works until his death, the artist is presented as a godlike figure, sometimes above and separate from the rest of mankind, at other times closely allied to the point of fusion.[28]

Throughout the 1860s Mallarmé continued to see all poets as kings who sit on thrones well above the level of the disgusting common crowd.[29] By 1875 in the prose poem "Un Spectacle interrompu" (An Interrupted Show), he seems neither to have changed his opinion of his own superior nature as compared to ordinary men, nor to have altered his scorn for mankind, sarcastically represented as a clown who cherishes a mythical belief in his superiority over animals.[30] In an 1886 letter to Mallarmé, in reaction to the label of anarchist given to the "decadent" poets by Louise Michel in a recent article, John Payne described the

27. *Ibid.*, p. 259.
28. Most of these images concern the poet's role and presentation of himself to a public in an ideal future society. At that time men will recognize the superior abilities of artists, with whom they will have communicated. In contemporary society, such a presentation is unknown because the poet remains so separate from men that he is not visible to most. This ideal situation will be studied in chapter 4.
29. Mallarmé, "Le Guignon," *O.c.*, p. 1410; "Symphonie littéraire," *O.c.*, pp. 264–65; "Igitur," *O.c.*, pp. 439, 442, 449.
30. Mallarmé, *O.c.*, pp. 276–78.

poet as he saw him: a refined conservative aristocrat who
hated the foul ambiguity of liberalism.[31]

Whether or not Mallarmé had altered his disdainful attitude toward men, he continued to appear to others as the
proud poet, placing himself on divine heights. In 1891 Jules
Huret interviewed him on the subject of literary evolution.
In an introduction to this interview, Huret offered his
readers a portrait of an artist who was revered by many fellow elitists: "a powerful charm radiates from the man in
whom one discerns an incredible pride, soaring above everything, the pride of a god or of an enlightened being, before whom one must mentally bow, as soon as one has
understood."[32] This superhuman pride may be interpreted
as implying hatred of an inferior mankind, or it may merely
signify Mallarmé's constant faith in artistic genius.[33] The
poet should be proud: with his abilities as a *voyant*, a clair-
voyant, he can raise himself above an earthly state. Other
men may not be so fortunate.

But Mallarmé was not certain whether mankind would
remain at a level below the divine-human poet. He could
never decide if the negative characteristics of men were
due to their contemporary situation or to innate deficiencies. In the explication by Robert Greer Cohn of
Mallarmé's difficult poem "Un Coup de dés" (A Throw of
the Dice), this critic interprets the eighth page of the poem
as a basic belief in man's stupidity because he is able to
laugh at himself. He is presented as the image of an in-
verted tree, reaching to heaven and yet rooted to the
earth.[34] Mallarmé continued his inquiry into the nature of
mankind in the unbound pages of his last work, the work

31. Stéphane Mallarmé, *Correspondance III 1886–1889*, ed. Henri Mondor et
Lloyd James Austin (Paris: Gallimard, 1969), p. 64.
32. Mallarmé, "Sur l'évolution littéraire," *O.c.*, p. 866.
33. Mallarmé, "Sur Poe," *O.c.*, p. 872.
34. Robert Greer Cohn, *L'Oeuvre de Mallarmé "Un Coup de dés,"* trans. René
Arnaud (Paris: Librairie Les Lettres, 1951), pp. 301–4, 335.

that occupied most of his life, Le "Livre" (The Book). One of five "myths" scrawled on these pages concerns man's general situation in life, a constant hesitation, not knowing whether or not to act.[35] Further on, Mallarmé observes that men have acted and have attempted to perfect themselves and the world, but that these deeds were accomplished or at least tried in the past. It is only in modern times that mankind is immobile.[36] Perhaps the answer to man's true nature lies in the discrepancy between his modern posture and his primitive or ideal state. His wavering between good and bad results in hesitation. Mallarmé found himself in a similar situation.

Given Mallarmé's belief in the baseness of politics and society, together with his low opinion of at least most contemporary men, life for a poet or for any literary man in such a world must also be deplorable. At times blaming society and at other times recognizing a voluntary desire for isolation on the part of contemporary poets, Mallarmé was continuously distressed about their social status. Instead of allowing these creative men to spend their lives in the true vocation of literature, society forced them to waste much of their time in unrelated occupations in order to earn a livelihood. One can easily see a reflection of Mallarmé's own ambivalent feelings toward teaching, which he regarded more and more as an encroachment upon his life as a poet.

The worst aspect of the contemporary poet's position in society was the mockery he had to endure from his fellow men. The young Mallarmé saw most poets as classless, leading the difficult lives of "ridiculous martyrs of a tortuous chance," who are the amusement of all the low classes

---

35. Jacques Scherer, Le "Livre" de Mallarmé: premières recherches sur des documents inédits (Paris: Gallimard, 1957), feuillets 12(A)–15(A).
36. Ibid., feuillet 24 (A).

of society, and who eventually "hang themselves ridiculously on a street lamp."[37] By 1895 Mallarmé still believed that society scorned poets as being lazy and that, if any poet were successful, the cause lay in a mistaken social destiny.[38]

Since the social fate of the contemporary poet was so rigid, one may just as well transform it into a positive cult, as the Romantics and Charles Baudelaire had already done, that is, the cult of the poor, misunderstood poet who, of course, is always superior to stupid mankind. The perfect example of this type of poet, in Mallarmé's eyes, was Paul Verlaine, and Mallarmé's tribute to him in 1896 was one of pity as well as of pride in his ability to withstand such a life.[39] In the fervently youthful attitude of "L'Art pour tous," Mallarmé had placed himself on heights for all men to see; now the poet retained such a position in his mind and in the eyes of his fellow poets of misfortune, not in the eyes of contemporary society.

If a poet is separated from other men because of his intellectual superiority, he is also apart from them because of his contemporary state of exile. A life of solitude and isolation is better than one subject to mockery and misfortune. The belief that Mallarmé and many of the poets of his day led their lives in an ivory tower largely stems from this advocacy of exile, physical if possible, and certainly as mental escape from the ugly world into a true poetic universe.

Mallarmé often described himself as a solitary figure who desired to isolate himself, especially at Valvins, from society and who had become the head of a poetic school despite himself and despite his general hatred of schools of literature: "In my opinion, the situation of a poet, in this society

37. Mallarmé, "Le Guignon," *O.c.*, pp. 1410–11. The 1887 revised poem depicts the same disgraceful situation. *Ibid.*, pp. 28–30.
38. Mallarmé, "Confrontation," *O.c.*, p. 409; "Solitude," *O.c.*, p. 405.
39. Mallarmé, "Verlaine," *O.c.*, p. 511.

which does not allow him to live, is that of a man who exiles himself in order to sculpt his own tomb. . . . For as for me, I am basically a solitary man. . . ."[40] A need for solitude and individuality for himself and in his art stemmed from a belief that a fragmented society, without stability and unity, inevitably fosters such an attitude. Every poet lives outside of society because of his own proud superiority, not bound by ordinary human laws, and because he can not exist in a world where people do not appreciate his innate gifts.[41]

Is this exile voluntary or forced upon him by society? Although Mallarmé believed that his isolation from men was self-imposed, almost as a duty to poetry, he may not have had a free choice in making his decision. Contemporary men exclude the poet from any official celebrations of art, regard him as a strange being, and treat him with scorn.[42] In order to escape from such a life, the poet retreats into exile, while claiming that it is he who scorns men and who desires and needs solitude. If a poet has high ideals for his work, and if a contemporary society can not raise itself to a level where it can understand either obscure thoughts or obscure language, that poet may refuse to compromise, withdraw from the world, and then present himself as a solitary and egotistical recluse. But it is possible that such a life may not coincide with the poet's original wishes.

From time to time, the poet needs to see what is happening around him in the outside world.[43] In this way, he

---

40. Mallarmé, "Sur l'évolution littéraire," *O.c.*, p. 869. See also Stéphane Mallarmé, *Correspondance II 1871–1885*, ed. Henri Mondor et Lloyd James Austin (Paris: Gallimard, 1965), pp. 153, 154; *Correspondance III*, p. 305; "La Gloire," *O.c.*, p. 289; "Bucolique," *O.c.*, p. 403.

41. Mallarmé, "Sur l'évolution littéraire, *O.c.*, pp. 866–67, 870.

42. Mallarmé, "Richard Wagner: rêverie d'un poète français," *O.c.*, p. 541; *Correspondance II*, p. 303. This was partially Mallarmé's own situation. He was treated like a god by his disciples in art, generally ridiculed by others, and unknown to most.

43. Mallarmé, "Le Genre ou des modernes," *O.c.*, p. 312; "Notes," *O.c.*, p. 856.

can also remain in touch with any changes occurring in society, changes toward a better period in which the artist and a public will be reconciled and will be able to communicate. One must not forget that, in this model, Mallarmé was essentially concerned with contemporary poets in nineteenth-century France, rather than with the general situation of all poets throughout the ages. If a separation exists between society and the exiled poet, he hoped that it was only temporary.

Mallarmé was a solitary man, but he believed that "poetry is made to be displayed in the supreme pomp of an organized society where the glory that men seem to have forgotten will have its place. The attitude of the poet, in a time such as this one, where he is on strike before society, is to put aside all vicious means that may be offered to him."[44] The poet remains uninvolved in contemporary society because it is beneath him. He continues to work in secret, while awaiting both the end of all that has been depicted as deplorable thus far and the dawn of a new era: "Basically, I consider the contemporary period as an interregnum for the poet, who never has to involve himself in it: this period is in such great disuse and preparatory turmoil that there is nothing else to do but to work mysteriously with the future, or never, in sight, and, from time to time, to send one's visiting card to those who are still living. . . ."[45]

If the poet has the misfortune, or luck, to be misunderstood by the vast majority of men, to whom does he send this reminder that he is alive and well? Throughout his life, Mallarmé tried to maintain confidence in the superior abilities of certain types of men. Generally one or more of the following labels were a prerequisite for Mallarmé's trust: literary elite of friends, aristocratic elite based upon

44. Mallarmé, "Sur l'évolution littéraire," *O.c.*, pp. 869–70.
45. Mallarmé, *Correspondance II*, p. 303.

family wealth, upper bourgeoisie elite based upon education, French as opposed to German but not as opposed to English, and, if French, Parisian, or at least cosmopolitan.

Mallarmé's high opinion and ardent support of his literary friends is well known. Entirely independent of his attitude toward the rest of humanity, such an opinion inevitably placed these men at the pinnacle of a progression of human qualities. In addition to the aiding of individual friends, Mallarmé spoke fervently for what he called a "literary fund," the profit from the sale of books on which a tax would be levied fifty years after the author's death. The writer and his immediate descendents would benefit from the profits derived from the sale of the book. The burden of the future tax would fall upon editors who now continue to enjoy the proceeds from reprintings. For years and centuries to come, the collected taxes would be placed in a fund for use by literary men of all countries.[46] Nationalism was generally not present when Mallarmé discussed his fellow artists.

In "La Musique et les lettres" (Music and Letters) of 1894, Mallarmé jealously compared the situation of English intellectuals to that of the French elite. The stable society of England allowed its literary intelligentsia to live in the exile of university towns.[47] This voluntary renouncement of an involved life did not result in the scorn of the remainder of the English citizenry. In France, the only means of separation was the "mental cloister."[48] Such an observation on Mallarmé's part may be interpreted in several ways. In one sense, the poet is continuing in the same vein of his early aristocratic attitude toward all but his elected few. He may also merely be offering a jealous description of the socially accepted intellectuals of England in contrast to the deplor-

46. Mallarmé, *Correspondance 1862–1871*, pp. 182, 199–200; "La Musique et les lettres," *O.c.*, pp. 637–42.
47. Mallarmé, *O.c.*, pp. 636–37.
48. Mallarmé, "Solitude," *O.c.*, p. 406.

able situation of their French counterparts. And physical isolation does not necessarily produce a cessation of communication among men who still have access to the publication of creative works.

Born into a family of civil servants and retaining the bourgeois position of English teacher, Mallarmé, already as part of the intellectual elite, longed to be aristocratic.[49] His consistent admiration of the former French nobility continued during his entire life, as is evident in 1895 when these aristocrats are considered as superior in intelligence to the vast majority of contemporary men.[50] During Mallarmé's early Parisian life and works, admiration for and desired complicity with the nobility are closely associated with a rather snobbish, cosmopolitan attitude. *La Dernière Mode* (The Latest Fashion), the fashion and literary magazine that he wrote and published in 1874, exhibits an almost distasteful clanishness between Mallarmé and his female readers, entirely composed of wealthy aristocrats and upper bourgeoisie living in Paris or familiar with its attractions.[51]

Given Mallarmé's hatred of contemporary politics and government, one can easily understand why most of his venom was directed at one particular social class, the bourgeoisie: "For whom, therefore, would we create a republic? For the bourgeois? Look at them in a crowd, in parks, and on the streets. They are hideous, and it is obvious that they don't have a soul."[52] Although Mallarmé did

49. An example of this longing is Mallarmé's use of the name de Boulainvilliers instead of his own at school as a child. See Mondor, *Vie de Mallarmé*, pp. 14–15.
50. Mallarmé, "La Cour," *O.c.*, p. 413.
51. Mallarmé, *O.c.*, pp. 707–847. See especially p. 733, where the poet labels all visitors to Paris as "foreigners" who should leave the capital. See also the names of subscribers in the various "Correspondance avec les abonnées" (Correspondence with subscribers).
52. Mallarmé, *Correspondance 1862–1871*, p. 94. See also *Ibid.*, p. 261 where the poet sarcastically announces the plan of a new book to be called "*Esthétique du bourgeois, ou la Théorie universelle de la laideur*" (Aesthetics of the Bourgeois, or The Universal Theory of Ugliness).

not often use the specific word *bourgeois* in his writings, one can state that, at least at the time of the Third Republic, it was bourgeois men who possessed political power and who were, therefore, responsible both for the sad state of political affairs and for modern warfare; it was the bourgeoisie who headed the organized church. It was also the bourgeois who disdained the intellectual elite.

As much as he may have disliked the truth, he also had to realize that most of the contemporary public was bourgeois. If the poet was scorned, it had to be by bourgeois readers and critics. Despite the 1881 laws providing for free lay public education in the Third Republic, the proletariat had not yet found the time nor developed the ability to read much literature or to attend most theaters and concerts.[53] Throughout Mallarmé's letters and works, one can find examples of his hatred of this contemporary reading public, an implied hatred, therefore, of the bourgeoisie. With such a long record of a belief in contemporary stupidity, it was easy for him to blame these men for yet another fault. As an attack against their charges of obscurity, he was able to retort succinctly: "contemporary men don't know how to read."[54]

In the poet's mind, monetary gold was the perfect symbol for this vast social class with its growing financial power. When, for example, bourgeois men want a railroad, they can easily exploit others to do the work because they possess the money with which to pay the lower classes of workmen.[55] Money is banal, grim, but universal. It is too impersonal and yet strikes the human race with its

53. Nicole Robine, "La Lecture," in *Le Littéraire et le social*, ed. Robert Escarpit (Paris: Flammarion, 1970), pp. 234, 238.
54. Mallarmé, "Le Mystère dans les lettres," *O.c.*, p. 386. See also "Solitude," *O.c.*, p. 408; *Correspondance 1862–1871*, pp. 93, 168; *Correspondance II*, pp. 76, 100–101; *Correspondance III*, p. 227.
55. Mallarmé, "Conflit," *O.c.*, p. 358.

omnipotence.[56] Money has become the god of most men,
not only of the bourgeoisie. Mallarmé wanted another god
to replace it.

Not all members of the bourgeoisie are in positions of
power. Stupidity in power can affect everyone negatively;
stupidity i weakness merely evokes pity. In this sense,
Mallarmé, in his later years, began to realize that the
bourgeois public's low level of taste and intelligence was all
too often the outcome of literary men's pandering to existing mediocrity. Journalists, bourgeois dramatists, and
novelists are the men largely responsible for the state of
bourgeois intelligence, as well as for the even worse situation of those members of the masses who have any desire
to better themselves. These latter men could move only
from the working to the bourgeois class, no great improve-
ment as Mallarmé saw it.

An attack against such influential men of literature should
be uncompromising. According to Mallarmé, these men
complain about the obscurity of other works of art. They
announce to the general public that, if they do not understand a work, no one will. Mallarmé believed that the mere
mention of obscurity implies a prior renouncement of the
ability to judge. But sadly enough, such men add to the
vast incomprehension of the reading public, which will
forgo difficult literature in favor of mediocre works.[57] In *Le
"Livre"* Mallarmé goes even further in his attack: the vil-
lainous novelists who pose as lay priests are responsible for
describing, maintaining, and imposing upon others the banality of contemporary social life. These men were odious to
the poet.[58]

---

56. Mallarmé, "Confrontation," *O.c.*, p. 410; "Or," *O.c.*, p. 398; "Or (Faits-
Divers)," *O.c.*, p. 1578.
57. Mallarmé, "Le Mystère dans les lettres," *O.c.*, pp. 383–84.
58. Scherer, feuillets 7(A)–8(A).

Hatred toward these men of literature must include a similar attitude toward popular literature, destined for the contemporary reading public. Part of Mallarmé's determination to search for an ideal art form was initially a reaction against much of the literature of his day, against, particularly, contemporary bourgeois novels, theater, and newspapers. Novels received the least amount of scorn, although the poet condemned their simple depiction of banal reality as offering the public no means of self-edification.[59] Because of his deep love for the theater, he was greatly distressed about the deficiencies of French contemporary drama. From his arrival in Paris, he attended the theater regularly and complained about what he saw as mediocre and pedantic.[60] The few worthy plays that were performed served to renew his hope for a better theater in the future.

Most of Mallarmé's disdain was reserved for the press, although great admiration for this modern form of art and communication accompanied any dislike. Essentially journalism consists of the crude, daily reporting of insignificant reality in an elementary form lacking any structured order. Mallarmé effectively uses his gift of sarcasm when he attacks newspapers as having the advantage of not interrupting one's preoccupations with other matters.[61] In "Solitude" there is a bitter satire against the press and its function of catering to the low level of its readers' intelligence. Mallarmé is requested by an interviewer to condense a long statement of his about the need for punctuation, a statement purposefully making no sense. He replies: " 'Wait. . .at least until I add a little obscurity.' "[62] Let him make it too difficult for the mindless reader of the ineptly

59. Mallarmé, "Etalages," *O.c.*, p. 375.
60. Mallarmé, "La Dernière Mode," *O.c.*, pp. 717, 750, 767; "Le Genre ou des modernes," *O.c.*, pp. 313, 315; "Crayonné au théâtre," *O.c.*, p. 297.
61. Mallarmé, "Le Mystère dans les lettres," *O.c.*, p. 386.
62. Mallarmé, *O.c.*, p. 407.

condensed newspaper to understand. In this way he can remain above such bourgeois mediocrity.

Even though the majority of the middle class was to be sarcastically viewed, Mallarmé did often show a sincere concern for the masses. His opinion of the emerging proletariat was, not surprisingly, rather ambivalent, but one general observation can be made: despite what many men have always stated about the poet, he was constantly aware of the masses and of their miserable existence as victims of social injustice. Beginning with a hostile attitude, Mallarmé then made a futile attempt to erase these men from his mind. He eventually emerged as a man deeply saddened by his thoughts of them.

Before any discussion of Mallarmé and the masses, two points must be stated to avoid any confusion. It has been seen that, especially in his youth, Mallarmé often referred to everyone except the elite as "the people." Second, one must also make a distinction between a contemporary crowd and an ideal future one; the two are presently separated but closely associated in many respects. According to Paul Bénichou, Mallarmé harbored only hostile feelings toward the contemporary proletariat and only optimistic ones toward an ideal crowd of the future.[63] For Mallarmé, however, such an ideal crowd was firmly based upon the present one, with most of its qualities already inherent in the proletariat. A more accurate interpretation can be described in this manner: awareness of the masses and their future power and abilities led the poet to love the people or at least to see in them certain great qualities that would soon be part of a vast public of art. There was no prerequisite of any true knowledge or understanding of these downtrodden men.

63. Bénichou, pp. 83–84.

After careful examination of Mallarmé's correspondence and works, one is surprised that most critics have been generally unaware of the poet's reaction to the masses. Dating from 1861 until his last works, examples abound that illustrate this deepening cognizance. Throughout his life, but especially evident in his earlier works, there exist sentiments of pity and disgust, later mixed with fear, toward the misery of these people. An 1861 poem, "Galanterie macabre" (Macabre Galantry), is the first such example where the masses in poverty are represented pitifully but as grotesque and ludicrous:

> And I saw a grotesque funereal scene
> Whose dream still haunts me, and here it is,
> A woman, very young, a poor woman, almost
> Laid out, was dead in a gloomy hovel.
>
> —Without sacraments and like a dog,—said her neighbor
> . . . .
>
> . . . .
>
> There it is.—Up until now nothing: One's allowed to die
> Poor, one dirty day, and have a choir boy
> Open his umbrella and, without even a dog's crying for you,
> Hurry up to a gallop your mocking funeral procession.[64]

An interesting example of his attitude toward the people can be seen in three early versions of the 1887 poem "Aumône" (Alms), versions entitled "Haine du pauvre" (Hatred of the Poor Man) in 1862, "A un mendiant" (To a Beggar) in 1864, and "A un pauvre" (To a Poor Man) in 1866.[65] In all of these versions, Mallarmé, or at least the speaker in the poem, violently reacts to a poor beggar with cries of hatred, disdain, and disgust, mixed with a sense of pity and guilt at turning his back on him. The 1862 poem, with its bitter title, characterizes the poor man as "servile

64. Mallarmé, O.c., pp. 15–16.
65. Ibid., pp. 1434–36; Bonniot, pp. 60–64.

and lowly," "the brother of the dog," "a jackal," who crawls on his belly and who should be "Down! . . .—on his two knees! . . .—his beard in the mud!" before the poet with his "simple scorn." And yet Mallarmé does have some pity for him. Seen in the total context of the poem, some of these hostile words are tempered by lines from the first two stanzas: "I love him, / Old specter, and that is why I throw you twenty sous. / Your servile and lowly forehead has no wan pride:/ You understand that the poor man is the brother of the dog."[66]

In both the 1864 and 1866 versions, the same confused feelings continue. Hatred of the poor man becomes simply a poem addressed to and about a beggar, and, lastly, without defining him, to a poor man. A general sense of shame and guilt pervades the two poems: the poet wants to give the man money, but he feels, perhaps, that such alms are wrong. His foolish condition is that the beggar use the money to supplement some dream or sin rather than for a useful purpose. Perhaps this is partially sarcastic and cruel disdain on Mallarmé's part, or perhaps, if the man forgets him, as the poet requests him to do, no one will remember that Mallarmé was even aware of the beggar's existence.

Certain revisions from 1864 to 1866 are interesting, but they illustrate no definite change in Mallarmé toward a greater sense of pity or disgust. The "foggy horizons" of 1864 become "dirty" in 1866; "the bright flash of a fanfare" becomes "oh evil fanfare!"; "the charming azure" is written as "the childish azure"; and while the "red feather" is transformed into a "black feather," the negative verse "And one throws, with a haughty eye, two sous to the boy" is somewhat assuaged by becoming "One throws a feast from the window to the beggar."[67]

If Mallarmé experienced a sense of guilt at helping a

66. Mallarmé, *O.c.*, pp. 1434–35.
67. *Ibid.*, pp. 1435–36.

poor man in the street, perhaps such a feeling stemmed from his inability to discover any redeeming qualities in the masses. Such a discovery had to wait until the 1870s when, in addition, he began to make a distinction between the haggard crowd on earth and their future selves.[68] In a discussion of the 1874 Salon of painting from which two of three paintings by Edouard Manet were excluded, Mallarmé firmly states his new faith in the public, whom he refers to as "the crowd," "the masses," "the people," or "the public." As stated previously, this public must have been predominantly bourgeois, but the use of such terms and further evidence in articles of the following two years do imply a generalization to include the proletariat. In "Jury," the public begins to show certain latent and instinctive tendencies, emphasized by the painter. This crowd, from which everything emanates, will finally recognize itself as the subject of art.[69] One must also admit the possibility that, in a fervent desire to support his friend Manet, Mallarmé may have overstated his case.

He does not go to any extremes in "Un Spectacle interrompu," when the crowd is described as being naive but jealously admired as being simple enough to enjoy and to find relaxation in banal myths.[70] By the time he writes his next defense of Manet in 1876, however, Mallarmé returns to the sentiments of "Jury." In an extremely benevolent frame of mind, the poet reminds his reader of the "true beauties of the people, healthy and solid as they are. . ." and of the graces even of the bourgeoisie as "worthy models in art. . . ." It is this "strange new beauty" in the masses that an artist such as Degas has so magnificently portrayed in his painting of poor washerwomen.[71] And it is this new

68. Mallarmé, "Toast funèbre," *O.c.*, pp. 54–55.
69. Mallarmé, "Le Jury de peinture pour 1874 et M. Manet," *O.c.*, p. 700.
70. Mallarmé, *O.c.*, p. 276.
71. Stéphane Mallarmé, "The Impressionists and Edouard Manet," *The Art Monthly Review* 1, no. 9 (September 30, 1876): 118, 121.

form of recognition of the proletariat that causes Mallarmé to bridge the gap between art and politics: "The participation of a hitherto ignored people in the political life of France is a social fact that will honour the whole of the close of the nineteenth century. A parallel is found in artistic matters, the way being prepared by an evolution which the public with rare prescience dubbed, from its first appearance, Intransigeant, which in political language means radical and democratic." The masses have become "those new-comers of to-morrow . . . the mighty numbers of an universal suffrage. . . ."[72]

During the period from 1885 to 1890, Mallarmé's attitude toward the proletariat continues to develop. He discovers new qualities in them while retaining the same ambivalent feelings toward their contemporary situation. He begins to perceive those admirable instincts in the people that he will soon make attributes of his ideal future crowd. Several prose works composed during these years clarify these newly found tendencies. For the masses, as for all men, "the era has exploded, legitimately seeing that in the crowd, or rather in the majestic amplification of each person, lies hidden a dream! There exists now in the multitude an awareness of its judgeship or supreme intelligence. . . ."[73] Mallarmé has become aware of the inner truths of the masses at the same time as the "jubilant throng" has begun to see a coarse image of its own divinity.[74] Instinctive and divine intelligence does not assure total maturity of such an attribute, especially since the contemporary crowd is still in its childhood. As a present-day group, the proletariat remains repulsive, but after germination, its multiple richness will be cultivated until it surges upward toward a golden future.[75]

72. *Ibid.*, pp. 121, 122.
73. Mallarmé, "Crayonné au théâtre," *O.c.*, p. 298.
74. *Ibid.*
75. Mallarmé, "Villiers de l'Isle-Adam," *O.c.*, p. 499.

In general, therefore, the masses that Mallarmé still sees around him in everyday reality deserve the same mixed feelings of sympathy and disgust that were evident in the early versions of "Aumône." If, in 1887, this poem reflects any change in attitude, it is one toward slightly more pity. Any negative implications of the former titles have been eliminated, and the poor beggar, formerly referred to as a "rogue," now becomes the "brother" of the poet.[76]

In a society with an unjust social organization, the masses usually have to endure a miserable daily life. But it is exactly this disdainful society that forces them to become self-aware and to commence some action toward a better future. Mallarmé sees the crowd as a closed circle with a mediocre exterior. Within this circle lies the mysterious virgin element of collective grandeur, something occult, significantly closed and hidden, that inhabits all common men. If the poet can help the people break its shell, they will both discover a new "Crowd (where Genius is included)."[77] By the 1890s Mallarmé had begun to place an extraordinary amount of faith in what he believed to be the instinctive intelligence of the people.

Given the social status of the poet and of the working class in the contemporary world, men like Camille Mauclair tried to unite artists and the masses in a common attempt to better their situation in life.[78] Given the newly perceived intelligence of the crowd as contrasted with the stupidity of most of the bourgeoisie, an additional rapport between the poet and the masses could be formed, united against mediocrity. Mallarmé had made the poor beggar his

76. Mallarmé, O.c., pp. 39–40. Aristocratic contempt mixed with pity and a desire to communicate with the masses is also evident in the 1887 "La Déclaration foraine," O.c., pp. 280–81.
77. Mallarmé, "Le Mystère dans les lettres," O.c., p. 383; "Plaisir sacré," O.c., p. 390. Another image is that of a sleeping people. Scherer, feuillet 23(A). Within this present sleep, however, are active dreams.
78. Mauclair, pp. 158–69.

brother in 1887; in that same year he had expressed a desire to "plunge myself once again . . . in the people."[79] By the early 1890s the masses, the majority, his compatriots had become his humble fellow men.[80]

Nothing concerning Stéphane Mallarmé can be simply explained. In the last years of his life any rapport with the working class remained complex, essentially because of his newly sensed duty toward these people. In the prose article "Conflit" (Conflict), Mallarmé tries to express his confused feelings by generalizing from a specific incident of 1895.[81] After talking about the masses for years, the poet is finally confronted by them and thereby given the opportunity to communicate with them directly. Mallarmé hesitates and then feels guilty.

At his vacation home at Valvins, the poet is disturbed in his creative tasks by the noise of workmen who are in the countryside in order to build a railroad near his property. The sight of these men from his window precipitates a flood of mixed emotions ranging from ardent admiration to deep fear. His initial reaction, perhaps based on anger at having been interrupted in his work, is one of long-standing disgust for these lazy but strong tramps. The poet returns to his youthful response of trying to erase from his mind the presence of the menacing proletariat, but it is "impossible to annul him mentally . . . this suddenly coarse and wicked colossus."[82] As usual, however, Mallarmé's scorn is imbued with a deep pity, though often condescending: the men are described as simple drunkards who have been reduced to

79. Mallarmé, "Crayonné au théâtre," *O.c.*, p. 296.
80. Mallarmé, "Diptyque," *O.c.*, p. 850; Scherer, feuillets 7(A)–8(A); "La Musique et les lettres," *O.c.*, p. 653.
81. Mallarmé, *O.c.*, pp. 355–60. See an exegesis of this article or, possibly, prose poem in Ursula Franklin, "The Prose Poems of Stéphane Mallarmé: An Exegesis," *Dissertation Abstracts International* 32 (1971): 6973A (Michigan State). Microfilm 72–16, 424, pp. 303–53.
82. Mallarmé, *O.c.*, p. 357.

an arduous task, because, "in contrast to the majority of more fortunate men, they have not had enough bread —they have first had to labor for a good part of the week even to obtain it. . . ."[83]

Then, perhaps recalling what he has been discovering about the masses during the past decade, Mallarmé expresses his faith in them, even as the simplest of human beings. In their elementary manual tasks, these workmen exhibit a deep sense of force and action, determined solely by themselves. They proceed directly from ideas to action. In a poetic manner, Mallarmé refers to these ideas as literature and to the action as the pure force of the worker who cultivates an unsown terrain. The poet is "overcome by a religious feeling. . .moved to the point of kneeling."[84] This sense of admiration is also evident in "Confrontation," the encounter of physical and mental labor, where one finds the same action of the workers' tools, striking toward some ideal summit. Once again "My look upon his [the worker's] . . . confirms, for the humble believer in this richness, a deference."[85]

Despite their social situation as victims rather than as officiants, the masses manage to glow in their pride of withstanding such a destiny and of extracting from their daily lives, by means of manual labor, an almost ritualistic sacredness of existence. This simplicity of task is exactly the germ of what will grow instinctively into magnificence. There is hope in the future for these now blind troops of men when their lucidity and brilliance will be "reduced to social proportions in eternity."[86]

Mallarmé had experienced these feelings and dreams be-

---

83. *Ibid.*, p. 359. See also p. 356.
84. *Ibid.*, p. 356.
85. Mallarmé, *O.c.*, p. 411. There is an obvious rapport between the physical striking of the workers' tools and the mental striking or blow (*heurt* and *coup*) in "Igitur" and in "Un Coup de dés."
86. Mallarmé, "Conflit," *O.c.*, p. 360. See also p. 359; "La Cour," *O.c.*, p. 414.

fore; what he sensed now in addition was fear of all that he was proposing and guilt about his own lack of action thus far. Actually confronted by the workmen, the poet recognizes the powerful strength of these men, both as an immediate physical danger to him and as an indication of their increasing will. The bright future becomes "alternatives . . . the season of understanding and of uneasiness. . . ."[87] One does not doubt the sincerity of Mallarmé's admiration for the proletariat, nor his faith in these instincts, but much of what the poet mentally tells these men does seem to have an overtone of immediate fear. If he complains about the noise, he does not want them to become angry. He does not want them to think that his sadly privileged state is a social barrier that could insult them. It is personal. He simply needs to be left alone by everyone so that he may continue his own work. When he scrutinizes one of these men, he does not find any differences because of class distinction; he considers the man to be a human being with a right to certain feelings of his own.[88] The supposedly "liberal" poet, in his persistent vein of elitism, does not want the workman to think that he considers him to be inferior.

These masses, whom the poet so deeply admires and for whom he prays for a glorious future, have also instilled a nagging fear in him. He does not know if he wants to avoid contact with them. He does realize that he cannot avoid such a contact. Stemming, therefore, either from fear or from a sincere awareness, Mallarmé experiences a deep sense of guilt about his lack of contact with them in the past, as well as during this actual incident: "I suffer from my indifferent silence which makes me an accomplice."[89] In a lack of action, or even communication, Mallarmé is re-

87. Mallarmé, "Conflit," *O.c.*, p. 357.
88. *Ibid.*, pp. 356, 357.
89. *Ibid.*, p. 357. The original title of "Confrontation" was "Cas de Conscience" (A Case of Conscience). Mallarmé, *O.c.*, pp. 1573, 1580.

sponsible for the plight of the masses whose mystery he should try to understand. From 1895 until his death, he will alter this situation: "I will, therefore, think only about them, these unfortunate men who close off the distant vesperal to me more because of their attitude of abandonment than, as before, because of their tumultuous noise. Watching these artisans of elementary tasks, next to a clear river, it is leisurely for me to look at the people. . . ."[90] One may notice, however, that Mallarmé still looks from a distance.

90. Mallarmé, "Conflit," O.c., p. 359.

2
The Function of Art

Given the banality and ugliness of much of contemporary life, escape into a world of art can provide a needed alternative either for an author or for a reader and spectator. Mallarmé's letters and works of 1863–1870 present the portrait of a man yearning for some refuge from life, but only during these same years did the poet specifically name art as this haven.[1] Throughout the later years of his life, he would not specify escapism as a proper role for his works; instead he would offer what he believed to be a more "realistic" substitute for present-day reality. Even during the 1860s when signs of actual escape from the world were evident, the trials of poetic creation and the discoveries made therein caused him to consider contemporary reality as a possible shelter from personal anxieties.[2]

1. Stéphane Mallarmé, *Correspondance 1862–1871*, ed. Henri Mondor (Paris: Gallimard, 1959), pp. 76, 90–91, 158, 180, 193, 195, 220, 245; Stéphane Mallarmé, "Les Fenêtres," *Oeuvres complètes* (Paris: Editions Gallimard, "Bibliothèque de la Pléiade," 1945), pp. 32–33; "Les Fleurs," *O.c.*, pp. 33–34.
2. Mallarmé, *Correspondance 1862–1871*, pp. 104–5, 111, 150, 324; "Las de l'amer repos," *O.c.*, pp. 35–36; "L'Azur," *O.c.*, pp. 37–38; "Brise marine," *O.c.*, p. 38.

A supplementary aspect of art's function as escapism can be seen, not when one creates, but when one approaches the work of another. This problem encompasses both Mallarmé, relating to the works of his fellow artists, and the public, confronted with any art form. A work of art can offer any man the possibilities of evasion, often with a dual purpose: art can hide the image of daily reality, and an escape into this art form can provide relief from the menacing world of absolute intellectualism, encountered, as in Mallarmé's experiences, during one's own processes of artistic creation.

Despite his persistence of a high level of intellectual poetry, there runs throughout Mallarmé's life a contrasting desire for art as simple amusement during one's leisure time. Given the contemporary situation of many men in society, Mallarmé often recognized the essential need of some form of artistic escape in order to withstand everyday misery. In his opinion, theater, as simple farces and vaudeville, was usually the art form best suited to this function. In theatrical presentations, as a compensation for social ills, he felt that there existed a superior refreshment for the tired worker.[3]

The poet himself loved this form of entertainment, but he could rarely find refuge and security in its charms. For him, the art forms best serving as a means of escape were poetry and, especially, music. As a youth he had ecstatically delved into the poetry of Gautier, Baudelaire, and de Banville as if it were opium. In Le "Livre," poetry as protection from the outside world remained prevalent in the poet's mind as that which cradled us in our infancy.[4]

3. Mallarmé, "Notes sur le théâtre," O.c., p. 345; "Le Genre ou des modernes," O.c., p. 314.
4. Mallarmé, "La Dernière Mode," O.c., p. 750; "Un Spectacle interrompu," O.c., p. 276; "Le Genre ou des modernes," O.c., p. 317; "Symphonie littéraire," O.c., p. 263; Jacques Scherer, Le "Livre" de Mallarmé: premières recherches sur des documents inédits (Paris: Gallimard, 1957), feuillet 142.

But if poetry were to retain such powers, it would have to rival the capabilities of music, universally used by most people as a source of emotionally soothing escape, almost as "the Sunday washing away of banality. . . ,"[5] and, in addition, by Mallarmé as a source of pleasant revery. The music of Wagner, especially, offered the poet this dual escape, "a hospitality against one's insufficiencies and the mediocrity of countries . . . like isolation, a rest for the spirit . . . as much as a shelter from the all too lucid haunting of this menacing summit of the absolute. . . ."[6]

The functions of art, however, are as numerous as its forms, and Mallarmé realized that this diversity was inevitable. Its desirability confused the poet because he could not definitely decide on the efficacy of certain functions. One such function was art as a mirror of contemporary life in various classes. It is clear that Mallarmé hated life in its banal and ugly guise, and that he despised literary men who did nothing more than depict this vulgarity, thereby suppressing any chance of public edification. And yet he did greatly admire the realistic novels of Emile Zola and often stated that art had to be the direct reflection of people and society.[7]

Beginning in 1871 with his arrival in Paris, one sees a distinct change of tone away from an earlier more serious and more egocentric Mallarmé. He becomes more cosmopolitan, preoccupied with life's attractions. From 1871 until his death in 1898, Mallarmé composed such works as *La Dernière Mode* and "Crayonné au théâtre" (Scribbled at the Theater), his numerous criticisms on contemporary theater, dance, and music. In 1875 he began a series of En-

5. Mallarmé, "Plaisir sacré," *O.c.*, p. 390.
6. Mallarmé, "Richard Wagner: rêverie d'un poète français," *O.c.*, p. 546.
7. Stéphane Mallarmé, *Correspondance II 1871–1885*, ed. Henri Mondor et Lloyd James Austin (Paris: Gallimard, 1965), pp. 146, 172–73; Stéphane Mallarmé, *Correspondance III 1886–1889*, ed. Henri Mondor et Lloyd James Austin (Paris: Gallimard, 1969), pp. 152–53.

glish contacts that were to result in his contemporary artistic "gossips" in the British publication the *Atheneum*. In all of these works, as well as in his letters, appears a mundane poet, himself reflecting at least a daily artistic world.[8]

It has already been shown in "Le Jury de peinture pour 1874 et M. Manet" (The Jury of Painting for 1874 and Mr. Manet) and in "The Impressionists and Edouard Manet" that Mallarmé considered both the bourgeoisie and the proletariat as "worthy models in art," worthy of the painter's time and effort, and recognizing themselves in all surviving art forms. Art, especially painting, has become a vision of the contemporary world with its look of the modern crowd.[9] It is the direct reflection of "our immediate, dear, and multiple life, with its serious nonsense" and of "types of individuals whom we see every day. . . . the apotheosis of the contemporary visage"; "nothing is to be neglected in the existence of an age. . . ."[10]

If art forms have an obligation to include all aspects of the contemporary period, these particular works still remain images of a select world where men have the leisure time to attend the theater and to gaze upon works of the Impressionists. Jacques Scherer has illustrated the point, however, that Mallarmé, in his own works, was less narrow, less of a purist than one usually assumes. By means of language, of what Scherer calls common or plebeian words, he not only refused to hesitate before the use of a vulgar, popular, or slang word, but he actually achieved with these words an effect of frank and surprising realism. For

---

8. Mallarmé, "La Dernière Mode," *O.c.*, pp. 707–847; "Crayonné au théâtre," *O.c.*, pp. 293–351; Stéphane Mallarmé, *Les "gossips" de Mallarmé "Atheneum" 1875–1876*, ed. Henri Mondor et Lloyd James Austin (Paris: Gallimard, 1962).

9. Mallarmé, "Le Jury de peinture pour 1874 et M. Manet," *O.c.*, pp. 698, 697.

10. Mallarmé, "La Dernière Mode," *O.c.*, pp. 718, 735, 719.

Scherer, Mallarmé believed that all aspects of reality could be the object of poetry.[11]

An apotheosis of contemporary mankind implies a present and an ideal being. Before he could be concerned with such a transformation for other men, Mallarmé had to discover some ideal world for himself. It is this function of art, and of poetry in particular, that has occupied most of Mallarmé's critics, but one half of all references made to such a concern in works and letters occur before 1871. The youthful poet, in an egotistical and narcissistic vein, turned toward the creation of poetry as a means of personal self-discovery leading to the existence of some ideal and absolute world for him alone. In his later years, such a search continued to occupy his thoughts, but the resulting goal would be achieved only with the active role of a public; the ultimate ideal world would include both the poet and other men.

While still living in the French provinces, Mallarmé could find no consolation in outside reality. He felt that, in order to continue to live, he had to find some other world more suitable to his needs. This new reality was to exist in poetic creation, and its development was to occur by means of a profound self-searching, a look into his innermost soul. Whether or not this new absolute poetic world was to be at all associated with social life has long been a subject of discussion. Most critics have stated that Mallarmé made himself a universal point of reference, rejecting all exterior inspiration, including his own memory. He based his poetry upon the intellectual idea, existing in a pure state within his own mind, and thereby surpassed his old self and created a new pure self in a new world. The origin of his

11. Jacques Scherer, *L'Expression littéraire dans l'oeuvre de Mallarmé* (Paris: Librairie A. G. Nizet, 1947), pp. 66, 68.

poems, therefore, can be found either in his pure consciousness or in an exterior Platonic world of pure ideas.[12] More realistic critics have observed that the poet, even if he denied much of outside reality, could not eliminate it from his thoughts. Even self-searching and self-discovery have to begin in a social being.[13]

No matter what the stimulus was for Mallarmé's attempt to create a new world for himself, this process involved an effort of self-creation where poetry was to become synonymous with life. As early as 1865, Mallarmé triumphantly proclaimed not only that he had begun to live for the purpose of composing poetry, but also that his very existence had become dependent upon this creation: "The artist *creates himself* before the paper."[14] If the poet performs an act of self-construction by means of poetic composition, he can also cause his own self-destruction. One of the prerequisites for the attainment of a new pure being in an ideal reality is the destruction of one's former impure self and the mental resurrection of an impersonal, universal, absolute self. Once again, the creation of poetry is the only means by which such a spiritual transformation can occur. Mallarmé's letters of 1866–1869 illustrate with moving emotion the famous crisis that the poet endured during this personal drama when, after mental death, he was reborn into the region of Eternity and Purity. "My distended thought, occupied with the fullness of the universe, lost its normal function . . ." but "having destroyed me will reconstruct me."[15]

12. Guy Delfel, *L'Esthétique de Stéphane Mallarmé* (Paris: Flammarion, 1951), pp. 34–41, 52; Emilie Noulet, *Suites: Mallarmé Rimbaud Valéry* (Paris: A. G. Nizet, 1964), pp. 11–15, 23.

13. A. R. Chisholm, "Mallarmé and the Act of Creation," *Esprit créateur* 1 (1961): 111–13; Georges Poulet, "Mallarmé," *Etudes sur le temps humain II: la distance intérieure* (Paris: Plon, 1952), pp. 303–4.

14. Mallarmé, *Correspondance 1862–1871*, p. 154. Also attributed to Mallarmé is the statement: "I exist . . . only on the paper." Camille Mauclair, *Mallarmé chez lui* (Paris: Editions Bernard Grasset, 1935), p. 131.

15. Mallarmé, *Correspondance 1862–1871*, p. 299. See also *Ibid.*, p. 240.

The poet, for himself alone and within his own mind, obviously desired to be godlike. What is perhaps more important is that, throughout his life, he was desperately attempting to assert his free will in opposition to a feared doctrine of determinism. The problem of man's liberty was one that deeply concerned Mallarmé. At times he seemed certain that man was fully responsible for all that happened to him, [16] at other times he complained bitterly that everything in life was predestined. [17] If man, and especially the poet, attempted to deny a supreme order, or the existence of Chance in "Un Coup de dés," the gods or some eternal power cruelly laughed at him. [18] And yet if the poet were godlike himself, he could partake in such Olympian laughter; and if all men were godlike, then man's free will might be ascertained.

The best example of Mallarmé's attitude toward determinism and free will can be found in the first "myth" of *Le "Livre,"* the "myth" of the call to mankind. Hesitation on the part of the man being called has already been discussed as a general reaction and fault of all men. It is an illustration of free man caught in the power of determinism. A human word is spoken, calling man, who lends his ear and leans forward to listen: "a little high as he who listens in order to obey/ for the word seemed to fall into profoundness, having come from above him/ somber/ where he is/ always while doing the opposite/ to obey and to begin again with his head leaning far away/ like a child contradictions/ a side opposite to the possible source of the sound/

---

16. Mallarmé, "Notes," *O.c.*, pp. 851, 852–53, 854; "Igitur," *O.c.*, pp. 427, 430, 441–42; "Crise de vers," *O.c.*, p. 363; "La Musique et les lettres," *O.c.*, p. 647; "Le Mystère dans les lettres," *O.c.*, p. 387.
17. Mallarmé, "Le Guignon," *O.c.*, pp. 1410–11, 28–30; "Symphonie littéraire," *O.c.*, p. 265; "Igitur," *O.c.*, pp. 450–51; "Hamlet," *O.c.*, pp. 300, 301; "Conflit," *O.c.*, p. 359; "Solitude," *O.c.*, p. 405.
18. Mallarmé, "L'Azur," *O.c.*, pp. 37–38; "Le Guignon," *O.c.*, pp. 28–30; "Autre Eventail," *O.c.*, p. 58; "Victorieusement fui le suicide beau," *O.c.*, p. 68; "Un Coup de dés," *O.c.*, pp. 466–67, 469, 470, 471.

enclosed—fearful—in the circle of a word."[19] The call from above is that of God, Destiny, or Duty to the poet or to any man below who first intends to obey, then childishly refuses, and, finally, fearfully remains indecisive. There exists a circular movement of determinism and free will where man has the ability to neutralize the call by acting within the exterior circle of fate surrounding him: "his free mind—he no not to the order, which, neutral, calls him and leaves him free." Or he can say Yes or No to this essentially neutral call and thereby take a definite stand. But "yielding to the order hidden in the firm and welcome neutrality of this word/ exaggerates the secret defiance of his act/ defiance/ it will not be he/ one time summoned by this word and knowing that it is/ the power of a well-spoken word."[20] Man hesitates; he is afraid to make a decision and to act. He is also afraid to defy or to rival God. Determinism prevails.

Such a pessimistic observation on the state of the poet and of humanity in a predetermined world, however, was not possible until the very end of Mallarmé's life. Before reaching such a conclusion, he had to endure much anguish and experience much intellectual stimulation. Mallarmé's well-studied crisis of 1866 occurred during the creation of the long poem "Hérodiade" (Herodias), a work that preoccupied the poet throughout his life. The mental peregrinations of the young poet led to his discovery of the world as *le Néant*, as Nothingness, and then as eternal Beauty.[21] They also led to the creation of a purely intellectual heroine

19. Scherer, feuillets 12(A)–13(A), pp. 131–32. See also a discussion of Mallarmé's intended play, *Hamlet et le vent*, where a similar image would have been evoked. Haskell Block, *Mallarmé and the Symbolist Drama* (Detroit, Mich.: Wayne State University Press, 1963), pp. 45–48.

20. Scherer, feuillets 14(A), 15(A).

21. Mallarmé, *Correspondance 1862–1871*, pp. 207, 208, 220, 225; "Hérodiade," *O.c.*, pp. 41–48.

who, denying all exterior reality, existed only by means of self-reflection. As a true narcissist, Hérodiade neither needed nor desired the presence of another. She would be able to surpass ordinary reality and enter into a pure world if she were to regard herself both from a distance in a mirror and from within. Hérodiade represented the youthful Mallarmé. The need for such reflections would undergo numerous transformations throughout his life.

If "Hérodiade" was Mallarmé's feminine heroine, then "Igitur" was her male counterpart.[22] This difficult piece adds more evidence to the image of a young Mallarmé solely concerned with the discovery of an ideal world for himself in art and with the mental torture and fear that he had to endure in order to achieve such a goal. The poet's letters of 1867–1869 continue in the same vein as those of 1866. The narcissist begins progressively to equate himself with the universe and to see himself as one whose pure consciousness will allow him to relive the entire life of humanity. Although still using totally self-sufficient and personal resources, the poet and Igitur have become ideal representatives in which an elite mankind could see itself reflected, if the poet so desired. Such a supreme role frightens Mallarmé, who fears that he may be committing a sin in overstepping his human bounds to rival God. And fear is also present in the form of horror at his necessary death and subsequent disappearance into a void in order to be reborn as an ideal pure being.[23] This is also the story of "Igitur."

Aspects of egotism and narcissism will persist in varying degrees in Mallarmé's own personality. They will also continue to be present in his fictional works. If Igitur has to

22. Mallarmé, *O.c.*, pp. 423–51.
23. Mallarmé, *Correspondance 1862–1871*, pp. 242, 243–44, 246, 247, 249, 259, 270, 301.

submit to the horrible end of death into nothingness in order to be resurrected with pure lucidity in eternity, the poet will make this process essential for every man. In "Igitur" this act is performed by a solitary figure in a personal drama. It is these dramatic qualities, especially, that link such an early work to themes prevalent throughout Mallarmé's life. Almost as a continuation of "Hérodiade," "Igitur" is the theatrical presentation of inner problems; it is the exteriorization of a personal tragedy, played before an elite audience of ancestors within the work. It is a monologue communicated to others. If Igitur is the sole hero of the play, he is also, as Mallarmé himself in his own letters, the representative of mankind. He belongs to a line of poets of genius and is the last hope of his race. If the hissing spectators within the play do not as yet undertake an active role, if they only witness the trials of Igitur's personal self-annihilation and rebirth, their unseen presence at least removes the poet from a purely solitary existence within the framework of the fiction.[24]

Communication of his innermost problems always remained a confusing question for Mallarmé. His admiration for Hamlet was for a hero who, like Igitur, looked only within to effect self-creation.[25] Even in 1895, Mallarmé made the poet a solitary actor in nature, personally creating and discovering his own intimate act, the work of art.[26] And finally, one can see numerous relationships between "Igitur" and "Un Coup de dés." It is evident that similar acts of personal suffering and egotistical creation and similar images of death, rebirth, or nothingness are involved in both works, but the attitude in the later poem will exhibit

24. Mallarmé, *O.c.*, pp. 427, 429 ("Préface"), 433, 439, 451. A distinction is being made here between the public in the work and the reader of "Igitur." Mallarmé never published this work.
25. Mallarmé, "Hamlet," *O.c.*, pp. 1564, 302.
26. Mallarmé, "Bucolique," *O.c.*, pp. 403, 406.

more of a concern for all of mankind. The symbolic hero will be a public of all men.[27] From the solitary self-discoveries of "Hérodiade" and the communication of such discoveries to certain others in "Igitur," Mallarmé will move first to an indirect use of other men for his own self-creation and finally to the mutual participation of both poet and public in his works. Once again, he found that he could not live alone.

If art is communicated to another and if the work endures throughout time, both the artist and the artistic subject attain a form of immortality. This may actually be an original desire on the author's part, or an indirect function of art. While Mallarmé vacillated between desires for fame or anonymity for himself,' he seemed determined to try to assure the glory of his fellow artists, either by their immortal works or by his tributes to them.

One of Mallarmé's most moving attempts to resurrect someone by means of art is his *Pour un tombeau d'Anatole* (For Anatole's Tomb), the fragments written by the poet upon the death of his young son in 1879. Mallarmé hoped to create a work that would serve as a monument for Anatole. The boy would continue to live in this poem and would, therefore, experience a form of glorious salvation.[28] But the distressed father could not bear to complete such a personal work; his son would not receive immortality by artistic means, at least not during his father's lifetime. Anatole had to wait until 1961 when Mallarmé's fragments, unfinished as they were, were finally published. Only then did he continue his existence in the minds of many others.

Such a method of assuring future glory was frequently

27. Mallarmé, "Un Coup de dés," *O.c.*, p. 473; "Igitur-Préface," *O.c.*, pp. 429–31.
28. Stéphane Mallarmé, *Pour un tombeau d'Anatole*, introduction de Jean-Pierre Richard (Paris: Editions du Seuil, 1961). feuillets A8, A46, A53, A117, A145.

used by Mallarmé in his shorter *tombeaux* (tombs or monuments), tributes to certain poets at their deaths, and in his *hommages* to fellow artists.[29] In these poems he stressed the belief that mortal death meant nothing to such men. Through their own works, they would live on forever. The attainment of immediate glory in contemporary society was impossible and to be scorned by these poets, who preferred eternal fame.

One can distinguish between two separate functions of art in an individual's attainment of glory or divine immortality: one's glory may be recognized by others, and either an artist or any member of his public may personally become aware of his own divine qualities. If Mallarmé was uncertain about the first function, the second continued to enforce itself in his mind, especially after 1885. In this role, a work of art becomes an active stimulus, causing a definite reaction on the part of its public. When an individual comes in contact with an art form, certain emotional and intellectual faculties should be aroused.[30] The work reminds the person of something that he has forgotten or of something of which he was not consciously aware. In all reactions to this artistic stimulus, the individual will experience what has been called "the moment of reflexive consciousness," that is, lucid comprehension of the world or of oneself.[31] There will be a change of consciousness or an awakening of consciousness on the part of men, away from dangerous lies, toward the total awareness of eternal truths.

Mallarmé had begun to discover these eternal truths very

29. Mallarmé, "Toast funèbre," *O.c.*, pp. 54–55 (to Gautier); "Le Tombeau d'Edgar Poe," *O.c.*, p. 70; "Le Tombeau de Charles Baudelaire," *O.c.*, p. 70; "Tombeau," *O.c.*, p. 71 (to Verlaine); "Hommage," *O.c.*, p. 71 (to Wagner); "Hommage," *O.c.*, p. 72 (to Puvis de Chavannes).

30. Mallarmé, "L'Action restreinte," *O.c.*, p. 369. Literary action signifies "producing movement on many people. . . ."

31. Jean-Paul Sartre, *Situations, II: Qu'est-ce que la littérature?* (Paris: Gallimard, 1948), pp. 196–97. See also Suzanne Bernard, *Mallarmé et la musique* (Paris: Librairie Nizet, 1959), p. 34; Jean-Pierre Richard, *L'Univers imaginaire de Mallarmé* (Paris: Editions du Seuil, 1961), pp. 267–68, 292.

early in life. It took several more years of maturing before
he was able to decide that these innate qualities were to be
found in all men rather than merely in the elite. The poet
also had to determine whether the proper role of art was to
communicate these truths, and, if so, to whom. Such deci-
sions paralleled Mallarmé's slowly evolving opinion of mankind in general and of the masses in particular.

It has already been noted that Mallarmé's earliest poems
reflect a strong belief in man's proximity to God. An ability
to communicate with a supreme power and the possibility
of resurrection after death imply that man, or at least the
young poet, is innately divine. If man was fashioned in
God's image, he may ultimately return to a primitive
heavenly state. When God disappeared from Mallarmé's
world, he needed to find some substitute. He instinctively
turned to man, although not necessarily to all men.

As early as 1864, upon contact with the poetry of
Théophile Gautier, Mallarmé discovered that he had become one with an inner supreme being and with the universe. When he became confused about the sensations that
he felt after reading this poetry, he wondered whether the
work had actually stimulated certain innate divine qualities
in him.[32] A similar reaction should ultimately occur with all
readers of poetry, but at such an early date he was too
egocentric to concern himself with these possibilities. A
godlike state, as a creator, would be retained in "Igitur,"
but this hero was also an aristocrat, offering his monologue
to an elite audience. Beyond this small public was a larger
one for whom Mallarmé did not yet intend his work. In
1866, however, when he decided to extol divine man poeti-
cally, he seemed to include all of mankind: "*Yes, I know it*,
we are only vain forms of matter, but how sublime to have
invented God and our soul. So sublime, my friend! that I

32. Mallarmé, "Symphonie littéraire," *O.c.*, p. 262.

want to offer to myself this spectacle of matter . . . singing about the Soul and all the similar divine impressions that have piled up in us since the beginning of time. . . ."[33] Although man was mortal on earth, he was sublime for having instinctively created the glorious lies of God and the Soul. The only possible divinity was man himself, the unifier of the universe in his own spirit.

A definite awareness of the instincts of all men occurred in the 1870s when Mallarmé began to suspect that a discrepancy existed between mankind's contemporary and natural posture. The purpose of art would be to describe this public both as it is at present and as it could be ideally in an ideal world. In this way, art would serve as a source of education to humanity. Even if certain eternal and innate truths exist within an individual or in nature, they may be so hidden, or the person may be so blinded by his contemporary state, that he may have to be taught to understand himself and the world correctly. Art as a form of education was advocated by the poet from 1876 until his death: "Bye and bye, if he [Manet] continues to paint long enough, and to educate the public eye . . . then will come the time of peace. As yet it is but one of struggle—a struggle to render those truths in nature which for her are eternal, but which are as yet for the multitude but new."[34] The ideal art form that the poet longed to create should retain a certain didactic quality, that of a lesson that will instruct the people. The public would then be cognizant of its own instinctive genius, which had recognized the true universe, and, in an intellectual sense, the work, with its lessons and discoveries, would cause all men to understand and justify their own existence.[35]

33. Mallarmé, *Correspondance 1862–1871*, pp. 207–8.
34. Mallarmé, "The Impressionists and Edouard Manet," p. 118.
35. Mallarmé, "Solennité," *O.c.*, p. 336; "Hamlet," *O.c.*, p. 1564; "Les Fonds dans le ballet," *O.c.*, p. 308; Bernard, p. 145.

Stemming from a personal experience of self-discovery by the poet, these discoveries made by all men will never lose their religious qualities. For Mallarmé, all functions of an ideal art form possess religious, social, intellectual, and emotional characteristics. Very often these qualities are so fused that they are no longer distinct. The role of art as education, for example, is often referred to as an initiation. The use of this particular word implies the introduction of an individual into some secret and mystical cult. Of course the original initiates, those who are first aware of the truth, are an elite, but eventually all men shall ceremoniously become members. It is the creation of this ceremony which, in Mallarmé's opinion, is the original function of French letters.[36]

While examining the various aspects of Mallarmé's works one begins to notice a particularly dominant theme, a cyclical or circular movement of everything existing in man and in the cosmos. If everything related to humanity can be seen as points along the circumference of a circle, two results are possible: the equality or identity of all things and the belief that there is nothing in this world or beyond that did not exist there initially. Man does not invent any truths about himself or about the world. As a creator of art or as a recipient of artistic communication, he merely rediscovers what, appearing as new to him, is eternally present and has been so since the very beginning of time.[37]

Mallarmé was persistent in his belief that, in order to effect any change of consciousness in man, the art form must

36. Mallarmé, "Deuil," *O.c.*, p. 524; "Richard Wagner: rêverie d'un poète français," *O.c.*, p. 541; "Plaisir sacré," *O.c.*, p. 390.
37. Mallarmé, "Catholicisme," *O.c.*, p. 394. One will discover that at times Mallarmé preferred a cyclical pattern, and at other times he used a circular one. Movement in the two is different, but repetition is essential to both, and, in a cyclical concept, equality exists at least among the crests and separately among the troughs. If, however, everything is seen as part of a circular format, there is implied the problem of no beginning and no end, not even of time. This will prove to be one of the most serious problems for the poet.

stimulate thoughts that will bring the individual back to his ideal origins, presumably before the advent of corrupting societies. No intermediary stage will suffice. Although the poet admired Richard Wagner for giving the German public an opportunity to witness the secrets of its origins as represented in operatic myths, he felt that the composer did not bring his audience back far enough in time.[38] Artistic myths should not describe the origins of any one particular race; they have a duty to present the sources of all mankind. Art must be seen as poems of humanity in its original state.[39] Only in this way can a general public attain true self-awareness.

The purpose of making man aware of his primitive origins and innate qualities is to erase the negative and superficial characteristics of his contemporary state. The ideal man of the future will be reborn through his contact with art. He will be primitive man before his present-day temporary corruption; the future shall exactly reflect the past. Everything that is eternally true of man and the world is circular and, therefore, equal.

Equality implies a total fusion so that a oneness, an identity reigns. In their present state, the multitude of men maintain a duality. Represented as a circle themselves, the masses possess a contemporary exterior and an inner natural soul. They do not see a reflection of their true selves in present-day life or art. They are forced to remain divided in two. If the crowd can see its image in an ideal art form, it will see its true being reflected. As savage beasts in the circus of the modern world, the crowd can jump through the mirror of art and, having returned pacified in a circular motion, can become one with its former self.[40]

38. Mallarmé, "Richard Wagner: rêverie d'un poète français," *O.c.*, p. 544.
39. Mallarmé, "Crise de vers," *O.c.*, p. 367.
40. Scherer, *Le "Livre,"* feuillets 23(A), 25(A).

Retaining a religious terminology, Mallarmé saw this action of man as death and rebirth. Such an image easily coincides with his cyclical and circular concepts of life. If there was any initial cause, in the beginning there was primitive man. Throughout the history of humanity, he has experienced a series of cyclical deaths and resurrections that have paralleled those of time. But these were merely intermediary stages. Now, through art, the ultimate action can be undertaken; after his final death, each man can be reborn ideally as he was originally. The future shall equal the past, and the circle can close. What occurs after this closing, however, was never fully determined by Mallarmé.

Although the poet himself had endured a painful experience of death and resurrection during his creating of "Hérodiade" and "Igitur," the public will generally undergo a pleasurable one, a delightful awakening baptism.[41] It is also possible that Mallarmé began to overlook any torment of death in order to emphasize a positive rebirth for man. This mental experience is, however, referred to as a Passion. An ideal drama would be a presentation of the Passion of Christ, having become that of man and, consequently, "a human assimilation to the tetralogy of the Year."[42] Reflecting once again a cyclical pattern, man, in his death and rebirth, would become part of nature's seasonal cycle. Every year there is repeated the same series of four seasons; each one contains the germ of the following one.[43]

The eternal truths to be rediscovered have always existed, therefore, not only in the universe, but also in man's mind. What has to be stimulated in order to effect a rebirth is an individual's memory, a *déjà vu* illusion of vaguely remembering scenes and events when they are actually ex-

---

41. Mallarmé, "Solennité," *O.c.*, p. 332; "Catholicisme," *O.c.*, p. 391. Possible references to a painful experience for the public occur in: "La Musique et les lettres," *O.c.*, p. 648; "Catholicisme," *O.c.*, p. 393.
42. Mallarmé, "Catholicisme," *O.c.*, p. 393.
43. Scherer, *Le "Livre,"* feuillet 182 (fin).

perienced for the first time. After a short period of time, one believes that this past has always been so. As stated differently, art serves as a catalyst to bring unconscious or subconscious knowledge to a conscious level.[44]

What will mankind consciously rediscover about itself? Mallarmé had already become aware of what he considered to be specific truths about man, and the masses were beginning to experience the same process of self- or collective-discovery without the aid of art. An ideal art form would further precipitate such a consciousness for all men. In his present state man does not truly know himself, that is, his essence or his soul. Initially, art will make him aware that something mysterious and occult inhabits his inner self, still hidden as his unknown intimate secret. Slowly this vague mystery will appear as a splendid golden richness. And finally each individual will realize that he alone "is the source for which he is searching," the origin of all these sensations of religious mystery personally placed within his self-created soul.[45]

Well before Mallarmé's own personal and artistic discoveries, Richard Wagner had already declared that art consisted of "the fulfillment of a longing to know oneself in the likeness of an object of one's love or adoration. . . ."[46] Throughout his prose writings, Mallarmé reiterates the same idea in different variations, clarifying, in addition, that man had originally invented this adored divine object. Man had created God in his own image. For centuries this creation had been displaced into an external heaven. It was

44. Mallarmé, "Richard Wagner: rêverie d'un poète français," *O.c.*, p. 541; "Crayonné au théâtre," *O.c.*, p. 298; "Planches et feuillets," *O.c.*, p. 327.
45. Mallarmé, "Conflit," *O.c.*, p. 355; "De Même," *O.c.*, pp. 397, 395; "Sur l'évolution littéraire," *O.c.*, p. 870.
46. Richard Wagner, *Wagner on Music and Drama: A Compendium of Richard Wagner's Prose Works*, trans. H. Ashton Ellis (New York: E. P. Dutton and Co., Inc., 1964), p. 89.

now time for every man to rediscover "the instinct of heaven in each person" and to recognize "the Divinity, which is always only Oneself. . . ."[47] As a supreme being, man shall enjoy his immortal attributes of genius and purity. And as God, he should be able to affirm his free will, his liberty in the world, and his power over the universe.

For if man is divine, and if he has created himself, then, as an omnipotent god, he has also created or has the ability to create his own universe and is one with it. Is this ideal cosmos a religious one after death and salvation; is it a reality existing only in man's mind; or is it to be an actual world in the future? This redemption shall offer mankind both a horizontal movement toward the future and a vertical rise toward heaven. In addition, salvation will be a nostalgia for the past, for Mallarmé's lost religious youth, and for humanity's lost primitive paradise. But where shall such a universe exist? Mallarmé states that this ideal world will bring the absolute reign of the mind or the spirit over reality,[48] but reality means the contemporary exterior world. The poet also emphasizes the fact that the new awareness on the part of humanity will be that of its "authentic earthly stay," of its "reconquered native life," and of "its joy . . . of perceiving itself as infinitely simple on the earth."[49] But once again, even if such a future world is earthly, it is ideal, a return to Paradise for "this civilized man of Eden,"[50] once only the poet, now all men. One can not yet, nor possibly ever, answer these questions. For now, this ideal world and ideal man will exist in Mallarmé's dreams.

47. Mallarmé, "La Musique et les lettres," *O.c.*, p. 653; "Catholicisme," *O.c.*, p. 391. See also "Crayonné au théâtre," *O.c.*, p. 298; "De Même," *O.c.*, p. 396. Here the public is identified as God and then specifically as Christ.
48. Mallarmé, "Sauvegarde," *O.c.*, p. 417.
49. Mallarmé, "Richard Wagner: rêverie d'un poète français," *O.c.*, p. 545; "Catholicisme," *O.c.*, p. 391; "Bucolique," *O.c.*, p. 405.
50. Mallarmé, "La Musique et les lettres," *O.c.*, p. 646.

It is evident that, from 1869 until his death, Mallarmé increasingly desired to communicate his own discoveries to every man, ideally educated or initiated. In addition, one can easily see another major difference between the elitist "Igitur" and "Un Coup de dés." Instead of a solitary personal drama "played" before an elite audience, the 1897 poem presents the image of the "Master" who is both the poet and humanity. The poem becomes the history of all men, and the "Master" is any man at any time in his life when he is about to act, as well as modern man trying to raise himself above his earthly state.[51] The poet had encountered obstacles during his attempted journey toward resurrection; man will be confronted with identical problems.

It is noteworthy that Mallarmé, after the attainment of his own true self, wanted mankind to be equal to him. He desired that "each person possess the same as I— he only has a right to it." Like "Un Coup de dés," Le "Livre" would be an "Iliad/Odyssey," the epic voyage of humanity.[52]

But this equality would present a problem for the function of art. If all men are divine, then equality is an eternal and innate characteristic among people. If Mallarmé's ideal future world exists only in the poet's mind or in the minds of his readers, the awareness of one's equality with all other men will be individually ascertained but may be at variance with an exterior reality. Like justice, equality is necessarily associated with social phenomena.

Even if a future divine mankind could be reborn, it would not be able to exist unless it were possible to resurrect a new universe, or rather an eternally true universe. Although it was clear to Mallarmé that the contemporary

51. Mallarmé, O.c., pp. 462, 475.
52. Scherer, Le "Livre," feuillets 132(A), 163(A).

world could neither mirror nor equal the ideal, he did not lose hope. He fitted the present period into a general cyclical theory of history and time and contented himself for awhile with the discerning of future characteristics as latent in the present.

Throughout his life, Mallarmé viewed the state of France as temporary, as an intermediary stage before the arrival of an ultimate, divine era. Such an observation implies only present stagnation and an optimistic belief in the progression of time toward the future. This concept of history and time was already evident in "Igitur," where Mallarmé began to refer to "the corridor of time" and where the present became merely an interval in a continual forward movement.[53] By the 1880s and 1890s this period of time was called an actual interregnum. Time was no longer a corridor but a tunnel that one had to traverse in order to arrive at some ideal future. Since the present was a mere waiting room for this future and a receptacle for the past, it had neither importance nor meaning for the poet: "There is no Present, no a present doesn't exist. . . ."[54] Mallarmé never abandoned this theory of time, and *Le "Livre"* offers the image of present inaction where the curtain of time falls for an intermission, awaiting the next act.[55]

Jean-Pierre Richard describes Mallarmé's theory of history and time as a cyclical one. It is a series of deaths and rebirths where there are strong and weak periods of time. Each epoch occurs independently without any transition from the past or to the future. What he defines as discontinuous revolution, therefore, is the abrupt passage from one period to another. Mallarmé himself corroborates this interpretation: "Everything is, in effect, interrupted in his-

---

53. Mallarmé, *O.c.*, pp. 439, 446, 447, 450.
54. Mallarmé, "L'Action restreinte," *O.c.*, p. 372. See also "Le Genre ou des modernes," *O.c.*, p. 314; *Correspondance II*, p. 303.
55. Scherer, feuillet 24(A).

tory, little transfusion. . . ." But he continues: "or the rapport is that the two states will have existed separately,
awaiting a confrontation by the mind."[56] A cyclical series of
deaths and rebirths may constitute historical or literary
time, but a link between past and future can be found in
man's memory, one of the sources for his awakening or
reawakening of consciousness.

The present period of time, therefore, although already
identified as meaningless, does serve as a transition, as the
instant before rebirth. In this period one can find the
genius poet and his work in preparation. Both the poet and
the work are links between the ideal past and future, just
as Igitur was part of a line of past and future elite poets
and, therefore, their present representative. Poets and
works together in the present will guarantee a progression
of time in the movement originally described in "Igitur": in
a forward motion, history and time march on in a series of
cycles or spirals, which ascend and descend like waves.[57]

But each individual cycle consists not only of a crest and
a trough, but also of a total return to its point of origin, in a
circular movement. Paralleling mankind's mental salvation,
each period of time will have its moment of birth and
death. The latter will contain the germination of a succeeding period waiting to be reborn.[58] In this way, one can envision history and time as the forward movement of an infinite series of circles contained within one large circle. This
major circle represents the totality of time where, in an

56. Mallarmé, "Catholicisme," O.c., p. 394; Richard, pp. 264–65.
57. Mallarmé, O.c., pp. 436–37, 449–50. See also "Solitude," O.c., p. 406.
One can see the same cyclical progressive movement of history and time in "Un
Coup de dés," O.c., p. 455. See also Robert Greer Cohn, Mallarmé's "Un Coup
de dés:" an Exegesis (New Haven, Conn.: Yale French Studies Publication, 1949),
pp. 10–11.
58. Mallarmé, "Catholicisme," O.c., p. 392; Scherer, Le "Livre," feuillet
191(A).

ideal future, man and his universe will return not to their historical past but to their primitive ideal source.[59]

A circular image of time implies a never-ending process where everything finishes at the beginning.[60] An ideal art form will, of course, mirror this movement in its descriptions therein, as well as in its structure: "a book neither begins nor ends, unless it pretends to do so."[61] And when the universe and all contained within it are described as circular, the return to a point of origin is inevitable. In contrast to a return to the purity of a white page in art, the world must travel back to its own particular origins in nature. Mallarmé explains the necessity of such a process in "Bucolique" (Bucolic) where every flight beyond returns like a river much in the same way as a round-trip train ride returns the passenger to his point of departure. Nature lies at the beginning of man's existence on a paradisaic earth; it represents the irreducible aspects of life.[62]

The importance of nature is specifically stressed by Mallarmé when he reverts once again to a cyclical description either of history and time or of the ideal universe to be mirrored in art. Despite the equality implied in a circular return to a point of departure, the poet, in his later years, states that each cycle will consist of an "end/ return/ of the same—but almost another."[63] Such a change away from total identity was present in Mallarmé's thoughts from his first observations that death, contemporary mankind, the

59. Mallarmé, "Un Coup de dés," pp. 466–67. The image is one of a whirlpool. See also "Igitur," *O.c.*, p. 442; "Les Fonds dans le ballet," *O.c.*, p. 308; Stéphane Mallarmé, *Propos sur la poésie*, ed. Henri Mondor (Monaco: Éditions du Rocher, 1953), p. 187.

60. Mallarmé, *Correspondance III*, pp. 375–76.

61. Scherer, *Le "Livre*," feuillet 181(A). See also feuillets 93–94(A). The last "un coup de dés" of the poem joins the initial one, thereby forming a circle. Mallarmé, *O.c.*, pp. 457, 477.

62. Mallarmé, *O.c.*, p. 404.

63. Scherer, *Le "Livre*," feuillet 78(B). See also feuillet 129(A) *(suite)*.

contemporary world, and all historical and temporal cycles contained latent signs of the future. Any succeeding period would be born from the temporary present but would retain its own particular qualities.

With nature at the basis of the universe, the prototype of such cyclical change is that of the four seasons and of the four parts of every day. If ideal-primitive man can be a divine creature acting in the elementary cycles of nature, an ideal art form must itself reflect these seasons. The number four becomes essential to this work of art, which must be a multiple tetralogy paralleling a cycle of years.[64] Presumably, each cyclical year or work, containing four seasons or four parts, will then become part of a larger cycle of years or works, perhaps of four years or four tetralogies each. These larger cycles will be infinitely repeated, themselves constituting the infinite circle of life and art. The actual structure and timing of communication of Le *"Livre"* find their origins in the four seasons: each meeting will consist of one orally read volume representing one season.[65]

Each cycle of nature will retain its own properties while preparing those of its successor. For the poet, autumn is the season before death in winter. But if winter signifies the death of nature, it is also the time of creation, when the poet prepares the birth of his artistic offspring, ready to make its entry into the world during spring. From the illustration of personal poetic creation, Mallarmé will transform the eternal return of the seasons into the history of all men and of the universe.[66]

If nature changes her form with each season, every group of four individual cycles will be equal. Once again one sees, in a progression of time, an infinite series of concentric cir-

64. Mallarmé, "Le Genre ou des modernes," *O.c.*, p. 313.
65. Scherer, feuillet 182(fin).
66. Mallarmé, "Sur le printemps," *O.c.*, p. 882; "Bucolique," *O.c.*, p. 404.

cles, each containing the same number of cycles. In this way, Mallarmé could envision a certain equality of time where the past, present, and future would be identical. An ideal art form, reflecting the ideal future, therefore, would reflect all time as unified, that is, as eternal.

As a result of his personal crises of the 1860s, Mallarmé had discovered the existence of what Igitur called the eternal present. For his youthful hero, this timelessness was contained within a single ideal moment, that of midnight, the death of one day and the rebirth of another.[67] The concept of absolute eternal time as that of one instant remained with Mallarmé throughout his life, for "time was annulled . . . he [Villiers] brushed it aside with a gesture. . . ."[68] The ideal minute was the goal of all men.

The time that the poet desired to negate by means of art was historical time, the duration that offered to man only the ugly exterior world and the existence of Chance or Fate. The time that Mallarmé would present to his public was an inner presence of accords and significances, unconcerned with and surpassing exterior historical contingencies.[69] A function of art would be to treat important subjects not historically but intellectually. In this way "the book suppresses time/ ashes/ toward a rapport in noncoexistence."[70] If exterior duration is annulled, and if an ideal future time returns to its origins in divine eternity within man, then the circle is once again closed. But the end of humanity and the universe has not arrived; absolute inner time will continue to exist within every individual who himself not only lives in but also understands the composition of this ideal cosmos.

67. Mallarmé, *O.c.*, pp. 435, 436, 438–40.
68. Mallarmé, "Villiers de l'Isle-Adam," *O.c.*, p. 495.
69. Mallarmé, "Solitude," *O.c.*, p. 405; "Le Mystère dans les lettres," *O.c.*, p. 384.
70. Scherer, *Le "Livre,"* feuillets 55–56(B). See also feuillet 147(A).

A description of absolute reality is a major function of art, for this eternal reality must replace the contemporary impostor. Even in his earliest letters, Mallarmé expressed a desire to create poetry that would represent the entire universe and imitate what existed eternally in nature and in its laws. One of the poet's most often quoted statements reaffirms this wish: "I have always dreamed and attempted something different. . . . What? It is difficult to say: a book. . . . I shall go further; I shall say: the Book, convinced that basically there is only one. . . . The orphic explanation of the World, which is the only duty of the poet and the supreme literary game."[71] This ideal book was to be a re-creation not only of the eternal earth but also of the entire cosmos as it is inscribed in heaven.[72] Its public would receive, therefore, an explanation and a justification not only of its own existence, but also of the ideal universe in which it would now live.

The use of the word *ideal* to describe this absolute reality in art has provoked many critical discussions in attempts to label the poet and his world as Platonic, idealistic, or escapist. Mallarmé himself consistently referred to the poetic re-creation of the cosmos as ideal, superior, and beyond, always detached from the historical contemporary world. But the primary importance of this reality would be its permanence as "the Opening of a Jubilee . . . in order to conclude a cycle of History . . ."[73] or, rather, to announce the end of historical duration and the beginning of an absolute totality and unity. With its goal of retransforming the complexity and multiplicity of the modern universe back into its original unity, the total structure reproduced in art

71. Mallarmé, *Correspondance II*, p. 301. See also *Correspondance 1862–1871*, pp. 222, 259, 279.
72. Mallarmé, "Richard Wagner: rêverie d'un poète français," *O.c.*, pp. 544–45; "Crayonné au théâtre," *O.c.*, p. 294.
73. Mallarmé, "Solennité," *O.c.*, p. 336.

would be one of "a thousand rythmic images" but "in its synthesis and illuminating all."[74]

In order to rediscover what can be called a universal analogy, the poet must first clarify certain relationships already existing in the world but which may seem obscure to most men. What Mallarmé wanted his ideal art form to reflect was "the totality of rapports existing in everything."[75] But a mirror of the totality of these relations was not sufficient to explain cosmic unity. A system of analogies must become a series of equations where the secret identities and equalities of the world can be placed on a circle in the name of one central purity.[76] Along this circle, all points become equal to one another and, thus, equal to a single point, or, as in "Un Cóup de dés," equal to a single, unique number, the summation of the cosmos.[77]

It is ironic that a poet as complex as Mallarmé should have had such a simple goal. With highly intellectual thoughts and in an obscurely difficult poetic manner, he merely desired to "simplify the world,"[78] to make men aware of the simple perfection that once glowed in paradise and that once again shall reign.

The hope for a return to the simplicity of paradise reminds one that Mallarmé's ideal universe may easily be interpreted in a religious manner. Whether or not the poet was trying to return to his religious dreams of childhood, he did believe, even in his later life, that nothing could be considered as exclusively secular.[79] Man's new awareness of

74. Mallarmé, "Sur Poe," *O.c.*, p. 872.
75. Mallarmé, "Crise de vers," *O.c.*, p. 368. See also "La Musique et les lettres," *O.c.*, pp. 647–48; "Le Livre, instrument spirituel," *O.c.*, p. 378; "Sur l'évolution littéraire," *O.c.*, p. 871.
76. Mallarmé, *Propos sur la poésie*, pp. 74, 182–83; Scherer, *Le "Livre,"* feuillets 6(A), 40(A)–40(A) (*suite*), 41(A), 88(A), 89(A), 91(A), 92(A), 104(A)–6(A), 147(A), 182.
77. Mallarmé, *O.c.*, pp. 462–63, 473, 477.
78. Mallarmé, "La Musique et les lettres," *O.c.*, p. 647.
79. Mallarmé, "De Même," *O.c.*, p. 397.

his divinity will transform him into the pure being who lived in a Garden of Eden prior to the appearance of original sin. The ideal paradise mirrored in art can be seen as a spiritual one where the tetralogy of the seasonal cycle may be interpreted as a religious or pagan ritual deifying nature, while representing the Easter Passion of Christ or of man.[80] In such an interpretation, the poet becomes the creator, or re-creator, of Genesis.

If the poet rivals or represents God, then the art form must be a bible or a religion. Even before any religion of poetry had been advocated by Mallarmé, there already existed a religion of music in the form of Wagnerian opera. By 1885 the poet had recognized the religious qualities of this art form; he was jealous of it, desired to rival it, and to surpass it in these powers.

According to his daughter, Geneviève, Mallarmé, before leaving every Sunday afternoon for a performance of the Concerts Lamoureux, would tell his wife and daughter: " 'I am going to Vespers.' "[81] He saw in these concerts not only a powerful art form but a sacred one, the modern form of religion. Richard Wagner had specifically intended his music to have such a religious function, and Mallarmé was painfully aware of this decision. In the poet's "Rêverie" (Revery), Wagner's music is described as "almost a Cult!" and as a means for discovering "ultimate salvation"; it "exalts fervent men" in "the finished voyage of humanity toward an Ideal" where one can taste sweet repose "in your Temple, half-way up the sacred mountain. . . ."[82] Throughout his life Mallarmé was to realize that music, in its self-

---

80. Mallarmé, "Catholicisme," *O.c.*, p. 393. See also Robert Greer Cohn, *L'Oeuvre de Mallarmé "Un Coup de dés,"* trans. René Arnaud (Paris: Librairie Les Lettres, 1951), p. 267, where the critic interprets the four stars at opposite angles of the constellation of Big Bear in "Un Coup de dés" as representing a cross and, therefore, the crucifixion.

81. Henri Mondor, *Vie de Mallarmé* (Paris: Gallimard, 1941), p. 458.

82. Mallarmé, *O.c.*, pp. 541, 546.

pronouncement as a humanly religious cult, offered mankind a needed baptism and resurrection from daily life.
Mallarmé had always believed that all art forms were in-
trinsically religious. His earliest letters and works describe
art in general and poetry in particular as sacred and
spiritual. Whether it be as an ideal theatrical presentation,
poetry, a book, or some ideal art form encompassing all the
arts, "let us penetrate the church with art."[83] Art, as the
basis and future for humanity's salvation, shall eventually
become the true religious cult, replacing all organized religions, all churches, and all cloisters.[84]
  Certain beauties of former religions shall be retained as
part of this new aesthetic cult. Mallarmé's love of the
Catholic ritualistic mass caused him to dream of his new religion as a similar ceremony, as a future festival with its
pomp and some of its liturgy. The written or permanent
form of this new liturgy shall be considered by all as the
new Evangels: "there would be only one—in the
world . . . bible as all nations simulate it."[85]
  Despite the spiritual nature of this future artistic religion,
it will play an essential role on earth and in society.
Mallarmé defines his ideal goal as "the staging of the state
religion," where every man will learn the necessity of "de-
votion to his Homeland" and "the authenticity of the words
and triumphal light of Homeland or of Honor, of Peace."[86]
The state religions described in "La Cour" and
"Sauvegarde" (Safeguard) are predominantly social and
literary ones, where the poet will evoke "the sovereign de-

83. Mallarmé, "De Même," *O.c.*, p. 395. See also *Correspondance 1862–1871*,
pp. 36, 250, 325; "Hérésies artistiques: l'art pour tous," *O.c.*, p. 257; "Symphonie
littéraire," *O.c.*, pp. 261–62, 264; *Correspondance II*, pp. 193, 258, 260.
  84. Mallarmé, "Sur le théâtre," *O.c.*, p. 875; "Solennité," *O.c.*, p. 335; "Conflit," *O.c.*, p. 359; "Catholicisme," *O.c.*, pp. 391, 392; "Sauvegarde," *O.c.*, p. 417;
Scherer, *Le "Livre,"* feuillets 21(A), 151(B).
  85. Mallarmé, "Crise de vers," *O.c.*, p. 367. See also "Notes sur le théâtre,"
O.c., p. 343; "De Même," *O.c.*, p. 396; "Catholicisme," *O.c.*, pp. 392, 394.
  86. Mallarmé, "De Même," *O.c.*, pp. 396, 397; "Catholicisme," *O.c.*, p. 394.

velopment of the forces of the country . . . or a spiritual
coup d'état. . . ."[87]

Although Mallarmé did not observe, or at least did not
mention, any parallels between art and society until 1874,
he consistently emphasized such rapports in his more socially aware prose writings of the 1890s. As a direct reflection of society, or rather as a direct refinement, art possesses not only its social counterpart, but also a duty to be socially concerned. Without this orientation, any advance-
ment in art is meaningless.[88]

The social function of art, for Mallarmé, will be its offering to humanity a social replacement for contemporary reality. As a substitute for the basic faults of governments, social classes, and industry, art, or literature in particular,
will exist above all things. It will provide mankind with a
doctrine, the needed forces in life, and a country as the
true city of man, "a beautiful homeland/ a divine urn/ the
earth."[89]

In this future social utopia where each man is divine, art
will reign supreme. It will rule politically, financially, and
religiously, if these terms can have any meaning when they
are superseded by a sole omnipotent power. If there is only
one Bible in this world, there will be only one law, the incorruptible law of literature.[90] In the 1895 prose article
"Sauvegarde," Mallarmé describes this law as being prom-
ulgated and enforced by an elite governing body, the In-
stitut de France. Within this group would be an even more
aristocratic institution, the Académie française, to decide
upon special or rare acts.[91] For Mallarmé, literary men

87. Mallarmé, "Sauvegarde," *O.c.*, p. 420. See also "La Cour," *O.c.*, p. 416.
88. Mallarmé, "Catholicisme," *O.c.*, p. 394; "Sur l'évolution littéraire," *O.c.*,
p. 866; "Solitude," *O.c.*, pp. 408–9. "La Musique et les lettres," *O.c.*, p. 656.
89. Scherer, *Le "Livre,"* feuillet 16(A). See also Mallarmé, "La Musique et les
lettres," *O.c.*, pp. 646–47, 649.
90. Mallarmé, "Le Genre ou des modernes," *O.c.*, p. 313.
91. Mallarmé, *O.c.*, p. 417.

were above all petty political problems and as incorruptible as the supreme law that they were representing. The poet's ideal government would obliterate bourgeois personal ambitions and interests. If art is to be a mirror of the ideal cosmos, and if society is to be based upon this art form, then "a government will reflect . . . that of the universe: which is monarchical [with one supreme God], anarchical [with all men as gods]. . . ."[92] In one sense, art and its creators would be king; and yet a form of peaceful anarchy would reign because each citizen of this ideal society would also be a monarch, a divine head of state.

Mallarmé was steadfast in his belief that justice should be a goal of social utopia, but his approach toward its attainment is highly questionable. In the contemporary world, the only equality that reigns is that evident in a work of art when an entire public may freely participate. Justice in contemporary art is, however, an indication of the arrival of a glorious future.[93]

The justice achieved through artistic means is an inner one, an awareness by each man of his divine equality with all others. An exterior just and social equality is another matter. Mallarmé's solution to this problem is obscurely explained in "La Cour." Despite his strong desires to create an art form that would reach all men equally to make them conscious of their innate beings, the poet still insisted upon the existence of social classes as indispensable to a national equilibrium and as a force against modern democracy.[94] It is possible that this form of society would temporarily remain during an initial indoctrination period, until all men could come into contact with the ideal art form that would change their lives and political state. From then on, aware-

92. Mallarmé, "La Musique et les lettres," *O.c.*, p. 656.
93. Mallarmé, "Richard Wagner: rêverie d'un poète français," *O.c.*, p. 545; "L'Action restreinte," *O.c.*, p. 372; "La Cour," *O.c.*, p. 415.
94. Mallarmé, *O.c.*, p. 415.

ness of inner equality would erase the importance of persisting monetary distinctions among men of different classes. Equal intelligence would be instinctive; formal education and, therefore, a correct interpretation of the ideal art form did not concern Mallarmé in this article.

Even in social utopia, a certain form of social class would remain. Just a few people would actually alter their social status. But despite the existence of these class distinctions, everyone would have the opportunity to become part of an elite when he became the auditor of the ideal art form. The number of this elite must remain constant at about a thousand because there can be no "temple" large enough to hold all men at one time while they learn the eternal truths taught by art. But the composition of this elite will change. In this way, there can be movement among classes; justice and equality can prevail. After having been an official member of the elite at a "concert" of the state art form, each individual can return to his original social class with the knowledge that he is divine. The new state social religion of art will, in one sense, replace the present ugly egalitarian system and, in another sense, will raise it to a higher level of true equality.[95]

According to Ernst Fischer, "Art is necessary in order that man should be able to recognize and change the world."[96] Mallarmé would have agreed with such a definition of a social function for art because, for him, that art, or the poet as its representative, is "the only idea in whose name social changes, revolution, are accomplished. . . ."[97] But the poet never explained exactly how art or man could effect these social changes, and the equality in his social utopias of "Sauvegarde" and "La Cour" is questionable.

95. *Ibid.*, pp. 415–16.
96. Ernst Fischer, *The Necessity of Art: A Marxist Approach*, trans. Anna Bostock (Middlesex, England: Penguin Books Ltd., 1963), p. 14.
97. Mallarmé, "La Cour," *O.c.*, p. 414.

Mallarmé saw art as the initial stimulus toward an ideal mankind and society, but, in some miraculous way, his art form would simultaneously reflect an innately equal humanity in an eternally just world. His public would not have to wait for an ideal society after a successful social revolution in order to see its true or new self. Despite his later statements that literature would cause men to "put the great machine into action," the poet never described his machine, nor clarified his means to set it in motion.[98] His circle of art and society naively remained at the departure point, reflecting the ideal end.

Despite this confused definition of art as social revolution, what should be noted is Mallarmé's belief that art constituted not only action, but the only possible action in this world. If ideal reality is to replace the ugly reality of existing social conditions, the means to achieve such an absolute world must be similarly aesthetic and social. Any violent action will never suffice.

Mallarmé did admire physical action if it had a useful purpose. His almost religious awe of the simple labors of the working class made him ashamed of his own physically lazy approach to life. But the antidote to his past laziness would never be found in direct physical revolution; the only true action could be limited or restrained. In chapter 1, "Petit Air (Guerrier)" was examined as an anti-militaristic poem. Now, seen specifically as an epigraph to the prose article "L'Action restreinte," it becomes not only an anti-bourgeois statement, but also a point of reference against which the succeeding article must be contrasted.[99]

Not living in isolation from the contemporary world, the poet was well aware of a need to act in order to effect any

98. Scherer, *Le "Livre,"* feuillet 30(A).
99. Mallarmé, *O.c.*, pp. 66–67, 369–73. See also "Confrontation," *O.c.*, p. 409.

changes in society. For him, however, the occupation of creating with words, literary action, was the only true one.[100] Until the end of his life, he insisted that "the act chosen by me has been writing."[101] His profession was far superior to that of a bourgeois soldier or politician.

Literary action was to replace not only military and political action but also all anarchistic methods. Mallarmé's attitude toward the French anarchists has already been described as sympathetic but pessimistic. Any contemporary social revolution is not the proper one; true revolution, literary, must await the future when the people are ready to accept social change.[102] But Mallarmé understood those who desired to hasten the arrival of such a time. He was greatly influenced by the anarchists and continuously used their revolutionary terminology to describe his own form of action.

After having heard about a bombing attempt by Edouard Vaillant, Mallarmé was quoted as having said: " 'I know of no other bomb but a book.' " His opinion of the 1894 incarceration of his friend Fénéon for anarchist leanings was one more of surprise than of pity: " 'Certainly there weren't any better detonators for Fénéon than his articles. And I do not think that one can use a more effective weapon than literature.' "[103] Literary action is again described as a bomb in Le "Livre," and, in "La Musique et les lettres," it becomes "the presentation, as an explosive, of a very pure concept to society."[104] A more frequently used term evokes

---

100. Mallarmé, "L'Action restreinte," O.c., pp. 371, 369. In a typically Mallarméan style, the poet emphasizes the importance of literature as action by placing the word *écrire* (to write) alone at the top of p. 370.
101. Mallarmé, "Sur l'idéal à vingt ans," O.c., p. 883. See also "Notes," O.c., p. 852; "Igitur," O.c., pp. 435, 441, 442, 451; "Solennité," O.c., pp. 334–35; "Un Coup de dés," O.c., pp. 457, 459, 464, 474–75, 477. Mallarmé consistently uses words like *act, gesture, striking,* and *blow* to stress this idea of literature.
102. Mallarmé, "La Cour," O.c., pp. 415–16.
103. Mondor, *Vie de Mallarmé*, pp. 670, 683.
104. Scherer, feuillet 168; Mallarmé, O.c., p. 651.

a similar image of explosion, but one implying less of a danger of total destruction: throughout his later works, Mallarmé often calls the literary act fireworks.[105] The underlying meanings of such a word are, of course, quite evident. Art is an artifice, fiction, or an imitation of reality. It is also an explosion of multi-colored lights, bringing the awareness of truth to man in the form of his pure lucidity. Art is the excitement of life as evidenced in the ceremonial celebration of joy exploding in the sky. And art is fire, the purifier of all things and a destroyer of the world.

The concept of literary action as fire implies, therefore, the problem of total destruction in order to effect a rebirth. It is the eternal condition of the Apocalypse and an essential tenet of anarchy. Although Mallarmé did desire the eventual destruction of the contemporary world and of modern man, he tried to emphasize the positive qualities of his ideal humanity and reality without mentioning any negative means to achieve this goal. As interpreted by Robert Greer Cohn, pages 8 and 10 of "Un Coup de dés," however, present doubts as to the efficacy of such an apocalyptic role for literature. After the destruction of the world, three negative consequences could follow. The ideal reality that the poet has been intending for mankind may become the negative *néant* originally discovered in "Igitur." Second, man's rise to divine heights may last only as long as the poet lives; with the latter's mortal death, mankind could fall back into its former contemporary state. And last, once an apocalypse occurs, the poet may fail in his attempt to re-create an eternal reality, or his public may fail to understand the truth. Nothing would remain except an empty place as a reminder of a useless act. But Mallarmé persisted

---

105. Mallarmé, "Villiers de l'Isle-Adam," *O.c.*, p. 499; "La Musique et les lettres," *O.c.*, pp. 652, 655; Scherer, *Le "Livre*," feuillets 72(B), 80(B), 81(B), 93(A), 168, 169(A) *(suite)*.

in his optimism even in this particular poem. Page 11 will reflect the hope of a new rebirth after total destruction. Literary action will be effective as a positive force.[106]

But is it true action? It is evident that all of Mallarmé's bombs and fireworks must be considered as metaphorical. Art can only figuratively explode. But one can also definitely state that, if an art form causes its public to act and thereby to effect some social change, that work of art does constitute at least indirect action.

But Mallarmé was never sure of how to begin such a movement, nor did he proceed directly from his social ideas to their practical fulfillment. The poet's only form of action remained within, much in the same way as the crowd with its sleeping exterior and active dreams. Thought was Mallarmé's revolution: "Every Thought emits a Throw of the dice."[107]

Can thought be considered as action? Once again the thought must produce an actual work of art which will in turn stimulate men to act. Good intentions are not sufficient. What is essential is the goal that one discerns and the degree to which this goal is achieved. Maurice Blanchot describes Mallarmé's limited action as that of pointing out the differences between his form of action and direct practical revolution and of emphasizing the conflict between the present period and an ideal literary reality.[108] Despite the truth of this interpretation, it is obvious that Mallarmé could discover neither within himself nor in his literary creations the means to link these two forms of action and these two worlds. Even if he sometimes saw a bridge be-

---

106. Mallarmé, *O.c.*, pp. 474–75, 476–77; Cohn, *L'Oeuvre de Mallarmé*, pp. 293–346, 371–86.
107. Mallarmé, *O.c.*, p. 477. See also Scherer, *Le "Livre,"* feuillets 20(A), 23(A).
108. Maurice Blanchot, "Recherches: ecce liber," *La Nouvelle nouvelle revue française* 5 (octobre-décembre 1957): 738–40.

tween the two, he hesitated to cross it. He remained in the immobile position of a dancer with one arm raised and the other arm lowered. Like man caught in the circle of determinism, he listened to a word being spoken; he thought; he did not move.[109]

Mallarmé's difficulty in creating action stemmed from his inability to relate an ideal reality that could exist perfectly within the mind to contemporary social life or to a miraculously attained social utopia. All of the functions of art examined herein result in the same problem for the poet. Do they all merely constitute different variations of escapism?

One must first distinguish among three general functions of art. A work of art may offer to its public a total escape from daily life in the form of pure fantasy, amusement, or emotional distraction. It has been seen that Mallarmé did love art of this type and recognized the importance of its role for many men in contemporary society; however, he also questioned the worthiness of art when used for these purposes. Such pure escapism can be considered as cheap entertainment, treating men as children, but not allowing them to better themselves.[110]

It is possible that a work of art as a means of personal self-discovery, of an awakening of consciousness of ideal mankind, of religion, or of the discovery and establishment of some absolute world of perfection could be considered as another form of escapism. Such an interpretation is related to the larger question of religion, philosophy, and metaphysics either as an escape from life, a means to cope with life, or a means to understand oneself and life in a fuller sense. It is evident that all of these inquiries originate in men who are born as social beings. But Mallarmé con-

109. Scherer, Le "Livre," feuillets 19(A), 12(A)–15(A).
110. Mallarmé, "Un Spectacle interrompu," O.c., p. 277; "La Déclaration foraine," O.c., p. 280; "Planches et feuillets," O.c., pp. 325, 327.

tinued these intellectual pursuits in search of a viable alternative to daily life. Does such a reaction against reality constitute a form of escapism? Although in Mallarmé's case an affirmative answer may be appropriate, this is a general question that can be answered only by one's individual judgment, or perhaps there is no answer at all.

Two facets of Mallarmé's beliefs on the role that art must play in the world can be treated as a third general function. It is evident that the initial reaction to an art form must occur in the mind and that the permanence of any discovery will depend upon man's allegiance to these thoughts. But for Mallarmé, an external social utopia must also exist on the earth as a direct reflection of man's inner world. In order to effect both this interior and exterior reality, art must serve as the initial catalyst. This third role of art is neither emotionally nor intellectually escapist: it is social; it is action. But Mallarmé's socially active literature would not change the world; it would in some unknown way destroy it in order to replace it with a better universe. If a totally practical function of art must be related only to the existence of contemporary reality, then the poet's desired works would not only be an evasion from this world; they would be a naive evasion.

If Mallarmé were to attempt to write or to rewrite the unique work of the world, his poetic duty would stem from the fact that "the world is made so as to end in a beautiful book."[111] Using his gift of sarcastic exaggeration to warn anti-literary men of literature's future dominant role, Mallarmé was able to declare that "literature exists, and, if you insist, it exists alone, to the exclusion of all else."[112] And yet, the poet was not exaggerating as much as one might believe. As a youth and for him alone, art did consti-

---

111. Mallarmé, "Sur l'évolution littéraire," *O.c.*, p. 872. See also "L'Action restreinte," *O.c.*, p. 378.
112. Mallarmé, "La Musique et les lettres," *O.c.*, p. 646.

tute life and everything within that life. With this belief in the omnipotence of art, Mallarmé would encounter a serious problem: if poetry, literature, or art equal life, they have no need for an outside reality. They contain within themselves their own proof of existence and can not be compared to an exterior world.

In addition to seeing Mallarmé's ideal world as a circle, one can also fit his unique work into a circular framework, reflecting this absolute reality. In order to be pure, this circle must be complete, and thus closed. A closed circle will allow no intrusion from the outside; to someone standing beyond its circumference it appears as a self-sufficient whole. The ultimate art form represents the unique, true world; therefore, it is equal only to itself: "the identity of this volume with itself."[113]

Self-proof must be found within the circle. Stated more accurately, the ideal work contains a reciprocity of proofs, a confrontation of terms and of successive identities that reflect the proof of its totality. If everything in the ideal world is first related and then equal, the various parts of the ideal art form must follow a similar pattern. The ultimate unity of the work is revealed by means of these comparisons. Each part of Le *"Livre"* must equal every other part and must equal the whole, or at least represent the "rhythm of the total—according to its fraction."[114] In this manner, each individual section can be self-sufficient and self-proving, while aiding in the self-proof of a totality. The entire work, like the entire ideal universe, can be reduced to a unique number.[115]

If the ultimate work in absolute reality has no comparison

113. Scherer, Le *"Livre,"* feuillet 192(A). See also feuillets 93–94(A), 96, 112(A), 200(A)–201(A). Mallarmé, "La Musique et les lettres," *O.c.*, p. 648.
114. Scherer, Le *"Livre,"* feuillets 171–72(A). See also feuillets 105(A), 173(A), 193(A); Poulet, pp. 343–44.
115. Jean-Pierre Richard describes this process of self-identification as one leading toward self-annulment. Mallarmé himself makes two references to such a possibility. Richard, pp. 573–74; Scherer, Le *"Livre,"* feuillets 100(A), 110(A).

with the outside world, it must similarly disregard mankind. From his earliest writings, Mallarmé had expressed the feeling that the work of art is self-creating and self-continuing.[116] But art that excludes man would imply that the world mirrored in this art also exists alone. With such an interpretation, Mallarmé would have to encounter two insurmountable problems: the roles of the poet and his public. Despite its existence in conjunction with ideal reality, the work of art needs an initial cause, or a re-creator; it needs the artist. And despite Mallarmé's observation that a work "does not require the approach of a reader/ . . . it takes place alone. . . ," he realized not only that an unknown masterpiece, communicated to no one, was useless, but also that he desperately needed the aid of other men in order to create his ideal work.[117]

A possible solution to these problems produces even more difficulties. Instead of placing all men, as well as himself, outside the circle of art, the poet could discover that humanity remains within and becomes a necessary part of this world. Such an interpretation is correct if one considers every man as one with an ideal universe. Once again, man can be seen listening to a call surrounding him. In this way, the source of the word being spoken can be found in Fate, Duty, God, or Art.[118] Does this ideal work of art constitute a mere description of absolute reality, or does it equal this reality; can it be considered as a means toward an ideal, or as this end itself; is the Book God or His written laws in the Bible? If an art form becomes a "Cult, a law—everything stops at the written work, returns to it," it

---

116. Mallarmé, *Correspondance III*, pp. 285, 316; "Symphonie littéraire," *O.c.*, p. 262; *Propos sur la poésie*, pp. 225–26.
117. Mallarmé, "L'Action restreinte," *O.c.*, p. 372. See also "Bucolique," *O.c.*, p. 401. Jean-Pierre Richard interprets Mallarmé's self-sufficient work as needing no exterior public once it is created. The poet himself never advocated such a position. Richard, pp. 569–71.
118. Scherer, *Le "Livre,"* feuillets 12(A)–15(A).

is the beginning and end of all things. If the work brings man the absolute reign of his inner soul as mirrored in "its mark, books," then art serves as a means toward a given goal.[119]

The inescapable answer to this question lies in the role and power of language, Mallarmé's choice of an artistic mode. Although he desired the word to equal ideal reality, to equal the essence of the Verb,[120] he was constantly reminded that his only means of expression was human language. A word is a sign; it can name, but it can neither create nor equal a unique, self-sufficient, aesthetic, and social reality.

119. Mallarmé, "Sauvegarde," *O.c.*, p. 417.
120. Mallarmé, "Notes," *O.c.*, pp. 853–54. *Propos sur la poésie*, pp. 181, 213–14.

3
The Ideal Art Form: Its Form

If Mallarmé were to present mankind with the possibilities of a new existence by means of art, he would first have to create or re-create a sufficiently powerful art form. A total preoccupation with such a kind of art dominated the poet's thoughts and much of his time from 1866 until his death. There is ample proof of this involvement in Mallarmé's writings and in the literary memoirs of his disciples, who often heard him refer to the great secret project that would encompass the supreme thought of universal meditation. They also saw some evidence of its progress in piles of notes on his desk.[1]

The first references to the fact that Mallarmé had begun working, or at least thinking, about a great ideal work appear in his letters of 1866. Faithful to a belief that a contemporary poet must work in secret while preparing his future masterpiece, Mallarmé first described his dream and

---

1. Henri de Régnier, *Figures et caractères* (Paris: Mercure de France, 1911), p. 133; Paul Valéry, *Ecrits divers sur Stéphane Mallarmé* (Paris: Librairie Gallimard, 1950), p. 14.

determination as personal, requiring twenty years to complete. By the following year, he erroneously thought that the work would be complete in ten years; however, in the early 1880s, still envisioning several more years of work, the poet then hoped to publish the first volume within a year.[2]

Mallarmé's famed autobiographical letter of 1885 includes a general definition of the scope of his desired work, but the poet also admits that although he may not be able to complete the entire work, he can at least indicate its totality by means of one finished section. He would then prove that such a book does exist and that he was aware of what he personally could not accomplish.[3] Emilie Noulet has interpreted these statements as a total renouncement by Mallarmé of his project, as mere speculations on organization, or as mere propaganda, rather than as any continued progress on its composition.[4] Although one can not know for certain the poet's deepest thoughts regarding the future of his great work, one can accurately state that his original desires never ceased. Whether creating a complete or fragmented work, his energies from 1885 until his death involved him in the investigation of all forms of art and religion, as well as the means of their communication to a public. The information to be learned from this research was to aid him in the creation of his own art form. He had already discovered the content of his unique work; now he had to decide how to explain it to others.

Despite signs of disillusionment in his 1885 letter, Mallarmé continued to plan his masterpiece, although

2. Stéphane Mallarmé, *Correspondance 1862–1871*, ed. Henri Mondor (Paris: Gallimard, 1959), pp. 222, 225, 243; Stéphane Mallarmé, *Correspondance II 1871–1885*, ed. Henri Mondor et Lloyd James Austin (Paris: Gallimard, 1965), pp. 220, 232.
3. Mallarmé, *Correspondance II*, p. 302.
4. Emilie Noulet, *Suites: Mallarmé Rimbaud Valéry* (Paris: A. G. Nizet, 1964), pp. 60–63.

teaching duties occupied much of his time. As of 1885, the date of his first desired public announcement, he hoped to spend the rest of his life on this project;[5] nevertheless, he had to wait until he was finally retired in 1894 in order to devote all of his time to the preparation of his secret. Even when the ideal art form was complete, its communication to a public would continue to involve the poet for an additional five to seven years.[6]

The dream and composition of this great work occupied most of Mallarmé's life, and he remained faithful to his early goals. The prose writings that compose most of his works after 1885 attest to his determination toward one unique subject of thought that would explain his doctrine.[7]

The specific identification of this desired work, as related to the known writings of the poet, will probably never be determined. Mallarmé himself usually referred to his project in general terms. His first interest in this lifelong endeavor was defined as an interest in all the literary works that compose the poetic existence of a man. And despite the early admission that his work was to be "The Work, the Great Work,"[8] this initial definition corroborates the belief that all of his writings, especially his poetry, are marked in some way with the essence of his unique goal.

As of 1876, Mallarmé was preoccupied with a great dramatic endeavor. Considering his deep interest in contemporary and future theater and his inquiries into the possibilities of a dramatic presentation for his own ideal art

5. Stéphane Mallarmé, *Correspondance III 1886–1889*, ed. Henri Mondor et Lloyd James Austin (Paris: Gallimard, 1969), pp. 216, 69.
6. Jacques Scherer, *Le "Livre" de Mallarmé: premières recherches sur des documents inédits* (Paris: Gallimard, 1957), feuillets 50(B), 112(A), 118(A), 129(A), 138 (*suite*), 143 (*suite*), 144(A), 174(A).
7. Stéphane Mallarmé, *Oeuvres complètes* (Paris: Editions Gallimard, "Bibliothèque de la Pléiade," 1945), p. 1538. *Correspondance III*, pp. 291, 313, 355; Scherer, feuillet 16(A).
8. Mallarmé, *Correspondance 1862–1871*, pp. 244, 226.

form, it is conceivable that, at least during this period of his life, the Great Work was to be "a vast popular melodrama."[9]

Pour un tombeau d'Anatole can also be linked, on an extremely personal level, to Mallarmé's dream of a unique work. In this tribute to his son, the poet explains that his "heart beat for projects that were too grandiose—and having failed/ it was necessary—inheriting from that marvelous filial intelligence, making it relive—to construct with his . . . lucidity—this work—too vast for me."[10] Mallarmé had hoped that Anatole would one day continue his task. Now that his son was dead, he would have to work alone. In addition to this specific reference to a great masterpiece, the *tombeau* itself is called a work, both a personal description of the death and desired immortality of his son and an orphic explanation of the destiny of mankind.[11]

One can relate at least four other works by Mallarmé to his ideal goal. The consistent importance of "Hérodiade" and the recent publication of *Les Noces d'Hérodiade: mystère* (The Marriage of Herodias: A Mystery) lend evidence to the possibility that this poem was to be an opening segment of the larger work. The similarities between "Hérodiade" and "Igitur" and between this second work and "Un Coup de dés" lead one to believe that "Igitur" was also in some way a preparatory exercise for Le *"Livre"*.[12]

But most critical controversy exists in regard to the choice of either "Un Coup de dés" or Le *"Livre"* as the true representative of Mallarmé's dream. Whether or not the

9. Mallarmé, *Correspondance II*, p. 108. See also pp. 101, 103, 105, 151, 154, 159.
10. Stéphane Mallarmé, *Pour un tombeau d'Anatole*, introduction de Jean-Pierre Richard (Paris: Editions du Seuil, 1961), feuillets 13–14.
11. *Ibid.*, feuillets 66–67.
12. Mallarmé, *O.c.*, pp. 41–49, 423–51, 455–77; Stéphane Mallarmé, *Les Noces d'Hérodiade: mystère*, introduction de Gardner Davies (Paris: Gallimard, 1959), pp. 18–19.

1897 poem was intended as the closest approximation to an ideal work, as a fragment of an entire future masterpiece, or as a first attempt in a shortened form of The Great Work, and whether or not the unbound pages of the poet's discovered "Livre" are serious calculations toward the fulfillment of a dream or mere games during hours of amusement, are questions of secondary importance.[13] One can accept Le "Livre" for exactly what it is, an unorganized compendium of fragmentary notes. Mallarmé was persistent in his desire to discover the particular art form that would create an ideal reality. All of these works are related to his dreams because his entire life was directed toward this sole end.

If an ideal art form were to be unique, in some way it would have to encompass all of the arts, either as a synthesis of the whole, or by borrowing from all art forms. In order to be successful in his task, a poet would first have to understand these complementary or rival forms of art. Mallarmé spent most of his life in this attempt.

The poet's interest, love, and jealousy of all means of artistic communication have been well studied. His knowledgeable interest in the painting of his day, stemming from his friendship with some of the most important contemporary artists, was particularly fervent.[14] Well before his move to Paris and his subsequent frequent contact with contem-

13. A. R. Chisholm, *Mallarmé's Grand Oeuvre* (Manchester, England: Manchester University Press, 1962), pp. 3–5. Chisholm says that Mallarmé's own ideal work, whatever it was, would be only a fragment of a future ideal created by all poets. He also rejects Le "Livre" as a valid example of this fragment. Robert Greer Cohn, "A propos du 'Coup de dés,' " *Esprit créateur* 1 (1961): 125–26. Scherer, pp. 149–52; Noulet, pp. 57–59. Considering the seriousness with which Mallarmé undertook his literary duties, an interpretation of the notes of Le "Livre" as mere games is very doubtful.

14. Wallace Fowlie, "Mallarmé and the Painters of his Age," *The Southern Review* 2 n.s. no. 3 (July 1966): 542–58. Daniel-Henry Kahnweiler, "Mallarmé et le peinture," *Les Lettres* 3, numéro spécial (1948): 63–68. This friendship, especially with James Whistler and Berthe Morisot, can be seen throughout Stéphane Mallarmé, *Correspondance IV 1890–1891*, ed. Henri Mondor et Lloyd James Austin (Paris: Gallimard, 1973).

porary theater, Mallarmé had expressed not only a deep love for the dramatic arts, but also a desire to create his own theatrical presentations.[15] "Hérodiade" was originally conceived of as a tragedy, hopefully to be performed at the Théâtre français. As a future drama, it elicited both hope and warning from Théodore de Banville. Both Mallarmé and de Banville desired to help the cause of poetry and drama by combining them into a single powerful art form. But an actual dramatic "Hérodiade" was soon abandoned by the poet who, nevertheless, never lost hope of composing a new play for his heroine.[16]

One of the causes of the change of "Hérodiade" from a drama to a poem was the painful rejection of his earliest version of "L'Après-midi d'un faune" (Afternoon of a Faun) by de Banville and Constant Coquelin for the Comédie française in 1865.[17] Although the poet had failed in two theatrical attempts, he continued to plan new dramas and to endow his works with dramatic qualities.[18] As of 1876, as already mentioned, he began to allude to his serious work on a vast new popular melodrama. These endeavors coincided with his increasing awareness of contemporary drama. Heightened, too, was his awareness of the role of dramatic criticism as a means for stimulating better theater and for

15. Henri Mondor, *Mallarmé lycéen* (Paris: Gallimard, 1954), p. 330; Haskell Block, *Mallarmé and the Symbolist Drama* (Detroit, Mich.: Wayne State University Press, 1963), pp. 6–8.
16. Henri Mondor, *Vie de Mallarmé* (Paris: Gallimard, 1941), p. 161; Mallarmé, *Correspondance 1862–1871*, pp. 154, 160, 174, 199–200; *Les Noces d'Hérodiade: mystère*, p. 16; Block, pp. 8–12, 17–20. In 1913, 1919, and 1937 theatrical presentations of the "Scène d'Hérodiade" were performed. Mallarmé, *O.c.*, pp. 1440–46.
17. Mallarmé, *Correspondance 1862–1871*, pp. 166, 169, 171, 174, 309; *O.c.*, pp. 1448–66; Block, pp. 21–27; Henri Mondor, *Histoire d'un faune* (Paris: Gallimard, 1948), pp. 101–4.
18. Mallarmé, *Correspondance 1862–1871*, pp. 343, 344–45, 347, 352, 354, 355; Block, pp. 33–43. Mallarmé never renounced his plans for a theatrical "Faun." In 1891 he announced a forthcoming new edition as a book and for the stage. Mallarmé, *O.c.*, p. 1463. For the plans of Paul Fort to stage "L'Après-midi" at the Théâtre d'Art, see Mallarmé, *Correspondance IV*, pp. 164–65, 188, 193–94, 235.

communicating his own dramatic concepts. These articles also give evidence of the poet's increasing love for the dance and for ballet in particular.[19]

But his own personal involvement in theater did not wane. According to George Moore, Mallarmé was planning to write a play entitled *Hamlet et le vent* (Hamlet and the Wind) to be performed throughout France at country fairs, and whose hero was to be played by the poet himself.[20] Mallarmé's love for the theater also included desires for his own theatrical participation. At his *Mardis* (Tuesdays) for literary disciples, at his lectures of the 1890s, and especially in his essential role as the "opérateur" (operator) at dramatic presentations of Le *"Livre,"* he loved the feeling of being alone on stage before an audience. He was afforded the opportunity of actual contact with theatrical performances in 1881 as the director of the Théâtre de Valvins, an attempt at popular theater made by his nephew, Paul Margueritte. Often after rehearsals, Mallarmé would talk about his own future desires for mass spectacles in which only the poet would star.[21] Such dreams would haunt him throughout his life.

Especially from 1885 until his death, Mallarmé would be haunted by another dream, the ardent desire to rival and surpass Richard Wagner. It has already been noted that the poet recognized the power of music to act as an escape from daily life and as a modern form of religion. He was

19. Mallarmé, "La Dernière Mode, *O.c.*, pp. 707–847; "Crayonné au théâtre," *O.c.*, pp. 293–351, 1561–62; Stéphane Mallarmé, *Les "gossips" de Mallarmé "Atheneum" 1875–1876*, ed. Henri Mondor et Lloyd James Austin (Paris: Gallimard, 1962).

20. Block, pp. 45–48. André Antoine also wanted Mallarmé to compose a play for his Théâtre Libre, but the poet, for an unknown reason, never offered such a work. Mallarmé, *Correspondance III*, p. 123. The poet's relations in 1890–91 with Paul Fort and the Théâtre d'Art are now documented in Mallarmé, *Correspondance IV*, pp. 164–65, 188, 193–94, 202, 209, 210, 235, 242–46.

21. Paul Margueritte, "Le Printemps tourmenté: souvenirs littéraires 1881–1896," *Revue des deux mondes* 51 (15 mai 1919): 241–80. See especially p. 246.

jealous of these powers, and he desperately wanted poetry to regain what he considered to be its innate attributes. Although Mallarmé knew of Wagner relatively early in his life, his serious awareness of a rivalry between poetry and music did not begin until 1885. Despite the fact that he had never yet seen a Wagnerian opera, he was then asked by Edouard Dujardin to write an article for *La Revue Wagnérienne*. From then on, in "Hommage," "Parenthèse" (Parenthesis), and in general remarks on music throughout the poet's works, Wagner, as a genius but never as the ultimate artist, would continue to occupy Mallarmé's thoughts.[22]

The relationship between Mallarmé and Wagner has often been carefully studied. Because of the interest in this aspect of Mallarmé and because of the poet's own concern for the power that music possesses, there has been a tendency to overstate the role of music in his life. More important, there has been an attempt to overemphasize his own technical knowledge of music in order to explain certain musical characteristics borrowed for his poetry. Calvin S. Brown has aptly stressed the point that much of the poet's intended borrowings, analogies, and jealousies stemmed more from his technical ignorance of the art form than from any ability to transform poetry into music or the reverse.[23]

From his earliest letters and works until the notes of *Le "Livre,"* Mallarmé often contented himself with the appellation of poetry as drama, painting, or music. In addition to

22. Lloyd James Austin, " 'Le Principal pilier' Mallarmé, Victor Hugo et Richard Wagner," *Revue d'histoire littéraire de la France* 2 (avril-juin 1951): 159–62, 180; Mondor, *Vie de Mallarmé*, pp. 296–97; Mallarmé, *Correspondance II*, pp. 289–90; *O.c.*, pp. 71, 322–24, 541–46.
23. Calvin S. Brown, "The Musical Analogies in Mallarmé's 'Un Coup de dés,' " *Comparative Literature Studies* 4 (1967): 67–79. Brown also explains the specific mistakes made by many other critics in attributing technical musical knowledge to Mallarmé.

the ease of such simple labels, these declarations were based upon a sincere belief and hope in the power of the word to fulfill all artistic functions. If the poet can rhyme, sing, paint, and sculpt in 1862, and if in 1865 dramatic verse must consist of a study of sound and the color of words in order to be poetic, Le "Livre" at the end of his life can be described as a "play/ symph./ ballet/ song/ poem/ Theater/ hymn/ opera."[24]

Although Mallarmé did continue to refer to poetry as dramatic and pictorial, music served as his major plane of reference. The poet is Orpheus who can not listen to a concert without seeing in his mind the innate poems of humanity, and whose duty it is, therefore, to succeed in creating "an art of achieving the transposition, to the Book, of the symphony or uniquely of regaining our property. . . ."[25] The true musical art form is poetry; music as one knows it, and especially in the form of Wagnerian music, has usurped the natural rights of literature. Language must reaffirm its power.

In an attempt to relate language to all other art forms and to cause poetry to encompass these rival or complementary artistic modes, Mallarmé immediately discovered a fundamental difficulty: either a distinction or a vague rapport among temporal and spatial arts. Guy Delfel defines a spatial art as one requiring an objective and physical structure; sculpture, architecture, and painting are spatial. Temporal artforms are more subjective. They are relived each time an interpreter re-creates them and rediscovers their necessary duration. Music is the most obvious temporal art.[26]

24. Mallarmé, "L'Art pour tous," O.c., p. 259; Correspondance 1862–1871, p. 168; Scherer, feuillets 102(A)–3(A).
25. Mallarmé, "Crise de vers," O.c., p. 367. See also "Symphonie littéraire," O.c., p. 265; "La Musique et les lettres," O.c., p. 648; Correspondance II, p. 286.
26. Guy Delfel, L'Esthétique de Stéphane Mallarmé (Paris: Flammarion, 1951), pp. 131–33.

It is evident, however, that there can be no definitive separation between temporal and spatial art forms. Dance, for example, the most physically spatial, requiring a material stage for its presentation, is also temporal in that it always necessitates an interpretation by a human figure; it always evolves in time.[27] Sculpture, architecture, and painting are spatial, but they could also be temporal if one includes as such the duration of time needed to communicate their essence to a public, the time used by an individual when he regards these works. The rhythm and rapports of structure could also be interpreted as temporal. Even the performing arts are based upon a written spatial structure: the symphony has its musical score; a play has its text; and a ballet has its permanent choreography. Dependent upon these structures, such art forms are then communicated in time and successively repeated by different interpreters. Literature also has its typographical form. It is then either performed orally or read individually. In both modes, a duration of time and a sequence of sounds are successively re-created.

Mallarmé himself was confused about his concepts of and desires for time and space in an ideal art form. It has been suggested that he wanted to deny historical time, both in the world and in the work of art, in favor of an intellectual timelessness, of a subjective and eternal moment. But his negation of duration involved him in the problem of the communication of his art form to a public and of the latter's method of interpretation. Even if an individual can understand a meaning instantaneously, it takes a certain amount of time to read or to hear a complete work. And despite an insistence upon mental images created by individuals constituting a public, Mallarmé also desired the power and permanence of the spatially written word as the initial

27. *Ibid.*, pp. 181–84; Mallarmé, "Le Genre ou des modernes," *O.c.*, p. 315.

stimulus for these thoughts.[28] Any art form is by nature both temporal and spatial. The initial moment of conception by the poet may be unique, but active creation and communication combine time and space.

If an ideal work is circular and suppresses the existence of time, in its essence it can be said either to equate time and space as one or to deny the existence of both. A circular art form representing a circular cosmos, which in turn equals a unique number, must open its closed structure so that its ideas can be explained to mankind. It becomes linear at each successive time of communication. When all men have returned to their origins as one with the work and the universe, the circle may close once again. Time and space can then be abolished, or rather can be equal to all else in eternity.

Mallarmé could easily theorize about the ideal concepts of time and space, but he could not deny the importance of the actual presentation of his art form. He was faced with a choice between the written text or the oral performance, and he could not decide which mode would be superior. He recognized the powers and weaknesses of both.

If he was uncertain about the supremacy of either the oral or written word, he did know that harsh, loud noises irritated his ears. Despite its religiously soothing sounds, music, to Mallarmé, sometimes seemed to be mere elementary tumultuous noise. These annoying sounds, however, are not to be found in all music, and the hated fracas of the "Hommage" to Wagner probably refers specifically to contemporary French music, or to music before Wagner.[29]

28. Mallarmé did desire a simultaneous rather than a successive form of reading, but he realized its impossibility. See especially Scherer, feuillets 200(A), 147(A), 179(A); "Le Livre, instrument spirituel," *O.c.*, p. 380.

29. Mallarmé, "La Musique et les lettres," *O.c.*, p. 469. See also "Crise de vers," *O.c.*, pp. 367–68; "Hommage," *O.c.*, p. 71; Austin, " 'Le Principal Pilier,' " p. 176.

Whether as music or as a word spoken aloud, aural or oral communication is extremely powerful. Mallarmé was well aware of this fact. Since an ideal art form was to return humanity to its origins in a simple paradise, the language used in this work of art should likewise reflect these beginnings of man. It can be said that the origins of communication are to be found first in sounds, and then in the oral word. To retain this initial sense of language, Mallarmé insisted that all written works be subjected to some oral proof by means of an exterior presentation. Oral communication is essential if one wants to explain one's thoughts. Every writer needs to speak in public so that, to counteract his solitude, he can rediscover the hidden conversationalist in him.[30]

There is much evidence to show that Mallarmé loved the conversationalist's role. He alludes in his writings to desires of simple oral dialogues among men. Others have often described him as having had a powerful yet musically sweet voice. His interest in the theater, his desires for acting in his own plays, his oral public lectures, his intimate *Mardis*, the possibility of reading aloud "Un Coup de dés," and his desired oral presentation of Le *"Livre"* all attest to his realization of the power and effect of the oral word.[31]

The spoken word can be considered to be superior to its written counterpart precisely because of its immediate effect upon an auditor. As music adds vitality to silence, language finds new life when it is pronounced aloud. The human voice, with its intonation, can easily communicate a thought that would require lengthy paragraphs to explain in

---

30. Mallarmé, "Notes," *O.c.*, pp. 855, 856.
31. *Ibid.*, pp. 851, 853; Mallarmé, "Crayonné au théâtre," *O.c.*, p. 295; "La Musique et les lettres," *O.c.*, pp. 637, 649–50; Mondor, *Vie de Mallarmé*, pp. 182, 354, 425, 581, 650. There is a controversy over the sincerity of Mallarmé's beliefs in the oral rendition of "Un Coup de dés," but, despite any technical impossibility, he did state in his "Préface" that the typography exists "for whoever wants to read it aloud like a musical score." Mallarmé, *O.c.*, p. 456.

written form. The notes at the end of "La Musique et les lettres," for example, are needed to replace what is lost from the oral talk. And last, both the human voice and the oral word have the power to rule or to entrap man.[32]

If a spoken word can affect man negatively, it can also create his immortality, while reminding him of his primitive past in an ideal world: "I say: a flower! and, out of the forgetfulness where my voice banishes any countour . . . musically arises, an idea itself and fragrant, the one absent from all bouquets."[33] Mallarmé had always hoped that a word could possess enough power to evoke the past, the eternal essence of an object, and the eternal glory of an individual, but he was not sure whether this word should be oral or written.

Despite the obvious differences between these two modes of communication, Mallarmé often tried to erase any lines of demarcation. In an attempt to embrace all art forms, an ideal artistic mode must first borrow from and then equate itself to all others; thus, the written word becomes oral in nature and in communication. It also becomes oral in tone. The poet's love for conversation was so deep that his written works also tend to have a similar style. This characteristic is especially strong in the prose works where poetic incantation is replaced by a tone of *causerie* (chat) in which intonation compensates for an apparent lack of liaison. Jacques Scherer has pointed out the possibility that many of the poet's devices, such as exclamation points, question marks, dashes, and parentheses, bring the written and oral sentence closer together by adding personal and subjective nuances that only the voice could otherwise truthfully render.[34]

32. Mallarmé, "Le Genre ou des modernes," *O.c.*, pp. 315–16; "La Musique et les lettres," *O.c.*, p. 654; Scherer, feuillets 12(A), 13(A), 15(A), 34(B), 131(A), 157(A), 194(A).
33. Mallarmé, "Crise de vers," *O.c.*, p. 368.
34. Jacques Scherer, *L'Expression littéraire dans l'oeuvre de Mallarmé* (Paris:

If poetry is the true form of music, it must be an oral music when spoken, but a visual, inner, silent music when read. It must be remembered that, although poetry is usually read, it can be said aloud, and, although music also exists in the written score, Mallarmé had to have music played for him. To the poet, therefore, music must be aural. Wagner's operas are golden trumpets too powerful to be reduced to the silence of musical notes printed on a page.[35] To someone skilled in music, however, these notes do represent sound, the silent inner sonority that Mallarmé desired for the poetic word.

When Claude Debussy composed the musical transcription of "L'Après-midi d'un faune," Mallarmé remarked to him in a surprised, although somewhat sarcastic tone: " 'I thought that I had already put it into music!' "[36] To the poet, the printed word exhibited not only its own sonority, but the true natural form of music: " 'I make Music, and call thus not what one can create from the harmonic proximity of words. . .but the superior world magically produced by certain dispositions of the word . . . like the keys of the piano. . . . but it's the same as an orchestra, except that it is done literarily or silently.' " Especially in the 1890s, after more jealous contact with Wagner's music, Mallarmé often continued to refer to written poetry as a silent and solitary concert.[37] But even silent or visual music uses some forms of aural communication. The reader hears the sonorities on the pages, through an inner voice, as mental sounds. Mallarmé was well aware of this process,

Librairie A. G. Nizet, 1947), pp. 53–62, 191–93. See also Robert Greer Cohn, *L'Oeuvre de Mallarmé "Un Coup de dés,"* trans. René Arnaud (Paris: Librairie Les Lettres, 1951), where this critic studies much of the 1897 poem in light of the visual forms of words used as reminders of oral sounds.

35. Mallarmé, "Hommage," *O.c.*, p. 71.
36. Mondor, *Histoire d'un faune*, p. 122.
37. Roger-A. Lhombreaud, "Deux Lettres de Mallarmé à Edmond Gosse," *Revue de littérature comparée* 25 (1951): 358; Mallarmé, "La Musique et les lettres," *O.c.*, p. 648; *Propos sur la poésie*, p. 198; "Le Livre, instrument spirituel," *O.c.*, p. 380.

and often one can not determine whether the voice or sound he refers to in his texts is actually oral or interior.

If the visual silent word and oral sound possess similar qualities, there is one characteristic of the written word that renders it superior: its permanence. As a spatial work, the written text can withstand time in its ability to offer immortality and to be communicated to future men without the aid of an exterior temporal interpreter. Any creative thought must be written down in order to be preserved. Once inscribed on a page, it will become as solid as a cathedral or a sculptured stone.[38]

But it is not only the visual word that remains eternally on the page; the empty white spaces among the notations in ink are also essential. Similarly, music has its silent rests. True music is not only visual; it is pure suggestive silence, implying, therefore, pure thought, that which is not uttered at all. If the poet was jealous of the powers of music, while decrying its aural nature, he was also envious of this poetry without words because "the modern meteor, the symphony, at the will of the musician, approaches thought; which no longer needs only current forms of expression."[39] The communication of music is pure in that it abolishes the text in favor either of an abstract, mentally visual image or mental poetry that in turn becomes silent music. It does not have to depend upon the mediocrity of ordinary spoken language.[40]

Mallarmé attempted to achieve this same form of communication by the creation of the purely poetic word,

---

38. Mallarmé, "L'Action restreinte," *O.c.*, pp. 369, 371; Scherer, *Le "Livre,"* feuillet 171(A).
39. Mallarmé, "Crise de vers," *O.c.*, p. 365. See also "Villiers de l'Isle-Adam," *O.c.*, p. 495; "Plaisir sacré," *O.c.*, p. 389.
40. Mallarmé, "Crise de vers," *O.c.*, p. 367. See also "La Musique et les lettres," *O.c.*, p. 649; "Bucolique," *O.c.*, pp. 402–3.

sonorous in itself, and placed upon a white page. Having rid his art form of any impure ordinary sounds actually spoken, and having discovered true music in the written word, he could now concentrate his efforts on the purity of silence, pregnant with meaning. The ease of including white spaces in literature stemmed from the obvious fact that "one does not write the alphabet of the stars luminously on an obscure plain. . .man pursues black upon white."[41] The significant silence of the white page represented for Mallarmé an artistic return to the ideal purity that he sought to restore. It is a return to pure essence whereby he could conquer the existence of chance while proving the existence of the pure idea.[42]

Mallarmé had been fascinated by the purity of silence and the white page since his early discoveries of *le néant* and of ideal beauty, but the pure essence of the page, as combined with the written word into typography, did not concern him until the late 1880s, after his first serious contacts with Wagnerian music. By the 1890s, he saw typography as being essential to a text as a physical reflection of the subject and of the author's thoughts, the presentation to the reader of certain concepts, and, with more practice, hopefully the actual rhythm of the poet's ideas.[43] If typography can mirror the subject according to its position on the page, it becomes not only a spiritual production where words represent actors on a blank stage, but also the written image of a ballet, a choreography dependent upon the sizes and types of characters chosen. Large Roman characters are principal actors or ballerinas and around them are

41. Mallarmé, "L'Action restreinte," *O.c.*, p. 370.
42. Mallarmé, "Le Mystère dans les lettres," *O.c.*, p. 387.
43. Mallarmé, "Bibliographie des *Divagations*," *O.c.*, p. 1576. See also *Correspondance III*, pp. 188, 236.

secondary groups whose size and relative position on the page are dependent upon their importance.[44]

An attempt at a written ballet is especially evident in "Un Coup de dés," where one can interpret each page, or parts of each page, as representing a painting or a design. Basing their observations on Mallarmé's interest in Oriental pictorial writing and sketches, some critics have seen particular ideograms on every page of the 1897 poem.[45] Much of this interpretation is subjective.

Mallarmé himself liked to consider this poem as a musical score based upon the overriding importance of typography and pagination. The size of the characters used would determine how loudly a particular word was to be pronounced, and its position on the page, at the top, the middle, or the bottom, would dictate the rising or descending intonation of the reader's voice.[46] Although Mallarmé's intentions have prompted many interpretations, their essential significance lies in the importance of a naive desire to rival music not only in its sonority, but also in its native rhythm and structure. One must not forget the poet's belief that an ideal art form is a reflection or an equation of the ideal universe. As a musical score, the written text of "Un Coup de dés" will have mobility. This movement will be that which is fundamental to the world. From one page to another, a sentence will imitate the essential rhythm of an

44. Mallarmé, "Le Livre, instrument spirituel," *O.c.*, p. 381; "Un Coup de dés: Préface," *O.c.*, p. 455.

45. In a letter to Paul Claudel, Mallarmé wrote: " 'Your sentence . . . reminds me of those Japanese designs where the image is sketched only by its whiteness. . . !' " Mondor, *Vie de Mallarmé*, p. 745. Examples of these ideograms can be found in Cohn, *L'Oeuvre de Mallarmé*, pp. 190–91, 287, 294–95, 347–48, 389, and Ernest Fraenkel, *Les Dessins transconscients de Stéphane Mallarmé: à propos de la typographie de "Un Coup de dés"* (Paris: Librairie Nizet, 1960), pp. 27–32.

46. Mallarmé, *O.c.*, p. 455.

action or an object. In this way, literature will regain its original purpose.[47]

Richard Wagner had compared the rhythm or beat in music to the accents of intonation in speech. Mallarmé went further in a definition of musical language: for him, music represented the rhythmic rapports among ideas.[48] Relationships among words and thoughts, observed as having mobility, remind one again of the fundamental rapports among all things in the cosmos. The ideal art form was to mirror the inner structure of this ideal reality in its analogies, identities, and equalities, circular and cyclical movement, and ultimate suppression of time into a unique moment summed up as a unique number. The self-proof of the work would be found within where the placement of words, fragments, and motifs would reflect or echo one another and the rhythm of the poet's mind.[49]

Although the complex but harmonious rhythm of these words will be reduced to a single unity, the poet was similarly concerned with the reverse process in poetic creation. A work grows from a single thought and a single word into a multiple whole, ultimately resimplified. According to Paul Valéry, Mallarmé began some poems by jotting down a few words on a page and then by connecting them.[50] In truth,

47. This description of typography is found in a letter to André Gide, where Mallarmé was referring to the incorrect printing of his poem in *Cosmopolis*, and to the necessary typographical format of a reprinting. Henri Mondor, *Autres Précisions sur Mallarmé et inédits* (Paris: Gallimard, 1961), p. 236. See also Mallarmé, "Un Coup de dés: Préface," *O.c.*, p. 455.
48. Richard Wagner, *Wagner on Music and Drama*, trans. H. Ashton Ellis (New York: E. P. Dutton and Co., 1964), pp. 196–203; Lhombreaud, p. 358. It has been suggested that, by adding a sense of rhythm and movement to a spatial, written text, or to any architectural structure, a temporal quality is implied. If each page of "Un Coup de dés" is seen as having mobility, then each one represents a unit of time presented spatially. Ynhui Park, *L'Idée chez Mallarmé* (Paris: Centre de Documentation Universitaire, 1966), pp. 121–22.
49. Mallarmé, "Le Mystère dans les lettres," *O.c.*, p. 386.
50. Scherer, *L'Expression littéraire*, pp. 77–80.

the poet's synthetically oriented mind allowed him to go back even further in the structure of his work. A book is the total expansion of the letter from which it gains a spacious mobility.[51] Literary creation follows a course from the alphabet, to the word, to the verse or line, to the stanza or paragraph, to the poem, page, or chapter, and finally to the unified book. Only in this way can individual parts be self-sufficient while being microcosms of the whole.

This totality of a work was paramount to Mallarmé's concepts of the architecture of a work of art. As every literary creation of his can be seen as leading toward and contributing to the ideal Work, every part of that particular work should be examined in light of a total unity. All of Mallarmé's thoughts were thus related or, as he himself explained, musically placed so as to form an ensemble. An isolated thought loses its true meaning.[52]

The structural organization of the ideal work always preoccupied the poet, especially in his later years. He knew that both the content and interior format would reflect a system of mobile relationships, but he continually changed his mind about the exterior architecture. At various stages during its conception, this Great Work was to be a single, unique masterpiece, a series of volumes numbering three, four, or five, three poems in verse and four in prose, three dramas, or a cyclically multiple work composed by many genius poets throughout the ages.[53] In addition to geometric considerations about the physical structure of the book, specifically, its height, width, and thickness, the pages of Le "Livre" show a confusion concerning the total exterior architecture. Mallarmé finally seems to

51. Mallarmé, "Le Livre, instrument spirituel," O.c., p. 380.
52. Mallarmé, "Sur l'Idéal à vingt ans," O.c., p. 883.
53. Mallarmé, Correspondance 1862–1871, pp. 225, 242–43, 244, 324; Correspondance II, p. 151; "Crise de vers," O.c., p. 367; "Solitude," O.c., pp. 406–7.

have decided upon a multiple structure: an ensemble of twenty volumes will consist of four groups of five volumes each.[54]

This complexity implies a specific order that is similarly evident in musical compositions, especially in the polyphonic works of the Baroque era. If Mallarmé was interested in poetry's exhibiting inner musical rhythm, he also admired the musical arts for their highly intellectual exterior organization. He desired to have literature use the same structural devices as the symphony, and the musical score of "Un Coup de dés" is described as being contrapuntal.[55] He found the same logical processes in nature and even in the internal movement of music. For him, a poet must "take back everything from music, its rhythms which are only those of reason. . . ."[56]

Whether as a musical score or as the direct reflection of a structured universe, therefore, the ideal art form must have a rational order, a determined architectural form, as well as inner logical mobility: "this spontaneous and magical architecture does not imply the lack of powerful and subtle calculations, but one is unaware of them; they themselves are made mysteriously. . . . The intellectual framework of the poem is hidden and holds itself firm—takes place—both in the space which isolates the stanzas and on the whiteness of the paper. . . ."[57] In a practical application to his twenty-volume Book, the poet would allow movement among the five volumes of each larger work, thereby offering the possibilities of interchangeable parts. But there

54. Scherer, Le "Livre," feuillets 175(A)–76(A). See also feuillets 39(A), 40(A)–40(A) (*suite*), 41(A).
55. Mallarmé, "La Musique et les lettres," *O.c.*, pp. 384–85; "Un Coup de dés: Préface," *O.c.*, p. 456.
56. Mallarmé, *Correspondance II*, p. 286. See also "Le Mystère dans les lettres," *O.c.*, p. 385.
57. Mallarmé, "Sur Poe," *O.c.*, p. 872. See also *Correspondance II*, p. 301.

would be no link among the four larger works composing the whole. Order would be assured.[58]

Throughout his life, Mallarmé had stated his preference for the book instead of what he called a mere album, devoid of any definite structure. But the mobile architecture of Le "Livre" was extended to include the use of loose pages, able to be read in any order, but fixed by the poet for his public. The interchangeable pages would form a book read in one order; they would then be reversed to form an album. The overall structure of twenty volumes would be determined in advance, but its musical rhythm would also be preserved.[59]

Music possesses another, perhaps stronger, aspect, which confused Mallarmé in his planned usurpation. Music is emotional. Wagner was well aware of this passionate, more subjective, quality inherent in his art, and he extolled it as a virtue in contrast to language, which had become devoid of any of the sensitivity and feeling needed by modern man. Although Mallarmé disliked the elementary, harsh sounds of music, he did appreciate its more lyrical nature and was jealous of the magical powers that could offer an emotional experience to large numbers of men. One must not forget that, to Mallarmé, music was a new religion that attracts converts because of its occultism and simple access to a state of ecstasy.[60]

The intellectual aspects of music are known generally only by those technically skilled in the art. The layman senses merely an emotional response. For the poet, pure

58. Scherer, Le "Livre," feuillets 119(A), 147(A), 157(A)–58(A).

59. Ibid., feuillets 51(B)–52(B), 100(A), 112(A), 113(A), 146(A), 160(A), 192(A); Mallarmé, Correspondance II, p. 302; "Bibliographie des Divagations," O.c., p. 1538.

60. Mallarmé, "La Cour," O.c., p. 416. As early as 1862, Mallarmé was jealous of the religious awe and emotion evoked by music. "L'Art pour tous," O.c., p. 257. See also Mallarmé, Correspondance II, pp. 73, 286; "Avant-dire," O.c., p. 860; Propos sur la poésie, pp. 195, 198; Wagner, pp. 151–54.

emotion would never suffice. In contrast to elementary musical sound, and as the true form of music, poetic language would add intellectual meaning to lyrical sonority. Music alone is seen as a mere vague but subtle cloud.[61] Wagner had added intellectual meaning to music in his operatic librettos, but Mallarmé seemed to desire only one artistic mode, encompassing all communicative characteristics.

Despite the essential role of intelligence in Mallarmé's own writings, he realized that some form of emotion was inescapable in an ideal art form. This creation was born from the genius poet's instinctive knowledge of himself and of the universe. In order to stimulate the innate intelligence of other men and to return them to their original state of being, a work of art must call upon an individual's native intuition. Vague inner emotions, also evident in the poetic work, are first actuated, leading, hopefully, to an intellectual understanding of multiple meanings.[62]

The emotions stimulated by religion and mysterious magic, already felt in music, are those specifically desired by the poet. Throughout his works, Mallarmé refers to the enchanting powers of poetry and of the ideal art form that will charm the people as well as instruct them. He felt that there existed a secret rapport between poetry and magic. Both the poet and the sorcerer can begin to evoke or create some unknown object or idea until they appear as real. The poetic verse has an incantatory quality in its circle of rhyme, similar to the magical rings of a fairy or a magician. A poet is a dispenser of charm.[63]

61. Mallarmé, "La Musique et les lettres," *O.c.*, pp. 656, 648; "Crise de vers," *O.c.*, p. 368.
62. Mallarmé, *Correspondance 1862–1871*, p. 351; "Villiers de l'Isle-Adam," *O.c.*, p. 481; "Les Mots anglais," *O.c.*, p. 902; "Notes sur le théâtre," *O.c.*, pp. 337–38; *Propos sur la poésie*, pp. 175, 182–83, 186.
63. Mallarmé, "Magie," *O.c.*, p. 400. See also "Solennité," *O.c.*, p. 336.

Since both music and poetry combine emotions and intellectualism in their own art forms, and since both can be either visual or aural, a fundamental discrepancy between the two must be found once again in the relative importance of oral or written modes of communication. Although an individual skilled in music can hear and then intellectually analyze a score, it was the written form that Mallarmé considered both as inspiring religious awe and as retaining an intellectual supremacy. In "L'Art pour tous," the poet expressed a deep jealousy of the ability of music, with its system of written notation, to be accessible only to an intellectual few, while poetry was being degraded by the multitude.[64] Mallarmé, of course, did not understand these written notes. It has been seen that later in his life the poet became jealous of the popularity of aural music in its emotional sway over a public, while his obscure poetry remained accessible to a highly educated elite. But music was still found in a written form, and Mallarmé never lost his desire to make language into a musically mathematical system of notation, first for initiates and finally for all.

To someone unfamiliar with their meaning, musical notes appear as something mysteriously unknown. They represent the gold of ancient missals or the hieroglyphics of Egyptian papyrus.[65] Since language is used by everyone, its written form possesses no religious mystery. Mallarmé was determined to change this deplorable situation. Poetic language must also represent magical symbols enclosed within a *grimoire* (a magician's book). The letters of the alphabet must themselves be seen as supernatural and divine, and the poet must affirm the existence not only of these verbal and hieroglyphic values, but also of secret pure signs confusedly indicated by orthography.[66]

64. Mallarmé, *O.c.*, p. 257.
65. *Ibid*.
66. Mallarmé, "Notes," *O.c.*, p. 855.

Art is not only an education; it is also an initiation. The youthful Mallarmé desired such an initiation into a secret artistic cult for a certain chosen few, ideally for artists alone.[67] As his social awareness enlarged, he would continue to describe art as a sacred ritual, but the number of its initiates would increase. The secret ceremony, however, would remain intact: even before deciphering the notes of language, an individual must cut the pages of a book; this act constitutes a brutal seizure of possession and an initiation into the mysteries to be discovered within the pages.[68]

One of the most essential characteristics of any art form, and especially of an ideal work, is mystery. This quality is to be found not only in music and in written poetic literature, but also in theater and in dance.[69] Whenever Mallarmé calls Le *"Livre"* a "mystery," he is referring to a combination of its theatrical, religious, and mysterious attributes. On the surface a work may appear to be obscure and impossible to understand, but within lies a clarity whose discovery warrants any amount of effort on the part of the initiate. The scope of this discovery encompasses, of course, an awareness of ideal-primitive man and reality.

In order to express this pure essence, a pure artistic mode is needed. If language is the chosen means, and if ordinary language is banal and impure, then the artist must create or rediscover a true language. Once again, the ideal word can be found at its original source.

If contemporary reality is complex and corrupt, one can similarly describe the state of modern languages. These languages are not only impure; there are too many of them

67. Mallarmé, "L'Art pour tous," *O.c.*, pp. 257–60.
68. Mallarmé, "Le Livre, instrument spirituel," *O.c.*, p. 381. The barbarous aspect of such an act caused Mallarmé to consider the unbound form of pages for *Le "Livre."*
69. Mallarmé, "Le Mystère dans les lettres," *O.c.*, p. 385; "Le Genre ou des modernes," *O.c.*, p. 313; "Richard Wagner: rêverie d'un poète français," *O.c.*, p. 545; "Ballets," *O.c.*, p. 305; "Crayonné au théâtre," *O.c.*, p. 297; "La Musique et les lettres," *O.c.*, p. 649.

in the world. Each one is individually related to its own particular history and, therefore, can never express the pure and supreme truth.[70] In addition to this diversity, there exists a distinction within each tongue between ordinary speech and poetic language. While the latter can evoke the essence of an idea, the former is coarse and immediate.[71] It must never infect the true poetic idiom. But rather than retain a separation between the two languages, the poet has a duty to perpetuate the use of one pure speech, in view of the eventual elimination of impure tongues.

Mallarmé desired to return man and his world to their unique source in or as God. At these origins can be found the common beginnings of all languages. During the course of history, a diversity was established; expansion led to deterioration. Pure poetic language would return to this ideal source and would be reborn as supreme. Individual words composing this unique language would themselves radiate the essence of purity. They would reflect the fundamental rhythm of the universe.[72] The poetic word constitutes this innate music specifically because of its return to a primitive source. As a pure notion, it can mirror the native purity of man; it becomes the immediate approach of the soul.[73]

Does the poet actually create a new language, or does he have to utilize existing words? Mallarmé has clearly explained his intentions: "The verse which, from several sounds and letters, recreates a total word, new, foreign to the language and as if incantatory, achieves this isolation of the word . . . and gives you this surprise of never having heard such an ordinary fragment of speech; at the same

70. Mallarmé, "Crise de vers," *O.c.*, pp. 363–64.
71. *Ibid.*, pp. 366, 368; Mallarmé, "Avant-dire au *Traité du verbe*," *O.c.*, p. 857.
72. Mallarmé, "Sur Poe," *O.c.*, p. 872; "Crise de vers," *O.c.*, p. 364.
73. Mallarmé, "Plaisir sacré," *O.c.*, p. 389.

time the memory of the named object is bathed in a new atmosphere."[74] Said more succinctly, "To give a purer meaning to the words of the tribe" is the poet's aim.[75] In one sense, an individual not attuned to the processes of poetic re-creation will not understand Mallarmé's use of ordinary words, and, in another sense, his innate intelligence will remind him of the truths inherent in the poem.

Since art is magical and mysterious in nature, a return of these attributes implies what Mallarmé has called a return to alchemy. Like an alchemist trained in a primitive science and mystical philosophy, he viewed his task as that of transforming ordinary matter into brilliant gold. On the surface the banal word, transmuted into its poetic sense, may appear either as ordinary to the uninitiated, or as totally obscure. With an ordinary exterior, the mystery may lie within; beyond that inner mystery or beneath an exterior obscurity are beautiful truths that hopefully will shine like the alchemist's gold.[76] But the poet will go further than the alchemist; he will not merely form precious stones by placing words on a page. Since true poetry consists of creating symbols, the poet must take the absolute, pure, and luminous jewels of man and transform them into a poetic manifestation of the soul or spirit.[77] These truths may be clear to the poet, but obscurity may be a problem for other men. Mallarmé was not even sure whether this symbol itself should be presented with a precise meaning or as a vague suggestion.

If the poet was jealous of musical notation as hieroglyphic, his reason stemmed from the fact not only that these notes are mysteriously unknown to laymen, but also that each printed notation represents a specific sign. Musi-

74. Mallarmé, "Crise de vers," *O.c.*, p. 368.
75. Mallarmé, "Le Tombeau d'Edgar Poe," *O.c.*, p. 70.
76. Mallarmé, "Magie," *O.c.*, pp. 399–400; "Or," *O.c.*, p. 399.
77. Mallarmé, "Sur l'évolution littéraire," *O.c.*, p. 870.

cal composition is built upon a mathematical foundation. The typography of a written text is to imitate a musical score but, in addition, can be seen as the choreography of a ballet. For Mallarmé, who deeply admired dance, each ballerina is also the notation of a hieroglyphic. As the symbol of the pure idea, she causes each individual to discover the nudity of his own mind. Dance consists of a system of visual essences; the dancer creates with a corporal writing that which would take paragraphs to explain in a written form. She (or he) becomes a poem without a scribe.[78]

An essential duty of the poet is to re-create a poetic work that can also represent a specific sign. Mallarmé was totally involved in this search throughout his life. The ideal universe exists to be re-created by the poet, who observes everything around him and within himself as symbols to be deciphered. After poetic re-creation, the genius poet can offer mankind this same system of signs, which will reflect or equal the simplicity of the cosmos. A fascination with equations for everything in the world led Mallarmé to consider language itself as a mathematical formula. The components of this formula are the letters of the alphabet, and the total equation becomes literature or poetry, the divine denominator and the summation and law of the world.[79]

As a summation of the simple ideal universe, language must ultimately equal a unique number. All of Mallarmé's attempts at the circular equality, in content and structure, of an ideal art form give evidence to his preoccupation. "Igitur" and "Un Coup de dés," especially, represent the search for "the unique Number which can not be Another."[80] As a supreme mathematical symbol, language

78. Mallarmé, "Ballets," O.c., pp. 304, 307. See also "Richard Wagner: rêverie d'un poète français," O.c., p. 541.
79. Mallarmé, "Solennité," O.c., p. 333; "Villiers de l'Isle-Adam," O.c., p. 481; "La Musique et les lettres," O.c., pp. 646, 648.
80. Mallarmé, "Un Coup de dés," O.c., pp. 462–63. See also pp. 466–67, 472–73, 477; "Igitur," O.c., p. 442.

would appear to be exact, dependent upon no subjective interpretations. An identical precision can be found in currencies, and Mallarmé did recognize the impersonal power of money, understood by everyone. But money fails to offer any abstraction whatsoever.[81] Despite its exactness, language as a number must allow some diversity of meaning.

If a ballerina corporeally writes the essence of a poem, she does not represent this idea in a definitive and lucid manner; she suggests. She is not a woman who dances but, rather, a metaphor.[82] In a similar fashion, if a word is a sign or a musical hieroglyphic, it not only possesses a specific number of connotations, but it is also subject to many interpretations, dependent upon the reader or auditor. Paralleling Mallarmé's desires for a mathematical language was a determined effort to use only allusion in his poetic creations: "*To name* an object is to suppress three quarters of the enjoyment of the poem which is composed in order to be devined little by little; *to suggest*, there's the dream. It is the perfect use of this mystery which constitutes the symbol: to evoke an object slowly in order to show a state of mind, or, conversely, to choose an object and, through a series of decipherings, to detach from it a state of mind."[83] If a word reflects the pure essence of an idea; if it equals a unique number or even a series of numbers, its clarity is only suggested through a veil of possible obscurity. The brightness of gold lies beneath a thick exterior.

The obscurity of his own writings and the possibilities of obscurity in his future ideal work were two of Mallarmé's greatest problems. Although he denied any obscurity in his poems, and although he said of Le *"Livre"* that "it is as clear as day," he knew that poetry, and especially his

81. Mallarmé, "Confrontation," *O.c.*, p. 410; "Or," *O.c.*, pp. 398–99.
82. Mallarmé, "Ballets," *O.c.*, p. 304.
83. Mallarmé, "Sur l'évolution littéraire," *O.c.*, p. 869.

poetry, did not have as wide a public as, for example, did music.[84] Because of the extreme difficulty of both his poetry and prose, there have been many attempts to explain the reasons for this frequent unintelligibility. It is possible that Mallarmé's original thoughts about art, man, and an ideal world were not totally defined in his own mind. A more plausible explanation can be found in the discrepancy between these thoughts and the means with which he expressed his ideas. Obscurity of expression can consist of a use of words suggesting too many associations or of the omission of certain words providing logical transitions. Words utilized in a new and unusual sense and the placing of words in a confusing syntax can also result in vagueness. Mallarmé used all of these devices in an attempt to make the word create and then equal an ideal that he felt and understood within himself. But words are signs, exact or metaphorical, and poetry requires these representational symbols. Endowing them with too many powers confuses the reader or auditor. The vague ideal universe suggested can not be real. Is it merely a myth?

The use of myths and legends was important to Mallarmé's concept of an ideal art form; however, it has already been seen that one of the poet's complaints regarding Wagner was the latter's employment of specific Germanic legends. These myths did not present a public with a picture of the origins of all men. But the poet's interpretation of Wagner must be seen in light of the musician's own statement that "the art work of the future must embrace the spirit of a free mankind, delivered from every shackle of hampering nationality. . . ."[85] Either Mallarmé had not

84. Scherer, feuillet 169(A); Mondor, *Vie de Mallarmé*, pp. 507, 645.
85. Wagner, p. 65; Mallarmé, "Richard Wagner: rêverie d'un poète français," *O.c.*, p. 544.

read enough by Wagner, or the latter's operas were not yet the art work of the future.

Despite this discrepancy, Mallarmé had his own criteria for the proper use of myths in art. The desired creation of suggestive symbols in language implies a complementary wish for an impersonal generality of content, accessible to all men as individuals. The mystery contained within an ideal art form should be abstract, but when each man discovers the radiant meaning, this vagueness becomes his personal hymn.[86] According to the poet, the French mind is abstract, imaginative, and poetic; as such, it dislikes art in the form of anecdotal legends seen as mere anachronisms rather than as eternal myths. Mallarmé had his own ideas about the true artistic myth. It must be a Fable, Poem, or Ode, independent of any particular time, place, nationality, and race. It is the myth of the universe as it is inscribed in heaven. Such a fable must mirror the multiple personality of mankind because it is of a general nature, reflecting original man in paradise.[87]

Mallarmé's use of the word *type* to define the artistic myth implies a desire not only of universal and eternal traits, but also of the reduction of men to their pure essences, to the simple characteristics inherent in humanity. An impersonal myth is aesthetic and religious; it represents and reminds men of their innate beings: "god, man—or Type."[88] Since every man is divine, art will suggest this notion generally for all and specifically for each individual.

A sense of divinity is an eternal feeling or understanding. An artistic myth must relate not only to all men at a specific time in history, but also to all men throughout the

86. Scherer, *Le "Livre,"* feuillet 105(A).
87. Mallarmé, "Richard Wagner: rêverie d'un poète français," *O.c.*, pp. 544–45.
88. Mallarmé, "Catholicisme," *O.c.*, p. 393.

ages. One of the criteria for a successful work of art is its ability to appeal to publics in different decades and centuries. In order to withstand time, art must eternally appear modern. Mallarmé desired such an attribute for his ideal work of myths.

Although he recognized the need of art to be both modern and eternal, he never explained how to modernize a work throughout the ages. The eternal myth has been evident since man's beginnings, but modernism implies change. What Mallarmé did envision was an art form appealing to nineteenth-century Frenchmen. He sarcastically describes the hat as a modern fashion that will continue forever. Styles of hats do change, but in Le "Livre" the contemporary style becomes an essential part of the modern presentation of the work. As the theatrical reader, Mallarmé must dress in a specific costume; "All modernism is furnished by the reader/The hat—etc."[89] Perhaps future styles of hats will be used in future presentations.

In general, Mallarmé concerned himself with the simple observation that his ideal art form, containing eternal myths, must appear as entirely modernized, "that is, within reach of everyone, currently applied." In this way a work of art becomes a modern Iliad or Odyssey.[90] The modern myth may be presented in many variations, but its general identification had been defined as of 1886. Theatrically portrayed as the drama of Hamlet, its sole subject will be the

89. Scherer, feuillet 148(A). See also feuillets 169(A)–69(A) (suite), 170(A) (suite), 171(A); Mallarmé, "Sur le chapeau haut de forme," O.c., pp. 881–82. Although the poet did seem to indicate a literal use of the modern hat, one could interpret this accessory in a metaphorical way. The hat represents the man; throughout the ages, modernism is added by individuals with their changing current ideas. Mallarmé's desired use of gas lights during this presentation is also a means toward modernism. Jean-Pierre Richard, L'Univers imaginaire de Mallarmé (Paris: Editions du Seuil, 1961), pp. 458–59, 502–3.
90. Scherer, Le "Livre," feuillets 103(A), 163(A). There are five "myths" in Le "Livre," each one specific while implying a general situation of mankind. Idem, feuillets 12(A)–15(A), 16(A)–24(A), 22(A)–26(A), 27(A)–33(A), 169(A)–69(A) (suite).

antagonism in man between his dreams and the fatality of his existence. It is the myth of the call to mankind and the drama of Mallarmé's own life.[91]

But if this pessimistic subject is even partially true, Mallarmé, in the same year, also believed that art represented the marriage between "desire and accomplishment, perpetration and memory."[92] Which myth is the true one, or can any myth be considered as the truth? Art is fireworks; it will represent an ideal under the guise of universal fables. This ideal shall replace ordinary reality with a representational one. Which world is real, and which one is pure fiction?

Considering what has been mentioned thus far, one can distinguish among three possible realities and, therefore, among three possible states of fiction. While defining pure artistic escapism solely as an illusion, the three realities or fictions can be found in contemporary daily life, in an ideal, absolute, perhaps Platonic world, and in Mallarmé's art, trying to create and to equal this pure concept. Each of these realities could be seen as fictitious in contrast to one or two of the others. A fatalistic possibility combines all three as inconceivable: if an ultimate Apocalypse occurs, all realities are illusory, awaiting an end in nothingness.

Mallarmé usually concerned himself with a more optimistic interpretation of reality and fiction. If the absolute universe consists solely of pure essences, then any reality on earth must be a simulation, unimportant when compared to its idea. The immortality of Théophile Gautier and the future apotheosis of mankind are the poet's concerns in "Toast funèbre" (Funerary Toast): "This hagard crowd! It announces: We are/ The sad opaqueness of our future

---

91. Mallarmé, "Hamlet," *O.c.*, p. 300; Scherer, *Le "Livre,"* feuillets 12(A)–15(A).
92. Mallarmé, "Mimique," *O.c.*, p. 310.

ghosts."[93] Life as one knows it has no meaning; one's true reality lies in a future glory. In an identical manner, the reality of states and governments in contemporary times is actually pure fiction. If one considers the ideal concept of a social state, one quickly sees that those on earth are not only mere artifices, but also "the brutal mirage" or a cruel, distorted reflection of the ultimate. Contemporary religion, too, is an evil Chimera, an illusion hindering man's true beliefs.[94]

If reality as one knows it in everyday life is a mirror of the ideal, the same must be said for art. It has been shown that the representational signs of art can neither create nor equal a supreme reality, but that they can imitate its structure and describe its content. Words, for example, can act as though they do correspond exactly to ideas and to things. But description is not sufficient enough to constitute reality; art is fiction.

Mallarmé had always recognized the role of fiction in music, dance, and painting, but most of his remarks concern the art of the theater, where the drama represents the succession of exterior acts without any reality. Ultimately, therefore, nothing occurs.[95] The illusion of theater is temporary; it can be broken during a performance. A pantomime is perhaps stronger in its powers since it can create a pure milieu of fiction, but even a pantomime is temporal. At the end of any performance, banal daily reality returns.[96]

Because of this constant intrusion, most art forms have to force their publics to submit to the power of illusion. If all

93. Mallarmé, *O.c.*, p. 54.
94. Mallarmé, "La Musique et les lettres," *O.c.*, p. 653; "Catholicisme," *O.c.*, p. 392.
95. Mallarmé, "Crayonné au théâtre," *O.c.*, pp. 294, 296. See also "Notes sur le théâtre," *O.c.*, pp. 339, 345; "Plaisir sacré," *O.c.*, p. 390; "Ballets," *O.c.*, p. 305; "Berthe Morisot," *O.c.*, pp. 536–37.
96. Mallarmé, "Mimique," *O.c.*, p. 310; "Les Fonds dans le ballet," *O.c.*, p. 308.

art forms can be defined as tricks or juggling, and if they all must conform to the laws of fiction, most of them employ only coarse forms of artifice. The modern public, scorning imagination but familiar with the arts, will submit only to a powerful form of illusion and even then with reservations.[97]

The concept of all art as illusion can be seen in the two words, *comme si*: art appears *as if* it were reality, but it is actually a powerful form of simulation, not a simple imitation.[98] Robert Greer Cohn has made an association between the word *si* and a twisting serpent. Whether or not this interpretation is correct, it does remind one of Mallarmé's use of the word *Chimera* to describe the fiction of art. This word can imply three meanings. The twisting serpent of *si* is an evil monster, the Chimera that causes suffering and leads to a fall of mankind; it is also the torture of fictitious art that the poet had to endure in order to experience a resurrection.[99] Second, a Chimera represents old organized religions that offer false illusions. And finally, a Chimera is good; it is the fiction of all art forms, and an ideal to be attained in a supreme work.[100] Poetry may be artificial, but the fiction that it creates is a serious one. It is to replace one false reality and to approach an absolute.

Despite his constant search to rediscover and to attain an ideal universe through artistic means, Mallarmé had always recognized the fiction implicit in language, poetry, literature, and in his supreme art form. The poet is a *jongleur*:

97. Mallarmé, "Notes sur le théâtre," *O.c.*, p. 341; "Richard Wagner: rêverie d'un poète français," *O.c.*, p. 542.
98. Mallarmé, "Un Coup de dés," *O.c.*, pp. 466–67; "Igitur," *O.c.*, pp. 436–37; "Ballets," *O.c.*, p. 305.
99. Cohn, *L'Oeuvre de Mallarmé*, pp. 225–48. Page 8 of "Un Coup de dés" presents the word *Si* and, further down on the page, the expression "in its twisting of a siren." This, of course, adds credibility to Cohn's association. Mallarmé, "Un Coup de dés," *O.c.*, pp. 470–71. Poetry is described as a "child of a siren" in "A la nue accablante tu," *O.c.*, p. 76.
100. Mallarmé, "Surgi de la croupe et du bond," *O.c.*, p. 74; "Quelle soie aux baumes de temps," *O.c.*, p. 75; "Plaisir sacré," *O.c.*, p. 390; "Magie," *O.c.*, p. 400.

he is a medieval poet, singer, or minstrel in the theater.[101] He is also a circus clown, a juggler, a trickster. But even with the implication in these words that the poet is a carefree actor, it is perhaps the seriousness of poetic fiction that makes it superior to other art forms as they now exist. In its cosmic metaphors, it becomes the ultimate artifice, and, as a supreme art form, "something special and complex results: at the convergence of other arts, and issued from but governing them, is situated Fiction or Poetry."[102] If the *comme si* of "Un Coup de dés" presents all art as artificial, it is specifically the poem and its content that exhibit such lies. Everything occurs hypothetically.[103] In a similar manner, the myths of Le "Livre" are fictitious: the description of a death by hunger in view of an ultimate rebirth is identified conditionally and literarily as such. Even the structure of the work only imitates an ideal: it merely pretends to have neither an end nor a beginning.[104]

A unique work of art may be a mere illusion, but it is a necessary illusion in order to free man from fictitious reality on earth. If it is a game, however, it must be recognized as such by everyone. Since all art forms must force a public to submit to the powers of fiction, the efficacy of any work of art depends upon the faith of its readers or spectators, upon their willingness to suspend disbelief.[105] In this way artistic fiction is voluntary; the spell of illusion can be broken at any time by the artist, the performers, or the public. When an individual refuses to continue to believe, he exerts some form of freedom: the art form can not determine the actions of its public.

101. Mallarmé, *Correspondance III*, p. 162.
102. Mallarmé, "Solennité," *O.c.*, pp. 334, 335. Language itself is fictitious. See "Notes," *O.c.*, pp. 851, 852, 853; "L'Action restreinte," *O.c.*, p. 370.
103. Mallarmé, "Un Coup de dés: Préface," *O.c.*, p. 455.
104. Scherer, feuillets 28(A), 181(A).
105. Mallarmé, "Richard Wagner: rêverie d'un poète français," *O.c.*, p. 542; "Notes sur le théâtre," *O.c.*, p. 341; "Catholicisme," *O.c.*, p. 394; Scherer, *Le "Livre,"* feuillet 70(B).

Mallarmé clearly explains the process of artistic faith in and sudden awareness of fiction. In "La Fausse Entrée des sorcières dans *Macbeth*" (The False Entrance of the Witches in *Macbeth*), the poet quotes from an article by Thomas de Quincey: " 'at no moment was my sentiment of suspense so complete and of a pause for human interest so full and so moving than at that moment when the suspense stops and the train of life suddenly returns. . . . and the reestablishment of the common facts of the world in which we live suddenly makes us deeply sensitive to the terrible parenthesis which had suspended them.' "[106] In addition to the artist's specific intentions of allowing a public to know or to feel in advance what will happen during a performance, an accidental awareness may occur. Mallarmé's example is that of the public's seeing by mistake a technician, the director, or the machinery behind the stage. Such a discovery causes an audience to laugh because they realize the fantasy of the entire work of art.[107]

This laughter on the part of a public can be associated with a moment of lucidity. When an individual begins to sense the fiction implicit in art, he smiles. Total clarity causes him to laugh. Mallarmé compares this natural reaction to the lights of a theater and of the stage: both laughter and light imply lucidity, an awareness of the processes of fiction.[108] Laughter is also a sign of superiority; it is a realization of one's power. If art exists as a serious illusion dependent upon a public's good will, man becomes a god over an aesthetic reality.

The creative god of fiction, however, is the poet. If his public becomes aware of the fact that all art can only be

106. Mallarmé, *O.c.*, p. 348.
107. The poet wants to add an initial extra-scenic section to *Macbeth* in which the presence of the three witches on stage will permit the audience to realize the future destiny of the play. By raising the curtain a minute too soon, one lets the spectators in on a secret. *Ibid.*, pp. 350, 351.
108. Mallarmé, "Crayonné au théâtre," *O.c.*, pp. 296–97; "Feuillets d'album," *O.c.*, p. 59.

fictitious, Mallarmé must compose his works with an identical realization. Even the "chance" that he desires to negate in an ideal universe is pretended.[109] The poet may not be able to rival a supreme God, but he remains the master over his own ordered creations.

There is, however, a possibility that no ideal God or universe even exists, and that the seriousness of artistic fiction is so necessary because it must fill the void beyond earthly reality. Mallarmé himself explains this need. As captives of an absolutely certain formula, men know that only that which is exists. But since man needs some pleasure in life, he turns to the beyond. The agent or motor of this other world is the literary mechanism of fiction. This fiction is, therefore, essential, but it is merely a game.[110]

Probably the most thorough interpretation of Mallarméan fiction and reality has been offered by Georges Poulet. If art is fiction because it can only simulate an absolute, it could also be considered an illusion because the absolute itself is mere fiction. According to Poulet, Mallarmé realized that only matter exists: the absolute formula of man admits only what actually is. The world of ideas and thoughts is pure illusion, the point of departure for the poet's mental and artistic inquiries. With such an interpretation, Mallarmé would have to accept as true the reality of the earthly world. This world, however, could not coincide with the poet's inner dreams. His artistic fiction would consist of a desire to believe that what is doesn't exist so that what isn't can exist. But the denial of what actually exists can take place only in the mind; one can doubt, pretend to deny, or mentally deny reality; one can never abolish it.[111]

109. Mallarmé, "Planches et feuillets," O.c., p. 328.
110. Mallarmé, "La Musique et les lettres," O.c., p. 647.
111. Georges Poulet, "Mallarmé," Etudes sur le temps humain II: la distance intérieure (Paris: Plon, 1952), pp. 323–24, 334–36, 341–43. Mallarmé's early discoveries of le néant as the truth also imply the existence of mere lies. His fears of disappearing into nothingness indicate that he was certain neither of an artistic nor of an ideal reality. Mallarmé, Correspondance 1862–1871, pp. 207–8.

If both the absolute and artistic worlds are fictitious, affirmed only in the mind, and if only material reality truly exists, then the possibility of all thought as escapism once again becomes a problem.

Another possible interpretation or solution can be presented: if one is aware of the fiction of the absolute idea and of the artistic universe, but if these two illusions are dominant in one's mind, can they not constitute an acceptable reality for that individual? Even earthly reality is seen through one's own eyes and is personally experienced and interpreted. If an individual has discovered happiness in fiction, then that fiction is, for him, a reality.

Despite any confusions regarding a definitive identification of reality or fiction, Mallarmé continued in his search for the creation of an ideal art form that would at least mirror some ideal universe or dream. He observed about him a diversity of art forms, each of which attempted to indicate the same real or artificial ideal, but each of which possessed its own particular mode of expression. Like the multiplicity of languages, the multiplicity of artistic means grew from a common origin in one instinctive art embracing all. A supreme art form should return this diversity to its unique source as a future ideal.[112]

This perfect mode of expression should, of course, contain all formerly diverse modes as one, and a total aesthetic fusion should result. But Mallarmé was uncertain about the means to achieve this synthesis and about the ultimate form that it should present. He was faced with two alternatives: a juxtaposition of genres where each one retains its own purity of expression, or a reciprocal fusion either where art forms borrow from one another or where the supreme work

112. Mallarmé, "La Musique et les lettres," *O.c.*, pp. 648, 649. After a description of the diverse, hierarchy of arts and sciences, p. 9 of "Un Coup de dés" presents a synthesis, and p. 11 shows the multiplicity as the One from which it emerged. *O.c.*, pp. 472–73, 476–77. Robert Greer Cohn, *Mallarmé's "Un Coup de dés: an Exegesis* (New Haven: Yale French Studies Publication, 1949), pp. 10–11.

borrows from all others and appears as one. He was also faced with the attempts toward a total art form already made by Richard Wagner.

Mallarmé's serious interest in Wagner as of 1885 caused a new awareness of an interrelation among the arts, especially among the theatrical arts. Wagner's operas presented to him the most comprehensive art of the times, but a contemporary total art form does not necessarily mean the ultimate form.[113] As a rival to Wagner, Mallarmé could still praise him for his theory of art and for his gift of assimilation in creating the marriage between two forms of beauty, personal drama and ideal music. But although Wagner's musical drama consisted of the synthesis of these formerly mutually exclusive art forms, Mallarmé felt that his German rival had so closely combined the two that their own properties were lost. The Wagnerian phase of theater theoretically juxtaposed drama and music, but in practice, rather than a true synthesis in view of a total art form, music overpowered all else.[114] Mallarmé's belief that the composer excluded dance from his works also stemmed from Wagner's attempt to fuse all arts into an overriding musical expression.[115]

As an alternative to Wagnerian assimilation in art, the poet advocated a concept of the purity of a genre. As early as 1876, he had recognized the intrinsic values of individual art forms. After his initial studies of Wagner for the 1885 "Rêverie," he became more insistent in this belief: drama and ballet may be allied but never confused. They become hostile to one another as soon as one forces their union. Each theatrical genre must remain distinct, but a com-

---

113. Mallarmé, "Parenthèse," *O.c.*, p. 323.
114. Mallarmé, "Richard Wagner: rêverie d'un poète français," *O.c.*, p. 543.
115. Mallarmé, "Planches et feuillets," *O.c.*, p. 328; "Solennité," *O.c.*, p. 335; *Correspondance III*, p. 83.

munication among them all must be found.[116] Mallarmé's goal would be to discover an art form as total as Wagner's synthesis, but adding more dance. If a purity of genre is to be maintained, and if a total aesthetic work is the aim, diverse art forms should be juxtaposed in order to form a proper fusion and communion.

From his initial interest in the composition of a vast dramatic work until his death, Mallarmé was fascinated with the possibilities of mounting a production that would in some way encompass the entire aesthetic spectrum, including gymnastics. There are frequent allusions in *Le "Livre"* that indicate a desire to create a work of multiple genres. The number of genres varies from page to page, from two to a possible eight. Most often the work is described as a totality containing an interchangeable drama, theater, mystery, and hymn, including poems, ballet, newspapers, a symphony, song, opera, and parade.[117]

But Mallarmé's confusion about the number of genres for an ideal work extended to his uncertainty about the method of juxtaposition in order to achieve a synthesis. He also describes *Le "Livre"* as "an intersecting of two genres, one into the other, so as to have the whole." From the combination of multiple art forms the poet can create a supreme mixed genre.[118] It must be remembered that, especially in "Un Coup de dés," he desired to compose one work that

---

116. Mallarmé, *Correspondance II*, p. 116; "Ballets," *O.c.*, p. 306. It has been pointed out that the separation between dance and pantomime not only pleased Mallarmé's sense of purity, but also stemmed from the state of ballet during the late nineteenth century. Not until the late 1890s and early twentieth century did such dancers as Nijinsky and Anna Pavlova, learning from Loïe Fuller and Isadora Duncan, integrate these two theatrical art forms. Mallarmé never saw this evolution. Grange Woolley, *Stéphane Mallarmé 1842–1898: A Commemorative Presentation* (Madison, N.J.: Drew University, 1942), p. 101.
117. Mallarmé, *Correspondance II*, pp. 116, 151, 159; Scherer, feuillets 87(A), 88(A), 102(A), 103(A), 104(A), 140(A), 148(A), 151(B), 180(A).
118. Scherer, feuillets 146(A), 106(A).

would simultaneously be a poem, symphony, painting, drama, and ballet. Everything that has been studied thus far emphasizes a need to borrow from other art forms in order to achieve one supreme genre, perhaps called poetry, but retaining all artistic qualities: temporal, spatial, written, oral, silent, visual, mobile, structured, emotional, intellectual, mathematical, and suggestive. The governing art form of Poetry or Fiction results from the convergence of all other arts, since everything that emanates from the mind ultimately returns as integrated.[119] Mallarmé explains that only then will the artist possess the reciprocal means to achieve the needed mystery in art. One must forget the former distinctions between music and letters since these two forms of art were born from and will return to a single source. The ultimate art form contains needed borrowed elements.[120] The concept of a purity of genre is a difficult tenet to defend in light of the poet's own statements.

Mallarmé will sometimes call this supreme genre Fiction or Poetry. At other times he will content himself with the use of the words *letters* and *literature*.[121] But a specific label is not important when compared to the poet's ultimate goal of rivaling the pretended supremacy of music with the just supremacy of the word. It has been pointed out that Mallarmé accused Wagnerian opera not only of assimilating diverse art forms, thereby leading to the eventual extinction of their individual properties, but also of subordinating all other modes of expression to the dominance of music. The poet had long doubted this pretended supremacy, but his specific complaint against Wagner was naturally the musician's attempt to reduce poetry, as dramatic theater, to a minor role in opera. According to one of his disciples,

119. Mallarmé, "La Musique et les lettres," *O.c.*, p. 645.
120. *Ibid.*, p. 649.
121. *Ibid.*, pp. 646, 656; Mallarmé, *Correspondance II*, p. 306; "Sauvegarde," *O.c.*, pp. 416–17, 419–20.

Mallarmé dreamed of a future "when Poetry, finally disengaged from the subordination to which Wagner had reduced it, would regain its primary role and, in turn assimilating the temporarily victorious Music to its power, would become once again the sovereign expression of thought."[122]

Even if total musical supremacy were temporary, some of its characteristics would always remain superior. In addition to its abilities to be intellectually structured and to represent mysterious but mathematical symbols, music, like dance, jealously guards its ideal purity as an art form without words. Even in its silent visual form, poetry needs representational signs that offer both specific and suggestive meanings. If the purity of silence is an ultimate goal, then the poet can offer the pure white suggestive page, but typographical words are still present. Total purity is achieved only in communication by thought alone.

But in order to make poetry rival music, Mallarmé had to stress the supremacy of language. Although he recognized the necessary influence of music, the poet emphasized the intellectual attributes of the word, adding meaning to an otherwise vague and emotional musical sound. If a total art form were to be a composite of all artistic modes, music would play an essential but secondary role, contributing its vitality and emotion to the work. Wagner's dramatic theory was operatic; Mallarmé's concept was poetic.[123]

As a poetic theory of drama, Mallarmé's dream remained constant. If the poet could state in 1898 that he had always been faithful to his goal,[124] he meant not only his goal of an

---

122. Henri de Régnier, *Proses datées* (Paris: Mercure de France, 1925), pp. 45–46. See also Mondor, *Vie de Mallarmé*, p. 705; Block, pp. 59–72; Mallarmé, "La Dernière Mode," *O.c.*, p. 817.
123. Mallarmé, "Crise de vers," *O.c.*, p. 365; "La Musique et les lettres," *O.c.*, pp. 648, 656; "Richard Wagner: rêverie d'un poète français," *O.c.*, pp. 542–43, 545; "De Même," *O.c.*, p. 396; Block, p. 69.
124. Mallarmé, "Sur l'idéal à vingt ans," *O.c.*, p. 883.

ideal and unique work, but also his unswerving lifelong belief in the artistic supremacy of literature.[125] Since the literary word is usually specifically identified as poetic, one must understand that, according to Mallarmé, all language should be considered as poetry, even under the guise of prose. As soon as there is an attempt at literary style, there is an attempt to create poetry.[126] Poetry is the unique source of all art; it shall once again reign as the ideal art form: "A contemporary French poet, excluded from any participation in the official displays of beauty . . . loves . . . to reflect upon the sovereign pomp of Poetry. . . . Ceremonies of a day that lies, subconsciously, in the hearts of the crowd: almost a Cult!"[127] Mallarmé, of course, is the contemporary French poet who will create and organize these future festivals. The ideal, official, artistic cult shall be musically poetic; as such it can be presented in a book, as mental theater, or on a stage. Both forms of presentation are theatrical, since "theater is of a superior essence."[128] Mallarmé had to choose between the two.

In 1894 the poet envisioned his supreme art form in this way: starting with music and letters, "One of the modes inclines toward the other and, disappearing in it, reappears with borrowed elements: a total but wavering genre is twice perfected. Theatrically for the crowd which, without awareness, is present at the audition of its own grandeur: or the individual requires the lucidity of an explanatory and familiar Book."[129] Mallarmé wants to forget the former distinctions made between music and poetry. His ideal does

125. Mallarmé, "Diptyque," *O.c.*, p. 849; "Igitur," *O.c.*, pp. 434, 437; "Les Mots anglais," *O.c.*, p. 901; "Solennité," *O.c.*, p. 334; "Villiers de l'Isle-Adam," *O.c.*, p. 507; "Or," *O.c.*, p. 399; "Le Mystère dans les lettres," *O.c.*, p. 386.
126. Mallarmé, "Sur l'évolution littéraire," *O.c.*, p. 867.
127. Mallarmé, "Richard Wagner: rêverie d'un poète français," *O.c.*, p. 541.
128. Mallarmé, "Le Genre ou des modernes," *O.c.*, p. 312.
129. Mallarmé, "La Musique et les lettres," *O.c.*, p. 649.

not consist of two separate art forms, one musical, theatrical, and emotionally vague, and the other intellectual and poetic.[130] Mallarmé would never have called music a pure and total art, and any ultimate genre must use certain borrowed elements. If everything in the world can be categorized either as aesthetics or as political economy, as Mallarmé so asserted, the first refers to all fiction and the second to "its social counterpart."[131] Eventually all will be reduced to aesthetics. In 1894 the poet dreamed of two complete and perfected genres as two modes of presentation, the theater and the book. Both would combine music and poetry, and both would be considered as alternative means of communication of a total art form that would encompass the world.

---

130. Suzanne Bernard, *Mallarmé et la musique* (Paris: Librairie Nizet, 1959), pp. 35, 49, 70, 71.
131. Mallarmé, "La Musique et les lettres," *O.c.*, p. 656.

4

The Ideal Art Form: Its Means of Presentation

The reign of poetry means the reign of the word, and since, for Mallarmé, a word must be written in order to be preserved, poetry's supremacy necessarily implies the power of the page and of the book. Mallarmé's belief in this superiority has already been mentioned in relation both to his desires to transpose the symphony into a book and to his exaggerated statements that the world will end in this beautiful form. But one should realize that the written text is the basis either for a silently or orally read work by an individual or for a theatrical presentation. If Mallarmé praised Maurice Maeterlinck for an art that included theater in the book,[1] he was admiring *Pélléas et Mélisande* as an actual drama, retaining certain superior qualities of the mentally read work and, as a play, able to be read in the privacy of one's home.

1. Stéphane Mallarmé, "Planches et feuillets," *Oeuvres complètes* (Paris: Editions Gallimard, "Bibliothèque de la Pléiade," 1945), p. 329.

Much of what has been discussed thus far leads one to the possible conclusion that the poet preferred the individually read work to the theatrical presentation. The power of the written word in its visual and suggestive silence, the importance of typography, and the written symbol as a mathematical note or number all lend support to such a conclusion. The printed word is also permanent. It is a spatially presented sign that could temporarily be lost or distorted in an oral performance. Any misinterpretation, however, could be primarily the fault of the inferior quality of contemporary bourgeois theater. According to Mallarmé, as soon as literary action is limited to the stage, the power of the written word disappears. A poet is uselessly precise in his work because the modern means used to present his ideal are defective and indirect. The work and its mode of presentation are currently contaminating one another.[2]

Mallarmé had originally desired actual theatrical presentations for some of his earlier works, but he failed in his attempts. Such failures may have caused him to revert to the written text as the sole means of communication. As of 1866, he had abandoned "Hérodiade" as an actual drama and had turned instead to the composition of a dramatic poem with an opening monologue, a major scene of dialogue, and a closing canticle, probably composed later in his life. *Les Noces d'Hérodiade*, dating from the end of the poet's life, also appears to be an intellectual and mental drama. It is a dramatic poem in both dialogue and monologue, including a prelude, two scenes, a canticle, monologue, and finale, all implying an inner movement or an intellectual ballet.[3]

2. Mallarmé, "L'Action restreinte," *O.c.*, p. 371.
3. Mallarmé, "Hérodiade," *O.c.*, pp. 41–49; Stéphane Mallarmé, *Les Noces d'Hérodiade: mystère*, introduction de Gardner Davies (Paris: Gallimard, 1959), p. 44; Haskell Block, *Mallarmé and the Symbolist Drama* (Detroit, Mich.: Wayne State University Press, 1963), pp. 17–20.

Although the earliest version of "L'Après-midi d'un faune" was intended for the stage and provided its single reciter with stage directions, the 1875 version, "Improvisation d'un faune," and the version most known today appear as dramatic monologues to be individually read.[4] "Igitur" is also mental theater in monologue. It is a tale addressed to the reader's intelligence. The mental action is not only staged by the individual reader but also occurs within the mind of the sole hero. In addition to these two forms of intellectual drama, there exists a third, related to the published work: the description of the mental action of Igitur will be found on the pages of a book within the tale. It is the volume of the hero's experiences, his monument to be opened and explained to other men.[5] Ten years later the poet would try to write another *tombeau* where printed characters would be on stage, dramatically recounting an actual tragedy transformed into the mind.[6]

During the 1880s and even after his first serious contacts with Wagner, Mallarmé continued to extol the virtues of the written book. According to Edouard Dujardin, the poet liked to imagine the German composer reading operas as though they were bibles; as a skilled reader, Wagner could see and hear within himself a theater of the imagination.[7] But Wagnerian operas were still compromises if the non-material stage were the aim. In "Le Genre ou des modernes" (The Literary Genre or the Moderns), Mallarmé states that a piece of paper, with its multiple personality, is sufficient to create theater. Each reader plays the drama in

4. Mallarmé, *O.c.*, pp. 50–53, 1448–66; Block, pp. 21–30; Henri Mondor, *Histoire d'un faune* (Paris: Gallimard, 1948), pp. 100–104, 107–11, 201–4.
5. Mallarmé, *O.c.*, pp. 433, 437, 438, 439, 446, 449.
6. Stéphane Mallarmé, *Pour un tombeau d'Anatole* (Paris: Editions du Seuil, 1961). See pp. 32, 35 of the introduction by Jean-Pierre Richard.
7. Suzanne Bernard, *Mallarmé et la musique* (Paris: Librairie Nizet, 1959), p. 77.

his own mind. Such individualized interpretation is never possible at an actual performance.[8] Working with existing texts, the best inner drama thus far may be a fusion of Wagner's works and *Le Forgeron* (The Blacksmith) of Théodore de Banville. Similar to a closet drama, to the "Spectacle in an armchair" of Alfred de Musset, *Le Forgeron* was a dramatic ode, not to be performed on an actual stage. For Mallarmé, it represented both an intellectual spectacle and an excellent mental exercise or game. It provided the poet with the opportunity of stressing the supremacy of the book over actual theater, often corrupted by the limitations of the physical stage: "What a presentation! the world is there, holding a book in its hand. . . . Admire . . . how a mind [*un esprit*], having found refuge in several pages, defies civilization, which had neglected to construct anything for his dream, so that this wonderful Theater and Stage can exist."[9] Whether the "esprit" mentioned above is de Banville, any genius poet, or individual readers' minds, the theater of the imagination seems here to be the ultimate goal.

In 1893 the volume is also considered to be a superior mode of communication, "A theater, inherent to the mind:" "an opera without accompaniment and song, but spoken; now the book will try to suffice, in order to open up the inner stage and to whisper its echoes. A versified ensemble invites an ideal presentation."[10] Mallarmé does seem to be uncertain in this article. He will try to make the book suffice as silent, mental, ideal theater, but it is possible that some oral rendition will be necessary. His uncertainty extended to the presentation of "Un Coup de dés" where, de-

8. Mallarmé, *O.c.*, pp. 315, 318.
9. Mallarmé, "Solennité," *O.c.*, p. 334; Block, pp. 72–73, 88–90.
10. Mallarmé, "Planches et feuillets," *O.c.*, p. 328.

spite the mental staging of words moving like actors, an oral "performance" may have been desired.[11]

The inferior state of contemporary theater and the desire to affirm the supremacy of poetry, however, reassured Mallarmé of the abilities of silent mental theater. "L'Action restreinte" was originally entitled "A l'éloge du Livre" (In Praise of the Book), and, a few months later in 1895, the book became a spiritual instrument where the silent solitary concert of poetry exalts the word's attributes as both true music and true theater. In "Catholicisme" the silently read book exhibits its abilities to inspire religious ecstasy, and, ultimately, the printed work shall rule the world.[12] In the future religious and social state, one will discover the absolute reign of the mind, as seen in books. In an impenetrable palace will be a library where on a throne one can see the apotheosis of the written word in a volume. Such a room, according to Mallarmé, exists mentally in the memory of every man.[13]

Many of the loose pages of Le "Livre" also indicate the possibility that Mallarmé's ideal work was to be in the form of a book, as mental theater. The action of the myths occurs in the imagination. One could offer the text as the theater and the page as the stage where individual readers can see their true selves reflected as mental actors.[14] But most of Mallarmé's notes concern a practical application of the printed work. There are numerous pages filled with the calculations for the number of copies to be printed and the

11. Mallarmé, *O.c.*, p. 455. It is difficult to answer these questions: if a book is read aloud by an individual for himself alone, does this constitute theater? If one person reads aloud to another, is theater involved, or is a larger audience necessary?

12. *Ibid.*, pp. 1572, 378, 380–81, 392.

13. Mallarmé, "Sauvegarde," *O.c.*, pp. 417–18.

14. Jacques Scherer, *Le "Livre" de Mallarmé: premières recherches sur des documents inédits* (Paris: Gallimard, 1957), feuillets 20(A), 32(A), 103(A), 100(A).

price to be charged for each volume. In contrast to a theatrical presentation, fragmentary or tediously long in its explanation of the multiple work to an audience, the printing of the book will allow an individual to purchase all twenty volumes. He can then refer to the printed text whenever needed or desired.[15]

Mallarmé had realized in "La Cour" that an actual performance of an ideal work was not practical, in that it could not easily and simultaneously reach all men. The printed work would not only offer a totality but would also be able to attain a vast public. A contemporary form of printed matter that already possessed a large following was the newspaper. According to Mallarmé, the absolute aspect of *Le "Livre"* would be so evident that its printed form would, perhaps, not be too important. The mental theater to be written in twenty volumes could be published as a book or could be inserted as poetry into a newspaper.[16] Despite his hatred of contemporary journalism, Mallarmé saw in it certain attributes that he wished to borrow for his supreme theater.

His first interests in journalism paralleled a persistent vein of elitism. *La Dernière Mode* was an attempt at the reporting of a select life-style for a small group of aristocratic women. In "Un Spectacle interrompu" the poet, distantly fascinated by the amusement in popular theater, dreamed of a higher form of newspaper, written by poets who viewed anecdotal events as dreams and people as ideal types. By 1887, the poet had recognized the power and need of journalism to speak in the name of a silent unanimity, but, in his aristocratic fashion, he continued to see a

15. *Ibid.*, feuillet 134(A). See also feuillets 130(A), 179(A), 75(B)–76(B), 81(B), 108(A), 113(A), 121(B), 122(B), 137 (*suite*), 167(A), 183(A), 202(A).
16. *Ibid.*, feuillets 171(A), 201(A), 66(B), 102(A), 104(A), 106(A), 132(A), 151(B).

disparity between correct and intellectual language, always poetic, and the language of newspapers.[17]

Jealousy of the vast public of journalism and dispersion of its vulgar characteristics remained present in Mallarmé's mind, but, in the early 1890s, he began to see signs of a new future, latent even in this contemporary form of mediocrity. His optimistic faith became the subject of an 1892 prose article, "Etalages" (Bookstalls). Although many newspapers were used for the propaganda of petty interests and opinions, peddled to the masses, there seemed to be a growing interest in making journalism a more literary art form. While contemporary books were becoming trivial, certain newspapers were allowing more space for the *feuilleton*, or serial. The large public reached by the newspaper was beginning to read the daily fiction that had finally appeared on principal pages and had replaced in importance what Mallarmé considered to be secondary articles.[18]

In its ability not only to offer popular literature but also to present each new day as if it were brightly new, the newspaper posed itself as a possible threat to the supremacy of poetry. Some members of the literary elite had become upset at journalism's parody of the sacred book and at its use of vulgar language; however, Mallarmé not only was aware of these occurrences but was excited about the prospects of a future that would bridge the gap between literature and the people. If elite snobs desired to hasten their steps, they were hurrying away from these events. If Mallarmé followed suit, he was anxious to partake in this

---

17. Mallarmé, *O.c.*, pp. 707–847, 276; "Crayonné au théâtre," *O.c.*, p. 295; "Sur l'évolution littéraire," *O.c.*, p. 867. Scherer believes that this distinction always remained in Mallarmé's mind: the two genres published as a book for Le "*Livre*" would be verse and journalism. Such an interpretation is credible since the poet did consider both forms for the printed work. Scherer, p. 36, feuillet 148(A).

18. Mallarmé, *O.c.*, p. 375, 376.

future. Considering the present increase in a more intellectual press, the poet felt that something decisive was occurring: a contest for the creation of a modern popular Poem, similar to *The Thousand and One Nights*, at which the majority of the reading public would marvel. Mallarmé advised artists to take part in this wonderful accomplishment. His entry for the contest would not be pure journalism, but it would borrow greatly from this modern changing mode of communication.[19]

After the publication of "Etalages" and until his death, the poet's opinion of the newspaper remained constant. The revolution of literary journalism was aided by men like Guy de Maupassant, who offered the mass public a high level of literature in daily doses.[20] Such occurrences caused Mallarmé to reevaluate his definition of newspaper articles, formerly separated from poetry. They became poems, "the only contemporary form because it is eternal." Eternal modernism was of prime consideration to the poet.[21]

Even the mediocre aspects of journalism were seen in a new perspective. The immediate and elementary coarseness and the lack of structured order in this parody of a book were now viewed optimistically as a first stage of or a departure point for the sacred form. By 1897 not only had poetic elements been inserted into the newspaper, but the latter had influenced all literature; no art form could nor wanted to escape from this influence.[22]

19. *Ibid.*, pp. 376–77. Marshall McLuhan, "Joyce, Mallarmé, and the Press," *Sewanee Review* 62, no. 1 (January-March 1954): 45, 46–50. An attempt is made in this article to limit Mallarmé's ideal work to journalism.
20. Mallarmé, "Deuil," *O.c.*, pp. 524–25. Mallarmé was always jealous of this ability of journalism to attract a vast public, charmed by the powers of a "popular fairyland." "Le Livre, instrument spirituel," *O.c.*, p. 379. The newspaper, therefore, was a good place to include not only his supreme work, but also his theories on art, developed in numerous articles published in literary reviews, themselves a high level of journalism.
21. Mallarmé, "La Musique et les lettres," *O.c.*, p. 655.
22. Mallarmé, "Le Livre, instrument spirituel," *O.c.*, p. 379; "Bibliographie des *Divagations*," *O.c.*, p. 1538.

Mallarmé's ideal work, therefore, could easily be presented in the form of a printed book or a newspaper. In an 1897 letter to Octave Mirbeau, the poet expressed a desire to condense his great work into a forty-page literary review article. Considering the length of the intended twenty-volume Book, one may possibly see in this statement an example of Mallarmé's gift of sarcastic exaggeration. A similar tone could have been intended when he said to Paul Valéry that, if there were a mystery to the world, it would be found in a copy of *Le Figaro*.[23]

If Mallarmé altered his opinion of newspapers in general, he followed an identical course in his views on the use of advertising in these popular art forms. When the poet had made a distinction between poetic and journalistic language, he had included in the latter the language of advertisements. But when he combined poetry and newspapers in 1894, he continued to see publicity as the separate and original language of the press.[24]

His fascination for the visual—the written word and the typographical page—understandably included an interest in the placement of printed words as used in posters and advertisements. According to Paul Valéry, Mallarmé carefully studied the typography of these printed forms before composing "Un Coup de dés."[25] He recognized the power of typographical resources that can emphasize the idea of principal and secondary motifs by catching the reader's eye without requiring prolonged concentration.

This interest in advertisement is also evident in the

---

23. Paul Valéry, *Ecrits divers sur Stéphane Mallarmé* (Paris: Mercure de France, 1911), p. 108; Robert Greer Cohn, "A propos du 'Coup de dés,' " *Esprit créateur* 1 (1961): 127–28.
24. Mallarmé, "La Musique et les lettres," *O.c.*, p. 655.
25. Such concerns had already been considered by Charles Henry and William Morris in a special issue of *La Plume* (15 novembre 1893) devoted to illustrated advertising. Suzanne Bernard, "Le 'Coup de dés' de Mallarmé replacé dans la perspective historique," *Revue d'histoire littéraire de la France* 52, no. 2 (avril-juin, 1951): 184–86.

fragmentary notes of *Le "Livre,"* although additional reasons can be perceived. Since newspapers and posters are important aspects of contemporary life, an imitation of their visual form brings the necessary quality of modernism to the work. In a more practical vein, Mallarmé envisioned the use of advertising for financial reasons: "advertising pays for the printing and paper/ poster/ book of magic/ folio."[26] If an ideal work can be presented as a book or in a newspaper, the inclusion of advertisements will not be detrimental to its appearance. It will actually add certain typographical effects, while covering acquired costs.

Advertisements will also appeal to the masses, or so believe the editors of a recent publication of a selection of Mallarmé's prose works. In 1969 there appeared a small volume containing sections from *Divagations* (Ramblings). This book, originally costing one franc, is part of a newly planned series called *Poésie I*, in which selected texts are presented on pages interspersed with paid advertisements. Throughout the book one sees advertising for other works and series, literary journals, records, guidebooks, newspapers, radio and television programs, banks, and perfumes. In a desire to see the marriage between poetry and the masses, Marcel Bleustein-Blanchet explains the ideas behind this book's publication:

> Advertising implies, above all, an act of choosing. To choose is to elect. To elect is to favor the development of a given production. Now, every advertising strategy provoking mass production inevitably involves mass consumption, putting within everyone's reach what was formerly reserved for a small privileged group.
> It is, therefore, a question of a truly democratic phenomenon which reaches not only what concerns our well-being but equally our spiritual values and culture in general.[27]

26. Scherer, feuillets 166–67*bis* (*suite*).
27. Stéphane Mallarmé, *Divagations* (extraits) (Paris: Librairie Saint-Germain-des-Prés, 1969), pp. 6–7.

It would have been interesting to hear Mallarmé's opinion of this attempt.

Despite all the evidence given above to indicate a preference for the book as mental theater, one can find throughout Mallarmé's life and works a parallel preference for the actual stage. The poet's own theatrical goals for certain of his works, his personal love of being on stage before an audience, and his belief in the power of the oral word and in the intimacy of the conversational tone all point to this fascination for theatrical presentations. According to Lugné-Poe, the poet loved to discuss and to dream about a future summer open-air theater where the stage would be on the banks of a river and the audience would sit on barges.[28]

It has been explained that "Igitur" can be seen as a dramatic tale, played within the mind of the hero and played to the mind of the intellectual reader. But more theatrical qualities have also been pointed out as occurring within the prose work. While employing actual stage directions, Mallarmé has created a monologue where the hero is on stage speaking to a theatrical audience of his elite ancestors who, although not visible, partake in the action by hissing.[29] The poet may have abandoned the idea of a dramatic performance for this work, but he was insistent on making theater an integral part of it.

Throughout the 1880s, Mallarmé continued to see the theater as possessing the excitement and ceremony needed by modern man,[30] but he began to confuse the distinctions between the book and actual theater. In his discussion of *Le Forgeron* by Théodore de Banville, he began to dream

28. Cited by Block, p. 106, from *Le Sot du Tremplin*, p. 223. Nature is described as the poet's theater, in Mallarmé, "Bucolique," *O.c.*, pp. 402, 404.
29. Mallarmé, *O.c.*, pp. 433, 438, 439, 442, 451.
30. Mallarmé, "Le Genre ou des modernes," *O.c.*, pp. 312, 314, 315, 318; "Crayonné au théâtre," *O.c.*, p. 295.

about a glorious future when the reason for assembling at official festivals would be to hear not ordinary theater or music but a dramatized ode, divided into heroic scenes, "an ode for several voices."[31] If this ode were silent, mental theater, Mallarmé could perhaps utilize dramatic voices in a written text, but a necessary gathering of people, as in theater or in a religious mass, would present a problem.

Possibly stemming from his own attempts at a vast popular melodrama, the poet deepened his interest in the actual assembling of people in a specific place. The magic of both theater and religion is partially dependent upon a feeling of togetherness when many people gather in a public place to witness a common event. The aesthetic place becomes religious; as such it must become the scene of future festivities. It must be remembered that the artist has to "display his fireworks on the public square" because the only true festivals are public.[32]

Mallarmé's own belief in the public domain, literary goods for all people, stresses the need for "the public square or building. The place depends upon the masses of citizens. . . ."[33] This edifice could already be seen in the building of Trocadéro: "The first theater that the Crowd possesses, the Palace of Trocadéro, is premature but interesting with its stage reduced to the floor of the platform (the trestle and in front of the choir), its considerable buffet of organs, and the public, jubilant to be there, undeniably in a building dedicated to festivals. It implies a vision of the future. One has unconsciously borrowed several elements from the church."[34]

The theater of Trocadéro resembles a church because art is to be the official religion of the future. One of the prob-

31. Mallarmé, "Solennité," *O.c.*, p. 335.
32. Mallarmé, "Villiers de l'Isle-Adam," *O.c.*, p. 499.
33. Mallarmé, "La Musique et les lettres," *O.c.*, p. 642.
34. Mallarmé, "De Même," *O.c.*, pp. 396–97.

lems of contemporary times is that men find neither the opportunity nor the place to be together; communication, especially among men of different social classes, becomes impossible. When people attend the theater, a musical presentation, or mass, they all participate together in a common experience; there is a communion between the work and the public, as well as among the spectators. The staging of Mallarmé's ideal art form will transform an ordinary place into a vibrating, infinite one until, as a purely virginal site, only the place remains. The theater becomes religious; the public is one with the divine place. Both are eternally saved.[35]

The Catholic mass, with its magical music, drama, complex ritual, public participation, and ultimate communion, became one of the prototypes for Mallarmé's future ideal art form. The drama would be a mystery, service, or the Passion performed in a majestic amphitheater.[36] The future social and aesthetic religion of the state described in "La Cour" would convoke at one time a thousand changing members of an elite present at a fervent rendezvous held in a temple. This public assembly can not be envisioned as a multitude of men where individuals silently and independently read a sacred work as mental theater in their own homes. It would be almost ludicrous to imagine such a huge gathering if individuals in the audience each read the new bible to themselves, without witnessing any actual performance or dramatic recitation. The ideal work must be organized and led by a conductor, the poet-priest.[37] In *Le "Livre,"* it requires the "opérateur."

Jacques Scherer describes the poet's great work in this way: "The total work is none other than a book, read aloud

---

35. *Ibid.*, p. 396; "Un Coup de dés," *O.c.*, pp. 474–75; "Catholicisme," *O.c.*, p. 391.
36. Mallarmé, "De Même," *O.c.*, p. 396; "Catholicisme," *O.c.*, p. 393.
37. Mallarmé, *O.c.*, pp. 414–16.

and commented on by Mallarmé in front of a particular public and according to a complex ceremony. It offers a lesson or a conviction of a metaphysical nature, destined to replace existing religions. This public reading is enough to give the name of theater to the work, and, besides, it is not without an analogy with the mass."[38] If many of the pages of *Le "Livre"* contain calculations concerning the printed copies of the work, even more pages describe what the poet calls "séances." In the intimacy of his living room, Mallarmé will play the role of the "opérateur" who reads, or rather acts out and explains the twenty volumes of this supreme work. These "séances" or "Readings" become the third mixed genre, derived from a combination of poetry and newspapers. They are so important that everything is contained within them, or, if the printed work can compete, they remain as the basis for the published form.[39] The theatrical presentation is the foundation for all future communication of the work.

Mallarmé had studied the possibilities of vast religious and aesthetic festivals performed in a public place. *Le "Livre"* continues in this manner as an application of the theater or public square. But in the privacy of his own home, the "opérateur" could only play before a small audience of twenty-four people.[40] If there could be no temple large enough to hold all of mankind at one time, Mallarmé's readings were to abandon the public place for the intimate salon. But at least the elements of theater could be retained.

The organization of the oral readings of *Le "Livre"* was very important to Mallarmé. He made numerous calculations about their frequency of repetition, the seating of the

38. Scherer, p. 37.
39. *Ibid.*, feuillets 34(B), 41(B), 42(A), 58(B), 59(B), 67(B), 90(A), 106(A), 107(A), 110(A), 113(A), 130(A), 131(A), 141, 188(A).
40. *Ibid.*, feuillets 102(A), 95(A).

public, the cost of entry, the length of time and composition of each performance, and the number of years needed to complete the entire work.[41] The supreme art form is described as a quadruple play of five juxtaposed acts. There will be twenty volumes, each one read in one "séance." The total time needed will be five years. Each presentation will last a total of two hours, with an intermission of fifteen minutes.[42] Mallarmé's love of drama will cause him to present not a mere recitation, but an actual performance, satisfying his personal desires of being on stage: "The seats—furniture./ curtain/ The reader [reader arrives, greets from the right] enters, through the empty space between the seats at the right and the left, and, a little bent over, goes directly to a piece of furniture—lacquered—obviously half-filled on a diagonal . . . each of the 6 diagonal racks, containing 5 sheets of paper (the number easily visible at a glance). . . . He knows, from then on, and places himself [turned in the direction from which he came, one turn made to what has become his right] under the sole electric lamp. . . ."[43] Mallarmé is alone on stage. His monologue may commence.

The poet's own gift for theatrics has been well documented. The *Mardis* seem to have been opportunities for him to discuss before his disciples what may have been prepared monologues. His Villiers de l'Isle-Adam lecture was dramatically read in Belgium and in Paris, and, at Valvins, before close friends, he delighted even more in his monologue:

"I shall read it to you; even better, I'll play it for you. . . ."
Mallarmé makes his entrance, smiles with thoughtfulness and

41. *Ibid.*, feuillets 41(B), 82(B), 112(A), 139(B), 143 (*suite*, 144(A), 184(A) (*suite*).
42. *Ibid.*, feuillets 175(A)–76(A), 194(A).
43. *Ibid.*, feuillet 195(A).

begins with the same ceremonial as though there had been two hundred people present. . . . he sits down right away in order to read, play, mime, whisper, and proclaim, in front of four people [Léopold Dauphin, Henri Roujon, Marie and Geneviève Mallarmé], for more than an hour, the long lecture. The public loses none of its beauty. The actor's game is so perfect that everything seems easy. "A sparkle of the eye, an intonation of the voice, a gesture of the hand, and the trick is played."[44]

During the 1894 lecture of "La Musique et lettres" at Oxford, Mallarmé experienced the same feeling of importance: " 'the staging was exquisite . . . enthroning Papa framed alone in light. . . . The applause at my entrance, at my departure. . . . the amateur of rareness in me was charmed.' "[45]

The poet's early poems exhibit a deep sense of narcissism where the hero, concerned solely with himself, looks only within or at a self-reflection in order to effect a mental rebirth. Even though "L'Après-midi d'un faune" was first entitled a monologue and, in 1891, planned as a recitation by a single actor,[46] and even though "Igitur" is a monologue played before a theatrical audience, another form of narcissism is still in force. Instead of a soliloquy to oneself, the poet turns to others in front of whom he will exteriorize his inner being. He still remains the sole actor.

The perfect example of man, or rather of the poet, as a unique actor can be seen in *Hamlet*, Mallarmé's favorite play. To the poet, this play represented a transition between former multiple action and the future monologue or

44. Henri Mondor, *Vie de Mallarmé* (Paris: Gallimard, 1941), p. 581. Léopold Dauphin recounts this experience. For more on the Villiers de l'Isle-Adam lecture in Belgium and in Paris, including Mallarmé's interpretation of the public's reaction, see Stéphane Mallarmé, *Correspondance IV 1890–1891*, ed. Henri Mondor et Lloyd James Austin (Paris: Gallimard, 1973), pp. 52, 53, 56–57, 58, 60, 62, 68, 69, 70, 74–75.
45. *Ibid.*, pp. 679–80. Mallarmé wrote this account to his daughter.
46. Mallarmé, *O.c.*, pp. 1450–53. See also Mallarmé, *Correspondance IV*, pp. 164–65, 188, 193–94, 235.

drama of the self. The hero, reading from a book about himself, becomes a living sign. He becomes the poet and ultimately every man, as he exteriorizes on the stage the sole character of an intimate and occult tragedy.[47] If Hamlet is the symbol of all men, he reminds one of the ballerina and of the mime who "recites" his role in a silent soliloquy. And Hamlet is Mallarmé who, in the theater of nature, acts out his role in order to present himself slowly to a public.[48] This exteriorization of one's self in a monologue can be played, of course, on an actual stage or on the stage of a printed page.

Is any dialogue possible on this stage? Although the Shakespearean play does present other actors, Mallarmé felt that all secondary characters were mere reflections of the central one. In a similar manner, the secondary dancers in a ballet can all be summed up in one synthesis called the prima ballerina.[49] At times, however, Mallarmé did stress a need for dialogue within a work of art: Le "Livre" is once described as a dialogue, and his ode for several voices does imply the use of several people in acting roles.[50] But the first reference may merely indicate a dialogue among the echoing and reflecting parts of an ideal work, and even several individuals presenting an ode must ultimately be seen as one with an ideal, unique, and divine universe.

Whether an ideal presentation of an ideal work were to be in the form of a book or a theatrical performance, its essence would be poetic, and its artistic vehicle would be the

47. Mallarmé, "Bibliographie des Divagations," O.c., p. 1564; "Hamlet," O.c., p. 299.
48. Mallarmé, "Mimique," O.c., p. 310; "Ballets," O.c., pp. 303–4; "Bucolique," O.c., p. 403; Scherer, feuillet 57(B).
49. Mallarmé, "Hamlet," O.c., p. 301; "Ballets," O.c., p. 304.
50. Scherer, feuillet 171(A); Mallarmé, "Solennité," O.c., p. 335. Paul Valéry recounts that at one time some people desired to stage "Un Coup de dés" as a polyphony of thirteen voices, based upon Mallarmé's ode. Valéry was very much against this idea. Valéry, p. 17.

word. This word must retain a mysterious and incantatory brilliance; it must imply and instill in all people a sense of ritual. In describing his future aesthetic religion, Mallarmé had compared it to the Passion of divine mankind, assimilated to the tetralogy of nature's seasonal cycle. A love and need for the pomp of solemn ceremonials, instinctive in all men, are manifest in pagan rituals of nature and in modern religions—specifically, for Mallarmé, in the Catholic mass. When Anatole Mallarmé was dying, the poet nostalgically returned to the security of religious funeral rites: he began to kneel, pray, and genuflect before his son.[51] Since all men possess this inner desire for ritual, an ideal art form must satisfy such a need. It will become the prototype of all ceremonials. It will offer all the necessary pomp of a cult and, above all, its dignified solemnity, as serious as the Catholic liturgy.[52] The somber ceremonies of art will be presented as a "Mass in Music or a Requiem"; whether initially as a book or a performance, they will eventually become a "solitary festival in oneself."[53] The divinity of each man is found within his heart.

But modern and future men need not only the seriousness of an aesthetic religion; they need its joy. For Mallarmé, some mystical link relates these two seemingly opposite desires.[54] The poet's interest in grandiose spectacles, performed like the drama of men and gods in the theater of nature, led him to dream of massive halls where the poet would stand before crowds of people, revealing aesthe-

51. Mallarmé, *Pour un tombeau d'Anatole*, pp. 51–53, feuillets 11, 74, 75, 178.
52. Mallarmé, "Catholicisme," *O.c.*, p. 394; "Richard Wagner: rêverie d'un poète français," *O.c.*, p. 541; "Le Genre ou des modernes," *O.c.*, p. 314; "Crayonné au théâtre," *O.c.*, pp. 296–97; "Parenthèse," *O.c.*, pp. 322–23; "Solennité," *O.c.*, p. 335; "De Même," *O.c.*, pp. 396, 397.
53. Scherer, feuillets 3(A), 20(A).
54. Mallarmé, "Plaisir sacré," *O.c.*, p. 389.

tic beauty to mankind.[55] The ideal art form is often described as this vast festival and, more importantly, as a jubilant celebration. The text is the basis; it grows into a public event or into a private celebration, sensed within as universal. Even a conversation by firelight can be defined as an intimate gala, oral and yet personal.[56] A love of public festivals implies a love and need for social ceremonies. Once again, the rituals of life can be personal, shared with close friends, or experienced with a large number of people. For Mallarmé, the intimate social ritual, similar to the small gatherings for the séances of Le "Livre," was exemplified by the toast at a banquet for personal friends.[57] The ideal work, however, is likened to the more universal ceremonies of life: baptism, engagement, marriage, and burial, as intimate and religious rituals, and banquets, balls, hunts, fireworks, and parades, as more festive and massive events.[58]

If any universal social ceremony is to be effective as an aesthetic religion, it must be official. In contemporary times, citizens have a right to demand from their state the building of an official theater and the organization of an official religion, both as compensations for mankind's deplor-

55. Mallarmé, Correspondance II, pp. 101, 103, 105, 108–9, 151, 154, 159, 260; "Les Dieux antiques," O.c., p. 1169; Paul Margueritte, "Le Printemps tourmenté: souvenirs littéraires 1881–1896," Revue des deux mondes 51 (15 mai, 1919): 246. This idea of an actual massive ceremony has caused some critics to see signs of totalitarianism in Mallarmé, a sort of Wagner-Hitler figure before huge gatherings of people! Albert-Marie Schmidt, "Mallarmé fondateur de religion," Les Lettres, 3 numéro spécial (1948): 111–12. Others have seen him at an international or Communist rally; today it would be Maoist! André Lebois, "Stéphane Mallarmé et la politique," Mercure de France 121 (1 septembre 1948): 75–78; Pierre Batistini, "Mallarmé, poète de la foule," La Revue moderne des arts et de la vie (1 avril 1949), pp. 16–17. It is interesting to note that all three articles were written in 1948–49.
56. Mallarmé, "Solennité," O.c., pp. 335, 336; "Symphonie littéraire," O.c., p. 265; "La Dernière Mode," O.c., p. 717; "Crayonné au théâtre," O.c., pp. 1562, 295; "Villiers de l'Isle-Adam," O.c., p. 499; "Sur l'évolution littéraire," O.c., p. 869; "Catholicisme," O.c., p. 392; Scherer, feuillet 104(A).
57. Mallarmé, "Salut," O.c., p. 27. All of the "Vers de circonstance" imply a deep sense of social ceremony. O.c., pp. 81–186.
58. Scherer, feuillets 69(B), 72(B), 80(B), 104(A), 105(A), 131(A), 168.

able existence. In the future, an official art form will be the sign of a stable society; it will become the staging of the state religion. It will be maintained by the state that fulfills its proper duty, since the religious and aesthetic festival will become synonymous with the functioning of this state and of life.[59]

It has been pointed out that, in 1894, Mallarmé envisioned two perfected means of presentation for an ideal art form. Both modes borrow from music and from letters, and both borrow from each other. But it has also been shown that the poet could not decide upon a preference for either the book or the theatrical performance; he vacillated from one to the other and often confused any distinctions between the two. A written text, assuring the permanent reign of poetry, is to be found at the beginning of all literature. If art is to be a stimulus to man, who then experiences a sense of mental theatrical staging, either the written work or the physical stage may serve as this initial catalyst. The theater of the mind goes beyond the physical limitations of both the page and the presence of an actor.

From 1864 until his death, Mallarmé vacillated between the use of the book or the theater for the presentations of "Hérodiade" and "L'Après-midi d'un faune." "Igitur" has been seen as a tale providing mental theater, as a theatrical monologue within the written story, and as an additional book within the staged drama. But if the poet still differentiated between two modes of communication in these works, while attempting to use both or to combine them, such a separation sometimes becomes indistinguishable in his articles of the 1880s and 1890s. Often a reader does not know whether he is defining a book as mental theater or as an actual theatrical performance.

It has been seen that in 1887 Mallarmé praised *Le*

---

59. Mallarmé, "Le Genre ou des modernes," *O.c.*, pp. 313, 314; "Notes sur le théâtre," *O.c.*, p. 345; "De Même," *O.c.*, pp. 395, 396; "La Cour," *O.c.*, p. 416.

Forgeron of Théodore de Banville as a masterpiece of mental theater in the form of a book, but that he immediately began to imagine a dramatic Ode, causing masses of people to assemble in order to hear several voices recite heroic scenes. In the same year, while lauding the plays of Alphonse Daudet, the poet explained that he was charmed by the type of art form that could establish a delightful ambiguity between the written and the theatrical work. The public would have the feeling of reading a book as well as being present at a performance.[60] "L'Action restreinte" describes the poet as the spiritual actor in a text, but as one who needs the intermediaries of the stage, the footlights, and the actual presence of spectators in order to offer the drama of every man.[61] The same confusion is extended to the "Presentation with a concert" of "Catholicisme" and to the mythical ceremony of books theatrically played by an elite group of actors in "Sauvegarde".[62]

Mallarmé has been quoted as saying, around 1896: " 'One must not give to the public what can not be offered under good conditions. Let us be content with enclosing ourselves in a book which is cloistered.' "[63] Contemporary theater is insufficient; one must be temporarily content with the mental theater of a book. But this form, too, may be a compromise, awaiting some future ideal means of presentation. It was Mallarmé's great work, however, that was to be the future ideal, but one will see that, even in the fragmentary notes for this perfected art form, he became confused and could reach no practical conclusion.

60. Mallarmé, "Notes sur le théâtre," *O.c.*, pp. 342–43.
61. Mallarmé, *O.c.*, p. 370.
62. *Ibid.*, pp. 393, 418. In *Le "Livre,"* the work is described as a play, a presentation with a concert, and a dialogued poem, scene, or symphony for stage and orchestra. Scherer, feuillets 171(A)–72(A). Once again, this play could be mental or actual. A similar controversy, although more distinct, has already been explained regarding the silent or oral rendition of "Un Coup de dés."
63. Mondor, *Vie de Mallarmé*, p. 728. Mallarmé was specifically discussing ballet in this passage.

It has been shown that, in Le *"Livre,"* Mallarmé had a choice between the printed book or newspaper and the intimate séance held in his own living room. Suzanne Bernard aptly observes that the poet seems to have hesitated between the cabalistic doctrine of initiation and the Catholic doctrine of universal diffusion.[64] Both means of presentation have their positive attributes: the elite oral readings provide a total understanding of the volume discussed because the poet-"opérateur" is present to explain and to act out all difficulties; the printing of the work allows everyone who so desires, hopefully all of mankind, to purchase all twenty volumes. In other words, the séances offer ideal, intellectual possession; the printed copies provide physical possession.[65,]

But if each form of presentation has its positive aspects, each one is also insufficient if used alone: the oral readings do not offer the totality of the work, and the purchasing of the twenty volumes may not necessarily produce correct understanding, since there is no knowledgeable person to explain the content or the structure of the loose pages.[66] In addition, if the oral word can have a magical power over an audience, the beauty of the written text may be lost for the crowd. In his examination of the various means of presenting a work of art, Mallarmé had considered a third possibility, the mass festival; however, in Le *"Livre,"* such a possibility is merely implied in the mention of a public place but never fully developed as a viable alternative. In this mode, the oral word is preserved; the "opérateur" is present; and a vast public is reached. But the poet considered only the

64. Bernard, *Mallarmé et la musique*, pp. 143–44.
65. Scherer, feuillets 108(A), 130(A), 131(A), 132(A), 134(A), 189(A), 192(A). Although all twenty volumes would ultimately be discussed at the séances, for practical reasons the poet states that each person could attend only two oral readings. Diffusion of the work in its totality was the concern of the press.
66. *Ibid.*, feuillets 111(A), 155(A).

elite séance for his oral explanation of Le "Livre." There may have been several reasons for this decision. First of all, vast assemblies were not feasible because the microphone was not yet invented; Mallarmé had to be satisfied with the attendance of twenty-four people in his home. Second, the poet may have preferred an initial public of an intellectual elite; these persons would hopefully understand more quickly and perhaps be more sympathetic toward Mallarmé's attempts.[67] And third, a small elite group could then serve as a means toward the future diffusion of the work; as disciples of Mallarmé, they could later spread the news of the publication and perhaps explain to others the meanings within Le "Livre.".

Doctrines of either cabalistic initiation or Catholic universal diffusion are not enough if each is used alone. They need each other. If every individual were ultimately to understand and to possess what Mallarmé had originally created or re-created, and now personally retained as supreme, he would have to attend all séances and purchase, read, and understand all twenty volumes. Both the book and the theater are necessary and are permanently inherent in the proper communication of Le "Livre." After the completion of the séances, Mallarmé will, if asked to do so, either have more copies printed, or even possibly continue the oral explanations that were dependent upon the presence of the "opérateur."[68]

As a result of the recognition of a need for both the séance and the book, and as a normal evolution from his earlier discoveries, Mallarmé often confused these two modes of presentation for Le "Livre." One of the myths is staged in this way: "to open upon a solitary milieu within oneself . . . preparation for the festival/ intermission/ confu-

---

67. Suzanne Bernard, *Mallarmé et la musique*, pp. 143–44; Block, pp. 78–79.
68. Scherer, feuillets 130(A)–30(A) (*suite*), 133(A).

sion between the two/ or [with spotlights] . . . raising of the curtain—lowering/ theater and background beyond . . . background = theater."[69] This myth could be presented as such in a book or on a stage. Ultimately the two are totally fused in the poet's mind: "identity of the Book and of the Play/ of the Book and a presentation of the Play . . . [thus ideal issued from juxtaposition]."[70]

If an ideal form of presentation grows from the juxtaposition of the silently read book and the orally recited monologue, then these individual means or their combination as considered by Mallarmé are mere compromises. If the poet's ultimate desire was the mass ceremonial, then the book compromises with its written text, and the elite séance compromises with its limited public. The true ideal may also be pure silence where thoughts are communicated and instantaneously understood by everyone without the aid of either an interpreter or the written word. Pure mental theater would be the ultimate goal.

But if this ideal presentation lay beyond those means already studied by the poet as feasible, its effective communication was still dependent upon the receiver of the supreme idea. The unique art form is destined for a specific or general public. Any participation by this public will be dependent upon the particular communicative process used. The public and means of communication chosen will also affect the proper response and interpretation desired by the poet. And finally, once a work of art is communicated, a rapport is established between the author and his public. A confrontation has occurred, and, hopefully, some ideal relationship, or reconciliation in Mallarmé's case, will result in the glorious future.

69. *Ibid.*, feuillet 20(A).
70. *Ibid.*, feuillet 129(A).

5
Communication Between the Artist and His Public

The act of creative writing usually implies the recognition of a public to whom the written or oral text will be addressed. In his critique of Mallarmé, Albert Thibaudet has suggested that a writer can choose among five alternatives when he begins his creative task: he may compose a work for everyone, for a particular group, for a single person, for himself alone, or, avoiding a decision, he may remain silent.[1] Although Mallarmé was often indecisive, all of his concerns for the publication of his works demonstrate a desire for communication. Three possible publics were available for his efforts: the elite, literary and intellectual or financially aristocratic; the masses; and the bourgeoisie that composed the majority of the average contemporary reading public.

Who composed Mallarmé's actual public during his

1. Albert Thibaudet, *La Poésie de Stéphane Mallarmé: étude littéraire* (Paris: Gallimard, 1926), p. 66.

lifetime, and who composes it now? This question can be answered by a single word, *elite*, or even by the words *intellectual elite*. Despite modern attempts to offer the poet's works to a wider public, it is doubtful whether most of his poetry or prose works can be understood by the average person or can even interest most members of a reading public. This public may have increased and may have become better educated since the nineteenth century, but Mallarmé's works have remained intellectually cryptic.

Mallarmé was well aware of his unpopularity and sometimes painfully so: in eight years, only 160 copies of *L'Après-midi d'un faune* were sold. When he concerned himself with the publication of his works, he concentrated on recognition by literary journals that were read, as today, by a small percentage of the total reading public.[2] He deeply appreciated the often fervent admiration by an elite public. At times this actual following fulfilled his desires, but dreams of reaching all of mankind increasingly haunted him.

The 1862 prose article "Hérésies artistiques: l'art pour tous" portrays the youthful poet as an aristocratic man of literature who scorns everyone but a highly literary elite. All other men are combined into one amorphous group labeled as the vulgar crowd or masses. At the age of twenty, Mallarmé felt that poetry was being debased in contemporary times because of its introduction into the schools and, therefore, its easy accessibility to all men. Although these men may have read some works of literature without ever having understood their true meanings, they

2. Henri Mondor, *Histoire d'un faune* (Paris: Gallimard, 1948), pp. 227–30; Stéphane Mallarmé, *Correspondance III 1886–1889*, ed. Henri Mondor et Lloyd James Austin (Paris: Gallimard, 1969), pp. 223, 237. For this concern in the number of copies to be printed, the price to be charged, and, therefore, the size of a public to be reached, see Stéphane Mallarmé, *Correspondance IV, 1890–1891*, ed. Henri Mondor et Lloyd James Austin (Paris: Gallimard, 1973), pp. 195, 213, 219–20, 237, 253, 295, 298, 301–3.

consider themselves knowledgeable enough to become experts. They would never attempt to judge other forms of art, especially painting.[3] Similarly, the mysterious hieroglyphics of musical notation, understood only by an initiated few and therefore protected from the vulgar public, provoked Mallarmé's jealousy. He wanted to present his art as a mystery whose solution should be attainable only by certain rare individuals. All other men should limit themselves to the reading of works on morality. Mallarmé is very specific about identifying this elite public. Not only the masses but also the educated bourgeoisie and even the aristocracy should abandon all attempts to understand the truths of poetry. Only one group is worthy of the poet's attention: fellow artists who will spend their last dime on the purchase of a book of poems.[4] The ideally desired public of 1862 would closely correspond to the actual public attained during Mallarmé's life.

In 1869 "Igitur" was addressed to two publics, one actual and the other theatrically within the tale. Once again the intelligence of a reader is specified at the beginning, while the hero of the work desires to communicate with his elite race of ancestors, each of whom presumably had tried and had failed in an attempt to write the ultimate volume.[5]

Despite these two examples of a desired elite public, one can discover a few early references to the greater aims of the poet. "Le Phénomène futur" (The Future Phenomenon) illustrates an attempt to relate to three different publics of poetry: those who are indifferent because they have no ability to understand; those who are emotionally moved; and fellow poets who become deeply inspired.[6] But at such an early date, the poet does not indicate whether or not these

3. Stéphane Mallarmé, *Oeuvres complètes* (Paris: Gallimard, "Bibliothèque de la Pléiade," 1945), p. 258.
4. *Ibid.*, pp. 259, 260.
5. Mallarmé, *O.c.*, pp. 433, 439.
6. *Ibid.*, pp. 269–70.

varying reactions to his poetry will satisfy his goals of reaching more men. By 1871, before his move to Paris, he hoped to interest a crowd, concerned with politics and war, in his new theatrical endeavors: "I have not lost hope in presenting at the beginning of October a small drama, adapting itself to the most varied curiosities of a crowd."[7] Perhaps because of his contact with the French capital as of 1871, or perhaps because of a normal process of maturing, Mallarmé began to turn away from his 1862 theory of pure elitism in art. He became more aware of a mass public behind his chosen few. In *La Dernière Mode* of 1874, while his actual public grew to include the feminine reader, still wealthy and socially elite, he democratically wrote that every man has a right to be part of a public of art, since this art should reflect a total reality.[8]

As has already been noted for the early 1870s, the poet's first real desires of communication with a larger public were related to his early theatrical attempts. Throughout his late 1870 and early 1880 letters, Mallarmé referred to his work on a vast popular melodrama as that which would dazzle the sovereign people.[9] His planned *Hamlet et le vent* was to be performed at country fairs, and his own involvement in the Théâtre de Valvins was in a theater whose public was described by Paul Margueritte as having consisted of "family, passing friends, and the people, peasants of the surrounding villages who, carrying chairs or benches, came into the large but narrow crowded room."[10] According to

---

7. Stéphane Mallarmé, *Correspondance 1862–1871*, ed. Henri Mondor (Paris: Gallimard, 1959), p. 354.
8. Mallarmé, *O.c.*, pp. 719, 744, 745, 765, 775, 827, 843–44. See also "Le Jury de peinture pour 1874 et M. Manet," *O.c.*, pp. 695–700.
9. Stéphane Mallarmé, *Correspondance II 1871–1885*, ed. Henri Mondor et Lloyd James Austin (Paris: Gallimard, 1965), pp. 159, 103, 108–9, 151, 236, 237, 256.
10. Paul Margueritte, "Le Printemps tourmenté: souvenirs littéraires 1881–1896," *Revue des deux mondes* 51 (15 mai 1919): 244; Haskell Block, *Mallarmé and the Symbolist Drama* (Detroit, Mich.: Wayne State University Press, 1963), pp. 45–48, 73–74.

Margueritte, Mallarmé considered only two worthy and intelligent publics for the theater: poets and the people. It would be before these men that the poet would stand, in great halls, revealing beauty to the masses.[11]

Richard Wagner had written in an 1849 essay that the perfect art work should be the "great united utterance of a free and lovely public life," embracing all of mankind.[12] Despite this recognition of the people as a needed force in art, and despite a desire as of 1876 for free access for everyone into the festival hall at Bayreuth, Wagner, like Mallarmé, was actually talking about some ideal future crowd. A great disparity lay between the musician's dreams and his actual popularity: Wagnerism was probably still an esoteric religion in 1885, a cult for an educated few. In a similar manner, the Concerts Lamoureux that so greatly affected Mallarmé, jealous of music's power over an audience, were in truth attended by an elite public of worldly men, musicians, and artists.[13]

But whether or not as a mistaken belief, Mallarmé's interest in and jealousy of Wagner as of 1885 greatly influenced his concerns for an art form's impact on a large group of people. The mysterious hieroglyphics of musical notation are still present in "Hommage," but now they are too powerful to remain silent on the page. They burst forth to be heard by everyone, while poetry, using common vocabulary, remains accessible only to the initiated. The poet's guarded admiration of Wagner in the "Rêverie" contains many references to a future ideal where a crowd, implying

11. Margueritte, p. 246.
12. Richard Wagner, *Wagner on Music and Drama. A Compendium of Richard Wagner's Prose Works*, trans. H. Ashton Ellis (New York: E. P. Dutton and Co., Inc., 1964), p. 64. See also p. 65.
13. E. Carcassonne, "Wagner et Mallarmé," *Revue de littérature comparée* 16 (1936): 348; Suzanne Bernard, *Mallarmé et la musique* (Paris: Librairie Nizet, 1959), pp. 23, 33, 50.

all men, will participate in the ceremonious and sovereign cult of Poetry.[14]

It has been seen that the ideal theatrical Poem or Ode will be composed of mankind's multiple self, diverse and yet unified. Mallarmé further studied this concept of a universal myth, relating to all men in their ideal but elementary state, when he decided that every member of an audience was reflected in the character of Hamlet and in the metaphorical symbol presented by the ballerina. If all men are originally and ultimately divine, and if art serves as a reminder of this eternal truth, then the poet's task must be the creation of a work that will reach everyone.

It has also been noted that *Le Forgeron* of Théodore de Banville prompted Mallarmé to theorize about a future ideal art form, either written or performed, that would charm the people. Similarly in his dramatic criticisms, he recognized the multitude of men as the public of the future.[15] Like Wagner, he would await a better time to change the composition of his own public. Although the contemporary masses do not seem to desire art, Mallarmé felt that this crowd would eventually shed its mediocrity and would then call the poet to its aid.[16]

It was precisely this contemporary mediocrity that angered and saddened Mallarmé. In his opinion, most contemporary men were not intelligent, and the masses in their present state were not yet ready for art. If there is any hope for an ideal future for art and for man, it is presently seen as a mere constellation far above the contemporary public, temporarily beyond its interest, and in a state of

14. Mallarmé, *O.c.*, pp. 71, 541, 542, 544, 545.
15. Mallarmé, "Solennité," *O.c.*, pp. 334, 335, 336; "Crayonné au théâtre," *O.c.*, pp. 1562, 294, 296, 298.
16. Mallarmé, "Villiers de l'Isle-Adam," *O.c.*, p. 499.

disuse.[17] The masses are unleashed onto art, but they remain tired children, neither understanding nor desiring to know the truth about themselves. Even the elite members of a concert audience do not possess totally lucid comprehension of the messages of music.[18]

As for the bourgeoisie, this majority of the reading public complains that poetry is too obscure. According to Mallarmé, charges of obscurity imply that the person who is complaining is either unintelligent or lazy.[19] Although the poet admired the ability of the Catholic religion to induce the general public to participate in its rituals without any true understanding, his ideal reader would possess more intellectual capabilities. In "L'Art pour tous" his desired public was an aristocratic literary one; in *La Dernière Mode* social class was of primary importance. Now he added a more specific qualification: "if someone with average intelligence and an insufficient literary education opens such a book [obscure] by accident and pretends to enjoy it, there is a misunderstanding. . . ."[20] Mysterious, obscure meanings can be discovered only after a great effort of deciphering and interpreting. Either an obscure exterior or a falsely simple appearance must serve as protection against an undesired public. The artist can thereby discourage the lazy reader who, upon an initial and cursory glance, is convinced that there is nothing in the text to interest him.[21]

From Mallarmé's point of view, a poet must await the proper time when the level of all men will be raised to an ideal height, but, despite widespread contemporary

---

17. Mallarmé, "Un Coup de dés," *O.c.*, pp. 476–77. See also Robert Greer Cohn, *L'Oeuvre de Mallarmé "Un Coup de dés,"* trans. René Arnaud (Paris: Librairie Les Lettres, 1951), pp. 387–420.
18. Mallarmé, "La Cour," *O.c.*, pp. 413–14; "Plaisir sacré," *O.c.*, p. 388.
19. Mallarmé, "Le Mystère dans les lettres," *O.c.*, pp. 382–83.
20. Mallarmé, "Sur l'évolution littéraire," *O.c.*, p. 869. See also "De Même," *O.c.*, p. 396.
21. Mallarmé, "Le Mystère dans les lettres," *O.c.*, pp. 382, 383.

mediocrity, laziness, and stupidity, certain signs of optimism were already evident in the present public. And despite his usual antipathy toward any intermediary compromises, he was pleased to see these changes being made
by the efforts of religion, music, the building of Trocadéro,
and, especially, the growing amount of literature offered to
an increasing public of the modern newspaper.

As for Mallarmé, he would continue to theorize and
dream about an ideal future when his public could consist
of all of humanity. His deep concern for the masses and
guilt about his lack of action in the past were suggested as
essential to an interpretation of "Conflit" and "Confrontation." The function of art as a catalyst to return men to
their original and ideal divinity implies the attainment of
such goals by mankind in general. The ideal religious,
aesthetic, and social state achieved through the ultimate art
form was to offer every man justice and equality. Even the
questionable society described in "La Cour" would allow
each individual to become a member of an elite when he
came into contact with the ideal work, often portrayed as a
vast and joyous festival for everyone. Mallarmé would not
lower his standards; he would expect every person to become intellectually superior to his present state. In addition, he would expect every person to desire both to
change and to read obscure poetry.

The unbound pages of Le "Livre" indicate a similar concern for a future mass public, while they present the alternative of intimate séances for a select few. In effect, Le
"Livre" will be an actual recitation only for the elite public,
at least until some future ideal means of presentation can
be discovered that will fuse both the book and theater. Although Mallarmé is not always certain about the number of
those whom he calls "assistants" at his séances, he most
often states that twenty-four people will be present at one

time to see and hear him recite and act out his work.[22] In a practical attempt, similar to that of "La Cour," to reach a wider elite public, the particular people composing the twenty-four "assistants" will change at each oral rendition. After the completion of the required twenty séances for the twenty volumes, 480 people will have had the opportunity to hear at least part of the ultimate Word.[23]

In order to attain a vast general public, Mallarmé had to make use of the written work either in the form of a book or inserted into a newspaper. Le "Livre" by right originally belongs to everyone, and the poet must give it back to the people in inexpensive copies. The entire effort to produce an eternally modern work of art was made so that it could be placed within everyone's reach.[24] Despite one mention of a desire for a published work with an infinite number of copies, Mallarmé usually decided upon the number 480,000 for the number of volumes to be printed.[25] If each person bought one volume, 480,000 men would learn the truths inherent in nature and humanity. Ideally, every individual would purchase all twenty volumes, and, if necessary, more copies could be printed at a later date.

It is obvious that, at least temporarily, Mallarmé distinguished between two types of publics for his Great Work. In contrast to his 1894 concept in "La Musique et les lettres," Le "Livre" would offer drama to the elite and the book to the masses. Whether or not one or both of these means of presentation were compromises has already been discussed. What is important is the fact that these two separate pub-

22. Jacques Scherer, Le "Livre" de Mallarmé: premières recherches sur des documents inédits (Paris: Gallimard, 1957), feuillets 51(B), 90(A), 95(A), 107(A), 188(A).

23 Ibid., feuillets 188(A), 192(A), 142(A). Mallarmé, however, also states that each elite auditor has the right to a double reading, to attend two séances. Idem, feuillet 184(A). Each volume is read through and then read in reverse to form a second interpretation.

24. Ibid., feuillets 62(B), 103(A).

25. Ibid., feuillets 69(B), 144(A), 170(A) (suite), 202(A).

lics will ultimately fuse into one: the séances can last only as long as Mallarmé lives. After the initial distinction in publics while *Le "Livre"* is being introduced at the poet's home, everyone will have to depend upon the printed volume. The elite will return as members of the crowd. Every person will then have the right to purchase all twenty volumes.[26] At times Mallarmé will continue to separate himself from his entire public, identified as the crowd, but finally everyone will have to possess the same knowledge as he.[27] From an original distinction among the poet, the elite, and the mass public, the elite will become part of the crowd, and all of mankind will eventually become equal to Mallarmé, that is, divinely equal.

In his biography of Mallarmé, Henri Mondor relates a well-known anecdote. When Berthe Morisot asked the poet why he did not write so that his cook could understand him, he was surprised. " 'What?' he cried, 'but I would not write any differently for my cook.' "[28] Although he would not simplify his poetry, one has seen that he did consider the possibilities of compromise in the modes of presentation described especially in "La Cour" and in *Le "Livre."*

Whether or not he should compromise in his actual works was a problem that Mallarmé could not always solve. When he considered only other men of literature as the proper public for art, it was easy to defend a refusal of compromise to the masses: "Oh you [fellow poets] are your own enemies, why . . . do you flatter and preach to yourselves this impiety, the vulgarization of art! You will, therefore, walk either beside those who, erasing the mysterious notes of music . . . open its secrets to the mob, or beside others who spread this music at any price throughout the

---

26. *Ibid.*, feuillets 130(A), 133(A), 134(A).
27. *Ibid.*, feuillets 132(A), 112(A), 124(B).
28. Henri Mondor, *Vie de Mallarmé* (Paris: Gallimard, 1941), p. 502.

countryside, happy that people are playing it incorrectly, as long as it is played."[29]

Upon his contact with Wagner and his investigations into the theater, Mallarmé altered his opinion. A vulgarization of art is a temporary necessity while awaiting an ideal future. In this way the contemporary masses can begin their journey toward the recognition of their godliness:

> It has always been necessary, considering contemporary infatuation, to erect between the gulf of vain hunger and future generations, suitable to an immediate need, a simulation, or official art which one can also call vulgar art; unquestionable, ready to contain by means of its basaltic veil of banality, the pushing of the jubilant crowd which only slightly perceives an unrefined image of its divinity. A temporary crude machine for the strengthening of what! an empty but lasting institution convincing me because of its opportuneness. . . . Heroic, so be it! Artists of today, rather than paint a cloistered solitude as the torch of your immortality or sacrifice yourself in front of your own personal idol, use your talents for this monument.[30]

Mallarmé wrote this surprising statement in 1887. Throughout the rest of his life, he vacillated between the inevitability of compromising to reach a vast public and a desire to retain a high level of art. Ideally speaking, a poet should reject all contemporary success and attempts at communication until a better future and a superior public can be achieved. But if an artist were to await the attainment of pure "lucidity" by all of mankind, his "concert" would never begin: "The sovereign bow marking the first measure would never fall, if it were necessary at that special moment of the year for the chandelier in the hall to represent by its multiple facets the public's lucidity with reference to what it is coming there to do."[31] The need to address oneself to other men prevailed.

29. Mallarmé, "Hérésies artistiques: l'art pour tous," *O.c.*, p. 260.
30. Mallarmé, "Crayonné au théâtre," *O.c.*, p. 298.
31. Mallarmé, "Plaisir sacré," *O.c.*, p. 388.

Many of Mallarmé's early poems express a sincere desire to rediscover himself in a pure form, only to find the absence of all things in nothingness. The method of self-discovery usually consisted of a search within himself or within his own reflection in a mirror, window, or body of water, all mirrored in highly personal poems. Throughout the 1860s, works such as "Les Fenêtres" (The Windows), "Las de l'amer repos" (Weary of Bitter Repose), "Soupir" (Sigh), "Hérodiade," "Igitur," and "Ses purs ongles . . ." (Its Pure Nails . . .) show the poet narcissistically regarding his own image, egotistically concerned with his own problems, and rejecting any exterior aid.[32] But Mallarmé soon realized that he could not effect purification solely by means of his own reflection in an exterior object. As already noted, he passed from this personal function of art to one that would encompass all men.

In the first step away from totally self-sufficient narcissism, he still remained an egotist. After having composed works presenting the image of the poet looking at himself, he began to write poems where he would see himself reflected in the eyes of one or many other people. With a growing concern for communication to a wider public, he also began to use this exterior body of men indirectly. Through his poetry he could present his own self to the eyes of his readers. In both cases, he was still searching for his own identity, but now he needed others if he were to expect any success.

In reference to this persistent egotism, Jean-Pierre Richard has stated that Mallarmé sought to see himself, to reassure himself, and ultimately to possess himself indirectly by means of his public.[33] Even in some of his early

---

32. Mallarmé, *O.c.*, pp. 32–33, 35–36, 39, 41–48, 433–51, 1488. The early version of "Ses pure ongles . . ." was called "Sonnet allégorique à lui-même" (Allegorical Sonnet to Himself).
33. Jean-Pierre Richard, *L'Univers imaginaire de Mallarmé* (Paris: Editions du Seuil, 1961), p. 347.

works, he began to view himself through the eyes of another person. The water in "Le Pitre châtié" (The Punished Clown) becomes the eyes of the poet's beloved. In them he experiences a drunken rebirth.[34] One is not certain of the exact composition date of "La Cantique de Saint Jean" (The Canticle of Saint John), but, as a later part of "Hérodiade," it serves as a reminder of a contrasting, or rather an additional, method of self-reflection. While the heroine of the "Ouverture ancienne" (Old Overture) and of the "Scène" of this long poem regards herself in a mirror and fearfully flees the look of another, the emphasis in "La Cantique" is upon the decapitated head of the saint with his pure regard. Although Hérodiade does not see her own image in the eyes of Saint John in this particular poem, Mallarmé obviously intended to confront her with the head of the saint when, in Les Noces d'Hérodiade: mystère, the two are wed in a union that will cause the young heroine's death and, hopefully, divine rebirth.[35]

With the two prose poems, "Le Phénomène futur" and "La Déclaration foraine" (The Strolling Declaration), and with the poem, "La chevelure vol d'une flamme . . ." (The hair, flight from a flame . . .), included within the second work, Mallarmé turned from a need of self-reflection in the eyes of another to that mirrored in the collective eyes of a crowd. In all of these works, he offers his work of art, in the form of a woman, to a large gathering of ordinary people at a fair. In effect, Mallarmé is offering himself to the crowd, and, in their nonlucid regards, he hopes to effect the same transformation that he had been attempting all his

34. Mallarmé, O.c., p. 31. See Richard, pp. 95–98, 130–31 for discussions of other early works relating to a reflection of oneself in the eyes of one other person.
35. Mallarmé, O.c., p. 49; Stéphane Mallarmé, Les Noces d'Hérodiade mystère, introduction de Gardner Davies (Paris: Gallimard, 1959), pp. 101, 116 117, 124, 135; Richard, pp. 204–8.

life. The look of the poet is projected from within onto the mocking but truthful multiple look of the people. In a return movement, this laughing collective mirror will expose the nudity of the heroic poet. Once again, Mallarmé is concerned solely with the attainment of his own pure self.[36]

When a person offers the image of himself to the eyes of a crowd, he is on stage before an audience. It has already been seen that Mallarmé loved the feeling of being an actor who recites a monologue, much in the same way that his favorite hero, Hamlet, acts out his personal and yet universal tragedy before all men. Mallarmé called the poet "the evil Hamlet" in "Le Pitre châtié" when he first began to see his reflection in the eyes of another.[37] Basing his proof on this poem and on the article "Hamlet," Wallace Fowlie has formulated an interesting theory that presents Mallarmé as a weak and egotistical actor, desperately needing to exhibit himself to others. According to Professor Fowlie, the poet was unable to understand and, therefore, to live his own life with its torments and dreams. In order to find himself and then to justify his own existence, he, like Hamlet, needed to create an art form, theater or poetry, in which he could act out his life before others rather than live it within himself.[38]

But the need to communicate to another and to see oneself reflected in another's gaze is not always entirely egotistical. Upon contact with an ideal work of art, the public will also benefit from the knowledge of the truths inherent in this art form. Mallarmé explains the force of literary action as that which philosophically causes in many people a cer-

---

36. Mallarmé, *O.c.*, pp. 53, 269–70, 279–83; Richard, pp. 98–99, 346–50. Richard explains this process as a transformation from *je* (i) to *Je* (I). Laughter has already been associated with a recognition of truth. For a similar use of a public for egotistical purposes see Scherer, feuillets 27(A)–32(A).

37. Mallarmé, *O.c.*, p. 31.

38. Wallace Fowlie, *Mallarmé* (Chicago: The University of Chicago Press, 1962), p. 244; Mallarmé, "Hamlet," *O.c.*, pp. 299–302.

tain movement that will in turn create for the initiator an agitation proving his own existence.[39] In other words, the poet creates a work of art; he affects others when he communicates his thoughts to them; in a circular return, this public will aid the poet in his own self-discovery.

Even in this more humanitarian concept of the function of art, Mallarmé makes the poet the initiator of creation and communication. There are times when he does place the source of inspiration for a poetic work not within himself but in the crowd: the poet becomes a child before his mother, who offers him truth and life.[40] Here, a public inspires a poet to show himself in his work to the world, but once again it is the artist who is purified to his most elementary and ideal self.

Despite this persistent vein of egotism underlying his humanitarian concern for mankind, Mallarmé will also at times seem sincerely interested in effecting the same transformation for his public as for himself. A truly reciprocal communicative process in art will then be his aim. Both the poet and his public could relate to each other and ultimately could become equal. In his terms, whether by means of an actual theatrical performance using a human intermediary or by means of the publication of a book in which a reader could see himself reflected directly, the active role of a public will be indispensable. Mallarmé's need for others will become the specific using of this other person or persons in a determined effort to benefit everyone.

It can be said that an essential goal of any artistic means of presentation consists of an attempt to discover some

39. Mallarmé, "L'Action restreinte," *O.c.*, p. 369.
40. Mallarmé, "Verlaine," *O.c.*, p. 511; "Notes sur le théâtre," *O.c.*, p. 342. Robert Greer Cohn interprets parts of "Un Coup de dés" as representing the crowd as the source of the poem. Ultimately both the multiple public and poem will return to the unique number from which they originated. Cohn, pp. 127, 159–61, 330–31, 349.

common plane on which men can communicate. A present lack of dialogue among men was one of Mallarmé's deepest concerns, whether the cause lay in the infrequent contact among social classes or in the imperfections of ordinary language. The poet feared that any true transmission of one's thoughts was impossible. Men are different; they view everything in the world and in art in a multitude of ways.[41] How can one expect them to relate totally to one another?

The closest human rapport that existed for Mallarmé and, in his opinion, for all men, was the intimate conversation where very often, among close friends, true communication is attained without the use of words. According to René Ghil, Mallarmé used to dream about an ideal type of watch whose face would present simple colored signs. These mobile symbols would silently speak to everyone and, being universally understood, would replace the need for ordinary conversation. One could nostalgically return to the language of the heart and of the eyes.[42]

What Mallarmé actually desired was pure, silent, and immediate communication among men where true thoughts would be neither misrepresented nor obscured by the imperfections of people and language.[43] It has been noted that the poet was jealous of music because it could relate to men without the use of words and could, therefore, communicate directly to an individual's mind and soul. Although a poet could re-create the purified poetic word, the ultimate purity, as the inevitable return to an original source, is silence: the white page or the pure thought. If both the book and the theatrical performance of the Great

---

41. Mallarmé, "Solitude," *O.c.*, p. 408; "Conflit," *O.c.*, p. 358; "Crise de vers," *O.c.*, pp. 363–64.

42. Mondor, *Vie de Mallarmé*, pp. 468–69; Mallarmé, "Diptyque," *O.c.*, p. 849; "Crayonné au théâtre," *O.c.*, p. 295; "La Musique et les lettres," *O.c.*, pp. 637, 642, 649–50.

43. Mallarmé, "Crise de vers," *O.c.*, pp. 363–64.

Work are compromises, the ideal means of presentation is mental. And if the ultimate circular work finally closes its circle so that eternal timelessness may ensue, the essential means of future communication of its truth to others would also be purely mental. Ideally, Mallarmé's desire was communication by thought alone.

The poet realized that in every-day encounters with others, man already uses certain forms of silent communication. At times he compared the silent exchange of thoughts to the silent exchange of money. Although he hated its impersonal and vulgar power, much in the same way that he hated the universal commonness of ordinary language, Mallarmé was jealous of its ability to render immediate and precise rapports among men.[44]

Men can also silently relate to each other by the use of gestures, visible signs, or physical contact. When Anatole Mallarmé was dying, his father desired to join hands with him in an effort toward some communion with his son during his son's journey into eternity.[45] Mallarmé believed that silent contact among men can express more sincere feelings than can ordinary language: "My look, clearly resting upon his, confirms a deference for this humble believer in richness, oh! how a silent handshake can be obvious—since the best of what passes between two people always escapes them when they are conversing."[46] A handshake, a sign, a smile can succinctly relate the same thought that otherwise would require an explanation of many words. Visual communication from a distance can also be used in place of actual contact among men: Mallarmé regards the country workmen from afar, while dreaming not only about an ideal

44. *Ibid*., p. 368; "Confrontation," *O.c.*, p. 410; "Or," *O.c.*, pp. 398–99.
45. Stéphane Mallarmé, *Pour un tombeau d'Anatole*, introduction de Jean-Pierre Richard (Paris: Editions du Seuil, 1961), pp. 51–53.
46. Mallarmé, "Confrontation," *O.c.*, p. 411.

rapport with these men, but also about simple advances toward them in order to express friendship.[47]

The poet had relied upon visual communication in order to effect self-discovery and self-transformation. Since all art forms are inherently theatrical, then the eye plays an important role, be it as a look at oneself in a mirror, a look at others, or among others. In *Pour un tombeau d'Anatole*, visual contact between two people is theatrically staged as occurring between the sole actor and a single spectator, Mallarmé. The eye becomes a symbol of prophetic lucidity, of pure consciousness not only of the present tragedy, but also of the eternal future, when the poet and his son will be reunited. Truth is reflected in Anatole's eyes, and, when his father fearfully looks at'him, a transference of thoughts occurs. Mallarmé, too, understands the future and can become one with his son: "purity/ double/—identity/ eyes/ the two equal points of view/ his eyes look at me, double/ and suffice."[48]

Another form of visual communication in the theater occurs when one attends a ballet. Each spectator regards the dancer and sees the visual form of the pure idea, a silent depiction of mankind's elementary traits, more effective and more instinctive because they are not explained aloud. Like the musician, the ballerina can communicate more truthfully to a public without the intrusion of language. If anyone were to speak during her performance, confusion would reign.[49]

This admiration for silent dialogues among men, dependent upon an optical procedure, also helps to explain Mallarmé's love of pantomime. In an article praising the

47. Mallarmé, "Conflit," *O.c.*, p. 358.
48. Mallarmé, feuillets 90–91. See also feuillets 123–24.
49. Mallarmé, "Ballets," *O.c.*, pp. 304, 306; "Les Fonds dans le ballet," *O.c.*, p. 309.

mime, Paul Margueritte, the poet compares his silent soliloquy, using only facial expressions and bodily gestures, to the concept of an unwritten poem, not yet placed upon the white page. While performing on the stage, the pantomimist actually becomes identified with the role that he is playing, and the public sees him as a work, a book being silently read to them.[50]

A similar form of silence does exist in the individually read book, but words are still used and, in effect, "spoken" in the mind of the reader. In poetry, language is necessary unless the writer can be content with an empty page, or at least until communication by means of pure thought alone can be attained. Silent dialogues among men may be the ideal, but they can occur only after mankind has reached the paradisaic state desired. Until that time, words are indispensable to the successful communication of a poetic art form.

In all of the above-mentioned examples of silent intercourse among men, there exists the actual presence of human beings, whether it be as friends on an equal level, or, in a more ritualistic situation, with an actor before his audience. If the ultimate work of art is to be presented theatrically as a monologue at an intimate gathering or at a mass festival, the physical presence of a human intermediary is needed in order to effect communication. Mallarmé's investigations into the theater either stemmed from or resulted in his fascination with the impact of a performance, interpreted by actors, on a public. He recognized the fact that even music that is sung by an individual is dependent upon the singer, who offers a musical mime in the form of a lyrical tragedy.[51] The same dependence upon a human interpretation of art before others can be found in

50. Mallarmé, "Mimique," *O.c.*, p. 310.
51. Mallarmé, "Sur Madame Georgette Leblanc," *O.c.*, p. 861.

instrumental music. Mallarmé's contact with Wagner involved him in a study of the relationship between a public and an art form played by musicians. Such music also possesses religious appeal: the attainment of communion in a ritualistic Catholic mass is successful because of the presence of a participating public, an officiating priest, at times a holy Book, and a spiritual being felt by all.

After an art form has been created by the artist, the theatrical communicative process begins with the human interpreter, the intermediary through whom a public will gain knowledge of the work and, presumably, of itself. In "Igitur" the hero not only recites his drama to an audience of elite ancestors, but also serves as a sort of stage manager, raising and lowering the curtains in order to let in light or to prevent this lucidity from reaching the public.[52] Anatole Mallarmé is the sole actor in his own real tragedy, but he becomes his father's teacher, offering a lesson that concerns the fate of every man.[53] It has already been seen that the dancer is the visual interpreter of the elementary instincts of all men; she is an impersonal and universal metaphor or sign that serves as a stimulus to a public's awareness of itself.[54]

But the most important role to be played by a human interpreter of art can be found in that of the priest, confused in Mallarmé's mind with the orchestra conductor and with the poet in his future vast ritual of art. In an 1892 article on religion and art, Mallarmé defines the poet-priest's role as that of an actor who officiates and points out a mythical presence with which everyone will become equated.[55] The

52. Mallarmé, *O.c.*, pp. 433, 439–40.
53. Mallarmé, *Pour un tombeau d'Anatole*, feuillet 66.
54. Mallarmé, "Ballets," *O.c.*, pp. 304, 307; "Crayonné au théâtre," *O.c.*, p. 296.
55. Mallarmé, "De Même," *O.c.*, p. 396. See also "Plaisir sacré," *O.c.*, p. 390, where the conductor of an orchestra has the same role.

officiating leader never presents himself as a particular actor interpreting the earthly presence of God; rather, he impersonally indicates the spiritual but invisible existence of a divinity. By 1895, however, Mallarmé realized that the public at a Catholic mass actually regards the priest as the impersonal but human manifestation of God. The actor becomes equal to the role he is playing. He becomes the real presence of a diffused but total and glorious being.[56]

The role of a human interpreter, leading a theatrical presentation of art, is more practically described in Le "Livre." As what he calls the "opérateur," Mallarmé is in total command of his elite séances. He alone possesses all twenty volumes of the Great Work; he reads them or acts them out before his audience; he distributes, and then redistributes in an inverse order, the unbound pages into his pigeonhole desk; he explains the numerous rapports and accords among the pages and among the different interpretations; he rereads the volumes; he alone furnishes the necessary modernism with his contemporary dress; and he alone sets an example for others to follow. As the "m.," presumably standing for maître or master, he will perform an "opération:" "The hero transforms Dr. [Drama] into mystery—restores dr. to mystery/ is played—of which he has the Idea . . . he restores it to a Hymn."[57] Only Mallarmé can transform ordinary theater into a performance of the ideal religious-aesthetic art form.

Any artistic work, if it is to reach a vast and universal public, must try to present ideas that relate to every man. And any human interpreter, be it an actor, dancer, mime, musician, conductor, priest, or poet-"opérateur," must become one with his role and with a universal concept in

56. Mallarmé, "Catholicisme," O.c., p. 394.
57. Scherer, feuillet 57(B). See also feuillets 61(B), 42(A)–43(A), 58(B), 90(A), 107(A), 113(A), 131(A), 148(A), 160(A), 178(A), 192(A), 193(A)–94(A).

order to communicate with everyone in his audience; he must become a mirror in which each spectator can see himself reflected. The wide appeal of the play *Hamlet* stems from the fact that the hero, who denies the look of others but who needs a public in order to live his own tragedy, represents the adolescence of all men, "the juvenile shadow of all. . . ."[58]

This public, however, does not passively see itself reflected in the image of a human interpreter of art. The true art form will involve the active participation, interpretation, and even creation by its public. There must be a collective communion among the author, the actors, and the audience. Ideally, everyone becomes an actor when he attends the theater or when he comes into contact with any form of art.

Mallarmé realized that there have to be numerous ways in which an audience can actively participate in the presentation of an art form. Only seldom do spectators become actual actors with their own oral or physical participation. In the Catholic mass anyone who so desires can mumble the Latin responses without any real comprehension. The miracle is that an individual still receives an exultant sense of participation as long as he sings or speaks.[59] But the poet's ideal work, like the Wagnerian opera, will offer its spectators the opportunity of silent communication.[60] Active participation will not necessarily be evident.

At times there would seem to be no involvement at all. It has been well documented that almost no participation occurred at Mallarmé's weekly *Mardis*. Whether or not because of the poet's preference, it was customary for his disciples to remain silent while the master spoke. The result

58. Mallarmé, "Hamlet," *O.c.*, pp. 1564, 299, 300.
59. Mallarmé, "De Même," *O.c.*, pp. 395, 396.
60. Mallarmé, "Richard Wagner: rêverie d'un poète français," *O.c.*, p. 545.

was that no one seems to have remembered exactly what Mallarmé ever discussed. Only a sense of awe remained.[61] The planned séances of Le "Livre" also appear to have been totally dominated by the poet. Only one time does he allude to the active involvement of his twenty-four "assistants" in a united effort toward lucid awareness.[62] But this participation on the part of a public does not have to be physically active or oral. An effort may be made in one's mind in order to understand what is being presented and in order to raise oneself to the level of intelligence of the human interpreter and intermediary. Based upon stimuli received from the performed work of art, a spectator participates by mentally interpreting suggested allusions. And, in its ideal role, a public will become involved when it mentally begins to create its own theater of the imagination.

On an elementary level, the audience of a play can actively participate when it knows in advance what is going to happen, or when, by accident, it becomes aware of the existence of pure fiction in the theater.[63] What is actually involved is the lucidity of the public. On a more complicated plane, the silent communication of a ballerina or a pantomimist to a spectator requires an effort on the latter's part to ask at every gesture or step " 'What can that signify' or even better, with inspiration, to read it."[64] The dancer interprets the choreography, and the public interprets the ballerina's interpretation.

When Mallarmé attended the weekly Concerts Lamoureux, he would arrive at the concert hall armed with

61. Camille Mauclair, *Mallarmé chez lui* (Paris: Editions Bernard Grasset, 1935), pp. 60–61; Mondor, *Vie de Mallarmé*, pp. 424, 425, 624.

62. Scherer, feuillet 110(A).

63. Mallarmé, "La Fausse Entrée des sorcières dans *Macbeth*," *O.c.*, pp. 348, 350, 351.

64. Mallarmé, "Ballets," *O.c.*, p. 307. See also "Mimique," *O.c.*, p. 310.

a piece of paper. While the orchestra was playing, the poet would compose poems. The music dictated certain feelings and thoughts to him; he saw them as mental images and transposed them into poetry, his own particular medium of expression. Visually or aurally stimulated by a human intermediary who interprets a work of art, any member of a public may subsequently become his own master of artistic illusion and may mentally create his own drama, personally related to his own tastes, background, and situation in life.[65] An author or composer may originally create a work of art, but the true meanings therein are merely suggested during a theatrical performance. There always exists an "ideal but absent piece of paper."[66] Mallarmé recites and interprets the Great Work. The effort made by his elite spectators may consist of their own re-creations of ideal pages, physically absent from the séances. The ideal theater is written and played in the souls of men and is latent in their imaginations. For Mallarmé, the development of spiritual symbols needs no other place than "the fictitious foyer of vision projected by the gaze of a crowd! Saint of all Saints, but mental. . . ."[67]

Maintaining all roles of the public on this mental level, one can see that others have become the receivers of artistic thoughts, the creators or re-creators of theater, the spiritual directors, and, ultimately, their own actors, mirrored and eventually equal to the impersonal characters portrayed on the stage. Mallarmé explains this process in the ideal but personal "test case" during the death of his son. Anatole is the original actor, a physical intermediary

65. Mallarmé, "Richard Wagner: rêverie d'un poète français," *O.c.*, p. 542; "Crise de vers," *O.c.*, p. 367; Grange Woolley, *Richard Wagner et le symbolisme français* (Paris: Les Presses Universitaires de France, 1931), pp. 108–9.
66. Scherer, feuillet 112(A).
67. Mallarmé, "Richard Wagner: rêverie d'un poète français," *O.c.*, p. 545. See also "Ballets," *O.c.*, pp. 304, 307; "Mimique," *O.c.*, p. 310.

equal to his tragic role and existing between the latter and his father, an active spectator. By means of the lucid regard, there will result a transfer of consciousness. The active public will assume the anguish and suffering of the sole actor, and Mallarmé will ideally and mentally die for his son.[68] Although an actual death is occurring, in contrast to fictional ones in Mallarmé's own experiences and in future artistic endeavors, the poet tries to view the situation intellectually. The mental tragedy created will cause the active spectator to interchange his role with that of Anatole, and the two participants will become one in a spiritual and fictional communion. At a mass or a concert, the same process occurs: "we [the spectators] do not remain mere witnesses: but from each place, through the torments and the brightness, each one of us in turn, in a circular movement, becomes the hero. . . ."[69]

Once again, Mallarmé returns to his favorite image of all things: the circle. Even before the poet consciously began to use another person or persons in order to effect his own purification, he inevitably began to include this other being in his ultimate goals, whether as a direct or indirect result of communication. He knew that "the amateur that one is . . . would no longer know how to be present, as a mere passerby, at a tragedy, if it were not to include an allegorical return back to him."[70] In "Igitur," the mental death of the hero is actually the martyrdom of a human intermediary through whom an elite public will become pure. This audience will hear an account of Igitur's life and goals; they will see themselves mirrored in the impersonal hero; and they, too, will be transformed.[71] In a similar manner, the iden-

68. Mallarmé, *Pour un tombeau d'Anatole*, feuillets 22–26, 62–64, 79–80, 106, 111, 118, 119, 139, 170–71, pp. 64–71, 76–78.
69. Mallarmé, "Catholicisme," *O.c.*, p. 393.
70. *Ibid.*, p. 394. See also Richard, pp. 354–55.
71. Mallarmé, *O.c.*, p. 442.

tification of the actor with the character of Hamlet will be followed by the fusion of the spectator, the actor, and the character.

The tragedy of *Hamlet*, however, needs the presence of a public in order to be performed; its hero needs the gaze of another so that he can live his life and fulfill his dreams. Just as the public is transformed because of its own re-creations based on the stimulus of the actor, the latter is mentally destroyed, eaten by the crowd so that he may be reborn.[72] The actor-poet and his public become reciprocal creators of one another in a rapport of mutual aid. They become mirror images, equal to one another, and equal to the fictional work or spiritual presence that represents all men: "The miracle of music is this penetration, in reciprocity, of the myth and the theatrical hall. . . ."[73] Like the spiral or whirlpool movement in "Igitur," the circular movement between interpreter and public will not remain on the same level; it will rise higher and higher until every man attains his ideal self. There will be a reciprocal motion between man and his true being until everything becomes "a function of festivals: the people witness their own transfiguration into truth."[74] Universal communion can then occur.

If the theatrical communication of art consists of a reciprocal or circular movement between a human interpreter and an audience, who is the initiator? In *Le "Livre,"* Mallarmé, as the "opérateur," was anxious not to appear to others as the originator of the work. He desired to be the simple reader or officiating interpreter. The work would

72. One sees here the myth of the poet sacrificed by his public, the host eaten by his invited guest, or the head of one's beloved served on a platter at a banquet. Robert Greer Cohn sees the relationship, "amour-mourir-nourriture" (love-to-die-nourishment-, on page 8 of "Un Coup de dés." Death, of course, will be followed by resurrection. Mallarmé, *O.c.*, pp. 470–71; Cohn, pp. 296–99; Scherer, feuillets 169(A)–69(A) (*suite*); Mallarmé, "La Cantique de Saint Jean," *O.c.*, p. 49; *Les Noces d'Hérodiade*, pp. 424–31.
73. Mallarmé, "Catholicisme," *O.c.*, p. 393.
74. Mallarmé, "L'Action restreinte," *O.c.*, p. 371.

seem to have been anonymously written by genius alone. During its oral rendition, it would cause the apotheosis of the first reader, that is, of the poet, as well as of the elite spectators.[75] But Mallarmé would have been the author, whether or not he admitted it to others. He would have initiated both the creation and the moment of confrontation for the communicative process. The myths of the work, however, would be poems containing truths inherent in all men and latent in their own imaginations. In this sense, the initiator is the crowd of divine men who, as has been seen, can inspire the poet. In other words, the public receives the knowledge of a work from an interpreter; this public then re-creates in its own mind a theater that corresponds to the needs and beliefs of each individual and, universally, of all men. What the actor is playing, therefore, is the role that the audience has created, just as the dancer offers the silent purity of man's inner being. In a third possibility, one can place the initiative of the process of communication in the actual confrontation between the author-actor and his public, whether it accidentally occurs, or because of a request made by either party.[76] Temporal communication may begin at that moment, but, as part of the eternal circle of life where everything is unique because equal, creation and communication neither ever began nor will end.

It should be emphasized again that, in all of the examples above describing the process of aural or visual artistic communication to a public, the actual presence of a human interpreter in a room is indispensable to an intellectual and emotional communion. Mallarmé's intonation, gestures, and facial expressions in his oral lectures were said to have caused any obscurity to disappear.[77] Theater can be per-

75. Scherer, feuillet 42(A).
76. Richard, pp. 358–59.
77. Mondor, *Vie de Mallarmé*, pp. 581, 599–600; Mallarmé, "La Musique et les lettres," *O.c.*, p. 654.

formed or read, but the presence of a brilliant actor not only aids in a correct presentation but also bequeaths an artistic immortality to the fictional character, while presenting a certain modernism intelligible to the contemporary audience. In his ardent praise of Mounet-Sully's interpretation of *Hamlet*, Mallarmé explains the importance of an actor's job: "A mime, a thinker, the tragedian interprets Hamlet as the plastic and mental sovereign of art and especially as Hamlet exists through heredity in the minds of the end of this century. . . . With solemnity, an actor bequeaths, clarified . . . to a future . . . an immortal likeness."[78]

Since the séances of the Great Work are the bases of all true communication, the essential reason is that Mallarmé himself is present to explain his work. He alone initially understands the total rapports; he alone can be identified with the work; he alone is essential to the oral readings: "or one among them—suffices—me/ they—passers by."[79] Mallarmé had already made many references during his life to the possibility that the poet himself, often identified as a clown or as Hamlet, would play the roles of actor, conductor, priest, and officiating leader of the sovereign ceremonies of Poetry.[80]

If these roles are filled by someone other than the poet, an inherent problem may occur: the human intermediary may incorrectly or badly interpret the work of art. The particular interpretation chosen may not correspond with the one being re-created in a spectator's mind. Pure communication suggested by the author's words is hindered. An additional problem may be encountered when the physical presence of a particular actor prevents a spectator from

---

78. Mallarmé, "Hamlet," *O.c.*, p. 302.
79. Scherer, feuillet 188(A). See also feuillets 58(B)–59(B).
80. Mallarmé, "Le Pitre châtié," *O.c.*, pp. 1416, 31; "Le Phénomène futur," *O.c.*, p. 269; "Igitur," *O.c.*, pp. 1581, 434, 442; "Bucolique," *O.c.*, p. 402; "Confrontation," *O.c.*, p. 412.

total mental re-creation and identification with the character being portrayed. The actor may not be able to be effaced behind the impersonal role played on the stage. The annoying result for the public is "the displeasure of an exact face bent over beyond the spotlights, onto my source or soul."[81]

Mallarmé was placed in the position of having to acknowledge the need for a human interpreter in some art forms, of desiring a physical presence for at least one means of presentation for his ideal work, and of disliking the cumbersome presence and incorrect interpretations of many actors. If he could not play the leading role at all times, he would attempt to deny or to minimize the corporal existence of another person on stage. A singer should disappear behind the pure song or source of sound, and an actor should blend with his role. Once again, what remains is the mental stage of the spectator's mind where nothing specific exists.[82] Purity exists in silence, whiteness, or in a void.

In his discussions of dance, Mallarmé's attempt to transform a human artistic interpreter into a nonrepresentational idea is fully evident. With her costume and movements, the ballerina first creates by herself any required stage decoration, another source of arbitrary interpretation otherwise forced upon a public by a set designer. Ultimately the dancer becomes a pure metaphor, the symbol of an idea that may be abstract and suggestive or mathematically precise.[83] Her corporal presence is minimized or, ideally, denied for the benefit of the pure mental thought.

But if a temporal theatrical performance of any sort is the initial stimulus for the creative imagination of a public, the

81. Mallarmé, "Le Genre ou des modernes," *O.c.*, p. 318. See also "De Même," *O.c.*, p. 396.
82. Mallarmé, "Sur Madame Georgette Leblanc," *O.c.*, p. 861; "Catholicisme," *O.c.*, p. 394; "Richard Wagner: rêverie d'un poète français," *O.c.*, p. 545.
83. Mallarmé, "Les Fonds dans le ballet," *O.c.*, p. 309.

physical presence of a human interpreter can never be totally eliminated. [84] The only way that Mallarmé could deny this human existence and avoid the problems of a bad interpretation was to turn to communication by means of the printed book, silently or orally read by an individual. A false interpretation would then be solely the fault of the reader. If a dancer can represent a sign on the empty space of a stage, a written word can similarly equal this symbol upon the white stage of the paper. It must be remembered as well that Mallarmé's favorite theatrical role, Hamlet, is that of a character whose tragedy may either be performed before the gaze of an actual public or be played before the mind's eye of a reader at home. The poet may be the "opérateur" at an oral presentation of his work, but, through the written version, he does remain as the "spiritual actor" in the "spiritual staging" of the text. [85] In many ways, Mallarmé's alternative for the presentation of *Le "Livre"* as a book or in a newspaper may provide the poet with more possibilities of success in the communication with his ideal public.

Throughout his writings, Mallarmé frequently discussed the various merits of relating to one's public by means of another human intermediary or himself and by means of the printed literary text. It has been noted that he often blurred the boundaries between these two modes of artistic presentation, at times to the point of identifying the two as equal. As a result, one can not always tell when the poet's mention of an intermediary refers to his actual presence on a stage or mentally on the pages of a book.

A definite choice between two communicative processes

84. It is interesting to note that modern technical inventions have changed this situation. Although human interpreters are still needed to perform a work of art, their actual presence is eliminated in television, the cinema, radio, and records. In the two latter means of communication, visual stimuli are also missing.
85. Mallarmé, "L'Action restreinte," *O.c.*, p. 370; "Un Coup de dés," *O.c.*, p. 455.

is not of paramount importance in view of three considerations. First of all, Mallarmé's ultimate goal was to inspire every man to rediscover his ideal and original self, unified with a perfect and divine universe and with a multiple humanity. The results to be achieved through the actual performance of an art form, that is, mutual communication, creation, and equality among the author, actor, spectator, and fictional work, should be synonymous with those attained when one reads. Second, if Mallarmé desired to see communion by means of a book, he was establishing literature as the supreme intermediary. With the exception of oral folk legends, the written text can be found at the origins of any literary work, whether to be read or performed. Even the temporal or performing arts possess their written, permanent, and spatial forms. And finally, it has been mentioned that the poet's ideal aim was to achieve communication, or rather intellectual, emotional, and spiritual communion, by means of pure and silent thought. If future intercourse among men is to be mental, then any intermediary, be it an actor or a book, is a temporary compromise. Mallarmé's considerations of the methods of artistic communication actually concern the selection of alternative stimuli. Even with the use of these catalysts, it is ideally the public's mind that must create or re-create a work of art that will be the theatrically representative myth of one's soul.

Despite these desires for the existence of a nonmaterial reality in an individual's mind, Mallarmé was fascinated not only by the use of the written text as the initial stimulus for mental re-creation, but also by the presence of the physical book as a sacred object for future communication. If a literary text is to be regarded as a new Bible, its exterior appearance becomes important to its effectiveness. Throughout Le "Livre," Mallarmé considered numerous possibilities for the physical proportions of his work. As a visible object on stage with the "opérateur," the unbound pages were to be distributed in a pigeonhole desk, but they must ultimately form a unified book with specific geometric properties of length, width, and depth or height.[86]

When the ideal art form is performed or recited before others, the public merely sees the holy physical object from a distance. In "Igitur," the book is first opened and then closed after the hero's act, but the elite audience does not retain physical possession.[87] Even when an individual does possess the sacred work, its presence in his home provides sufficient inspiration, with the knowledge that he can return at will to its mysterious pages: "On the table, as an altar holding up the offering of the place, it is fitting that the volume . . . be there—simply—with the air of a leafed-through companion—one doesn't know when—and when needed . . . this partially open spiritual coffer of one hundred pages. . . ."[88]

Mallarmé recognized the need of physical possession of the ultimate work as one of the attributes of presenting his art form as printed matter.[89] A closed book with its folded pages contains a secret, as yet not communicated to an individual. The active reader opens the book and cuts the pages in order to read the mysteries within and in order to gain physical and then intellectual possession. Ideally, the pages should not have to be cut so brutally, especially if the Great Work borrows the unbound form of the newspaper. The reader becomes the re-creator and master of the book simply by opening and closing it or by turning the pages according to his own will.[90] Presumably each individual is

86. Scherer, feuillets 39(A), 40(A), 41(A), 77(B), 195(A).
87. Mallarmé, *O.c.*, pp. 435, 442.
88. Mallarmé, "Villiers de l'Isle-Adam," *O.c.*, p. 500.
89. Scherer, feuillet 134(B).
90. Mallarmé, "Le Livre, instrument spirituel," *O.c.*, p. 381.

his own master, but the poet still remains the original creator who offers the written text to his public.

Just as the corporal presence of an actor or conductor is eliminated, the author should disappear behind an impersonal text and replace his own respiration with that of the lyrical verse. As a stimulus to the creative mind of a reader, the author and his text are universal and ideal mirrors: "responding to all—who can remain there . . . and the book is for this reader a pure block—transparent—he reads in it, guesses it—knows/where it is—what will have to be—accords—rapports."[91] Communication to a public is more direct when the work is the sole intermediary.

When the written work is the source of mental drama, optics are again of paramount importance. The eye sees a physical object with black symbols on a white background; it will transform these images into the mind's eye for theatrical staging and interpretation. It has been seen that the visual regard is a sign of silent communication, truth, and total awareness. Mallarmé was fascinated by the action that occurs when one's eye follows the line of a printed text. Total and almost divine lucidity is contained within that look and will remain as permanent in one's memory as upon the page.[92]

Vielé-Griffin recounts an anecdote about Mallarmé that may not be totally accurate, but that serves as an example of what the poet intended his reader to see on the printed page. The younger poet found Mallarmé one day working at his desk and holding one of the numerous pages upon which he jotted down his ideas and polished works. The poet was talking to himself: " 'I no longer even dare to write that for them because I am giving them too much.' As I was near him, I read on the sheet of paper this single

91. Scherer, feuillets 42(A)–43(A). See also "Crise de vers," *O.c.*, p. 366.
92. Mallarmé, "Le Livre, instrument spirituel," *O.c.*, pp. 378, 380.

word: 'What.' "[93] If Mallarmé's poems are obscure, their hermeticism lies in the fact that the poet considered his works as enigmas to be deciphered by the intelligence of the individual reader. Words are in one sense precise mathematical numbers, but they are also mere allusions to a total reality vaguely suggested to a reader. The meaning that one immediately discerns is banal; through an obscure cloud can be seen the unspoken truth.

Silent communication can be suggested by the printed word, but it also exists in the blank spaces among the black symbols. It has been seen that typography was essential to Mallarmé's concept of the book. He realized that, by placing words upon a page, he could emphasize the contrasting whiteness as an additional and perhaps more valid means of communication, thereby coming closer to his ideal of pure silence in mental thought. He increasingly wrote about the importance of this silent whiteness that represents either the poet's unexpressed thoughts or the end of a specific image written on the page.[94] The reader's own mental images should then continue when the poet becomes silent. Through the intermediary of the pure white page, a meeting of minds takes place; a transference of thought occurs, or a silent stimulus activates the creative mind of a public. In both cases, language is eliminated.

Pure mental communication among men is supreme because it is immediate. But, as has been noted, with the use of the book or actor as a visual intermediary, Mallarmé required his public to expend a great amount of effort in order to understand and to re-create its own drama. Until such time when man is his ideal self, only a labored effort will result in discovering as clear the mysterious thoughts

---

93. Mondor, *Vie de Mallarmé*, p. 740.
94. Mallarmé, "Sur Poe," *O.c.*, p. 872; Stéphane Mallarmé, *Propos sur la poésie*, ed. Henri Mondor (Monaco: Éditions du Rocher, 1953), pp. 185, 189–90, 208.

presented by the poet. Paul Valéry states that Mallarmé created the concept of the difficult author who demands from his reader an often painful intellectual task, that of re-learning how to read.[95] The reader can not simply react to a poetic stimulus; he must undergo the same act of creation that the poet had experienced.

From "Igitur," written for the active intelligence of the reader, until the last works of Mallarmé's life, examples abound that illustrate the poet's desire to make his reader an active participant, the mental "opérateur" of the art form. The role of the reader can be described in this way: a poem offered to an individual possesses no significance unless the reader projects his own thoughts into the work. Once he sees himself in the poem and makes it intellectu-ally his own, he may be united to it and to the poet in total communion. The reader then finds and understands himself.[96] In re-creating the poet's text, thoughts will create or re-create one's own existence, and self-creation implies a godlike state.

The divinity of humanity is innate, having always existed in every man. A work of art will stimulate an individual's memory; during artistic re-creation, he will remember his anterior state, common to all of mankind, and will conse-quently re-create his original being. In a similar manner, a reader will remember the original meaning of a word re-created and purified by the poet and appearing as new and shocking in a contemporary work. Ideally, since the poetic word is used in its elementary pure sense, and since a reader will be reminded of his own native self, a confronta-tion between the public's mind and the work will result in

95. Paul Valéry, *Ecrits divers sur Stéphane Mallarmé* (Paris: Gallimard, 1950), pp. 36, 44, 45.
96. Georges Poulet, "Mallarmé," *Etudes sur le temps humain II: la distance intérieure* (Paris: Plon, 1952), pp. 354–55; Mallarmé, "Igitur," *O.c.*, p. 433; "Le Genre ou des modernes," *O.c.*, p. 318; "Solennité," *O.c.*, pp. 334–35; "Notes sur le théâtre," *O.c.*, p. 343; "Mes bouquins refermés," *O.c.*, p. 76; "La Musique et les lettres," *O.c.*, p. 647; "Le Livre, instrument spirituel," *O.c.*, pp. 380–81.

a total understanding through innate and instinctive intelligence.

But Mallarmé had to realize that only in an ideal universe, once men have already attained their pure selves, can such a rapport occur. In contemporary times, the poet is faced with a public whose levels of intelligence and education vastly differ. As in a conversation among close friends, a similar mental plane of reference can serve as a basis for communication only between the poet and an intellectual reader with a common educational background. Even with the labored effort required by Mallarmé, a less educated or less intelligent reader may never comprehend the true meanings in a work.

Art ideally activates a person's memory of his original pure being, inherent in all men, but it will also stimulate a reader's or a spectator's individual memory. Remembrances are based upon one's background, family, social class, and education. These variables can differ as greatly as the number of men in the world. Every individual brings his own memories, often latent, to a work of art. Communication to a public by means of the written book does eliminate the problem of a false interpretation by a human intermediary, but it can not escape the hazards of each reader's individual interpretation.

Does this public actually form its own interpretations and thereby create its own thoughts and self, or does it merely re-create the author's original ideas? Despite his belief in an impersonal poet and work, Mallarmé admitted that individual members of a public do not possess as much free will as one would believe. They are directed by another's thoughts. The book becomes a perfidious god over its readers. [97]

The exterior architecture of Le *"Livre"* is limited to

97. Mallarmé, "Notes sur le théâtre," *O.c.*, p. 343.

twenty volumes, but its interior structure and its unbound pages provide a mobility that can alter an interpretation. By changing the order of a series of pages, one re-creates a varied text, and by reading one particular page in a reverse order, one arrives at an alternative meaning.[98] Mallarmé states quite clearly in his notes that the ultimate work will contain ten different possible interpretations.[99] The limited number of interpretations will, therefore, be determined by the poet and explained to an elite audience during the séances. Even if the "assistants" mentally participate in the presentation of the Book, they are entirely led by the "opérateur" and can not go beyond his restrictions.

When the printed form is sold to a general public, no "opérateur" will be present. Men may be unaware that there are a limited number of interpretations to the work. They will also be ignorant of the contents of these determined meanings. Even in a given period of time, a common sense of modernism is not sufficient to negate individual remembrances and backgrounds. If each person in a general public of art makes an effort to understand a particular work, there can result as many different interpretations as men in the world.

Despite Mallarmé's awareness of the existence of specific ideas in any work of art, he did believe that every individual should interpret art in his own way and as related to himself alone. Such a belief stems from a recognition of the fact that each man is unique: "Every soul is a melody which must be renewed; and because of this, there exists the flute

---

98. Scherer, feuillets 44(A), 91(A), 92(A), 104(A), 146(A), 147(A), 154(A).
99. *Ibid.*, feuillets 107(A), 108(A), 111(A), 155(A). Scherer believes that the existence of ten different interpretations is that of a series of pages or of one volume, not of the entire work. Since pages and volumes can be ordered differently, provided that each group of four remains intact, many more combinations are possible. Scherer arrives at the maximum number of 9,864,100 interpretations. This number, however, is still restricted by Mallarmé's original creation, and his public can not freely and infinitely create. *Idem*, p. 87.

or the viola of each of us."[100] Since every person possesses
personal secrets, often unknown even to himself, art will
offer men the key to their souls.

If Mallarmé were to accept an individual's personal interpretation of an art form as sufficient, he would encounter
an essential problem: an infinite number of these interpretations may prevent the pure communication among men
that is one of art's primary goals. The poet often referred
specifically to the written text as offering mankind a solitary
concert with the discovery of solitary truths, but at the end
of his life he extended this description to all art forms:
"art, in its supreme forms of expression, implies a solitude. . . ."[101]

Both the creation of a work of art by a poet and the re-
creation by a public are egotistical processes. Just as
Mallarmé was concerned with self-discovery by means of
others, every individual is similarly involved. The reciprocal mirrors of actor and audience or of poet and public
exhibit the reflections of an infinite number of narcissists,
each identifying himself with an impersonal character and
with God. A prima ballerina and Hamlet are both unique
actors on the stage, despite the physical presence of others.
Mallarmé will present his drama in the form of a
monologue. In a similar manner, every man will see an ultimate work of art as his own private monologue. Multiple
interpretations could result in multiple islands of one in-
habitant each and no communication among them: "I truly
belive that two mouths—neither her lover nor my
mother—have never drunk at the same Illusion. . . ."[102]

Since the myths represented by art are impersonal and
universal, relating simultaneously to individuals and to all

---

100. Mallarmé, "Crise de vers," *O.c.*, p. 363.
101. Mallarmé, "Sur Madame Georgette Leblanc," *O.c.*, p. 861.
102. Mallarmé, "Surgi de la croupe et du bond," *O.c.*, p. 74.

men, a reader or spectator who sees himself reflected in a work or in a character may at first see only himself. But since every man can relate to the same myth, the individual reader or spectator should eventually see all of mankind in the same mirror. According to Mallarmé, every person possesses his own personality, equal to every one else's: art "evokes, to the soul, the existence of a multiple and single personality, mysterious and totally pure."[103] Each member of a public represents mankind as part of himself.

It has been seen that Mallarmé viewed the contemporary masses as an amorphous group with a hard exterior and mysterious movement within its shell. Composed of many men, this crowd already showed signs of its glorious future collective grandeur. If each man can contain the multitude of humanity within him, that multitude can similarly be seen as one. The concept of total unanimity among men implies reciprocity: "Our communion or part of one to all and of all to one. . . ."[104] Despite the numerous interpretations of a work of art by different men, and despite the original thoughts of the author, they are all part of the unified and multiple whole of life and of the universe. Communication among men can be achieved since all of mankind is equal. God is a multiple and collective one.

The realization that one is an individual, part of humanity, and yet reflecting all of mankind often occurs at a religious gathering, when masses of men join together in experiencing the same feelings. Paul Valéry described the Concerts Lamoureux in this way: a group of auditors who "experience the same rapture, feel as though they are alone with themselves, and yet, because of their intimate emo-

---

103. Mallarmé, "De Même," *O.c.*, p. 395.
104. Mallarmé, "Catholicisme," *O.c.*, p. 394. See also "Plaisir sacré," *O.c.*, p. 390.

tion, are identical to so many of those near them, and have truly become their fellow men—form the perfect religious state, the sensitive unity of a living plurality."[105] Mallarmé had attended these concerts on a regular basis; he had also read and had praised Emile Zola's *Lourdes*.[106] In both religious pilgrimages and masses, and in musical concerts, the actual presence of a vast number of people often serves to stimulate what otherwise may have remained a latent but unfelt communion among men. Unanimity can produce miracles more effectively in the theater-church than through the written Bible.

The reciprocal movement between a multitude and one can be related to a favorite image used by Mallarmé: that of the *lustre*, the chandelier or, at times, the electric and gas light. The many crystal lights composing a chandelier are united into one source of brightness and are then dispersed. When the "opérateur" of the séances of Le *"Livre"* places himself under the single electric lamp in the room, he and the light represent the lucid consciousness of twenty-four people united and yet individual. As a representative of collective awareness and with his superior intellect, the poet is surrounded by a golden luster that signifies artistic genius.[107]

Mallarmé described the ideal art form as fireworks, a source of light, truth, and lucidity brought to mankind. He extended this concept of light to include, especially, the theater, easily identifiable with its actual use of spotlights on the stage and additional lights within the room. The heavy chandelier can represent the multiple ideas or motifs

105. Valéry, p. 127.
106. Stéphane Mallarmé, *Dix-neuf Lettres de Stéphane Mallarmé à Emile Zola* (Paris: Jacques Bernard, 1929), pp. 60–61. Emile Zola, *Lourdes* (Paris: Fasquelle Editeurs, 1954).
107. Mallarmé, "Villiers de l'Isle-Adam," *O.c.*, p. 492; Scherer, feuillet 195(A); Richard, pp. 571–72.

presented in a drama. When the harsh gaslight, generally used outside, is used inside, it reminds one of those public places where the poet desired to hold his mass festivals. It becomes the "modern dispenser of ecstasy, alone, with the impartiality of something elementary. . . ."[108]

But the fireworks of art are only artificial fire in the sky; they must contain within them the demonstration that art is fiction. Like the gaslight, betraying this truth to men, the chandelier in a theater reminds the spectators that nothing real has occurred during the entire theatrical presentation.[109] It has been suggested that the moment of a public's awareness that it is witnessing mere fiction occurs when that public begins to smile and then to laugh. For Mallarmé, even if an individual is moved by a work of art to the point of crying, his tears will remain suspended like the chandelier, seldom falling, seldom submitting to the power of artistic illusion. Eventually his tears will turn into the laughter of awareness and of complicity with the author.[110]

In its ideal sense, therefore, the *lustre* will represent by its multiple facets the public's lucidity. Through the intermediary of light, one can be assured both of the equivalence between the theatrical myth and a public's resurrected spirit and of the total awareness of truth; the crystal chandelier is also an eye and a mirror.[111] Jacques Scherer rephrases Mallarmé's famous dedication to literature: if the world were a theater, it "would exist in order to end in a

108. Mallarmé, "Le Spectacle interrompu," *O.c.*, pp. 277–78. See also "La Dernière Mode," *O.c.*, p. 736; "Catholicisme," *O.c.*, pp. 392–93.
109. Mallarmé, "Crayonné au théâtre," *O.c.*, p. 296; "Le Genre ou des modernes," *O.c.*, p. 315.
110. Mallarmé, "Crayonné au théâtre," *O.c.*, p. 296; "Sur la Fausse Entrée des sorcières dans *Macbeth*," *O.c.*, p. 350.
111. Mallarmé, "L'Action restreinte," *O.c.*, p. 370; "Plaisir sacré," *O.c.*, p. 388; Scherer, feuillet 86(B).

chandelier."[112] One can again rephrase: the world is made so as to end in the lucidity of the public.

Mallarmé generally used the image of the *lustre* when he was referring to the art of actual theater. In a similar manner, Valéry's description of the phenomenon of unanimity of a multitude of men concerned the actual gathering of a public witnessing a theatrical presentation, be it musical or religious. The response elicited in these spectators is often essentially emotional, leading to a vague sense of communion rather than to an intellectual comprehension of an artistic work. A suspended tear may be as transparent as a truthful mirror, but it is also a symbol of feeling.

The contemporary theater public, as seen by Mallarmé, usually responded to a play in an elementary and emotional way. An additional cause for such a response may be found in the parallel that the poet often made between a theatrical presentation and a religious mass. A public at a religious ceremony often participates without any true understanding of what is occurring. Its Latin responses are pronounced either by rote or from a deep sense of mystical emotion, usually exultant. Such emotion constitutes sufficient participation for a public at a religious mass.[113]

This same sense of emotion is also sufficient at a concert. It has been noted that the poet's complaint with and jealousy of music often concerned this art form's emotional aspect and ability to arouse mystically religious responses in a public. The written form of music in "L'Art pour tous" was for the intellectual mind, but, in its aural presentation, accessible to a vast public, its aesthetic value becomes re-

---

112. Scherer, p. 66. Mallarmé wrote: "the world is made so as to end in a beautiful book." "Sur l'évolution littéraire," *O.c.*, p. 872.

113. Mallarmé, "Plaisir sacré," *O.c.*, p. 389; "Parenthèse," *O.c.*, p. 322; "De Même," *O.c.*, pp. 395–96; "Catholicisme," *O.c.*, pp. 391, 392, 393.

ligious. According to Richard Wagner, music can immediately display the essence of a world, whereas in all other arts this essence must first pass through the public's intellect before being exhibited. The listener to music, through his most receptive organs, the senses, can fall into a dreamlike state "essentially akin to that of hypnotic clairvoyance."[114]

Such a lucid visionary state was also Mallarmé's goal for the public of poetry, but he feared that any mystical response would be too vaguely emotional, and he could not decide upon the extent of the role that these emotions should play in developing total awareness of oneself and of humanity. When the young Mallarmé read the poetry of Théophile Gautier, he reacted emotionally with tears that represented primitive diamonds, in other words, elementary, crystal mirrors. But his initial response led to intellectual lucidity as the knowledge of pure beauty. In "La Musique et les lettres," a book is seen as offering lucidity to an individual, while a theatrical performance can not stimulate its public's intellectual understanding.[115] The opposite was true for Le "Livre," where the oral presentation, usually for an emotional, vast crowd, was to be destined for an intelligent elite, and the printed form was to be distributed to the general public. Whether dependent upon the mode of presentation, the presence of a human intermediary, or the composition of a particular public, what constituted ideal lucidity for Mallarmé? Was the lustre to be equal to an emotional or intellectual interpretation, both with the possibilities of being incomplete or false?

114. Wagner, pp. 183–84, 186, 188–91; Mallarmé, "Plaisir sacré," O.c., p. 388; "Hérésies artistiques: l'art pour tous," O.c., pp. 257, 258.
115. Mallarmé, "Symphonie littéraire," O.c., p. 262; "La Musique et les lettres," O.c., p. 649.

In her thorough critique of Mallarmé and music, Suzanne Bernard states that the young poet searched only for sonorities and emotional sensations in his early poems, but that, with "L'Après-midi d'un faune," both intellectualism and vague feelings became essential. After 1885 Mallarmé struggled to create purely intellectual poetry. In contrast to Wagner's desired state of mystical dreams, eventually leading to the hypnotic clairvoyance of his listeners, he sought to reach his public's lucid soul directly, thereby stimulating an intellectual awareness of the Absolute.[116]

Considering Mallarmé's desired elite public during his early periods of creativity and considering his heroine, "Hérodiade," and hero, "Igitur," one can see a definite concern even at that time for intellectualism in poetry and in the public's proper interpretation of this art form. It is true that the poems, mostly sonnets, composed later in Mallarmé's life are increasingly hermetic, but, in a contrasting vein, after 1885, the poet also began his serious investigations into theater, Wagner's music, and religious ceremonies. Desires for an intellectual response and interpretation by a public of poetry may have been a determined reaction against the mystical emotionalism of music, but the poet merely wanted to add this preciseness to an inevitable existence of one's senses. As late as 1897, he was able to write: "The fusion between the song, every thought, and exterior evocations is a vague and rich mixture where, while one can not put his finger on anything specific, he remains enchanted. I truly believe that this is poetry."[117] Since poetry only suggests certain ideas, they must first be vaguely felt by a reader and then intellectually understood

---

116. Bernard, pp. 69, 97–100, 113, 114–15.
117. Mallarmé, *Propos sur la poésie*, p. 208.

after a labored effort.[118] Once again, only after men have attained their ideal selves and can communicate by pure thought alone, can intellectualism be supreme, and can people relate directly and lucidly to each other's souls.

But the majority of men may not desire or may not be able to go beyond their initial emotional sense of communion in order to reach an intellectual communication and interpretation. If an individual gleans what he can from a work of art, be it sensory, intellectual, false, or incomplete and superficial, and if, after a period of questioning and examination, he is convinced that what he has extracted constitutes a correct perception of the absolute, as Mallarmé so desired, has this person sufficiently attained his ideal self? Faced with these problems, Mallarmé had difficulty in deciding upon an answer. He did realize that if he were to wait for the attainment of pure intellectual lucidity on the part of his public, he would never be able to begin his distribution of the Great Work to mankind. If he were to reach the vast public of all men, he would have to renounce some of his principles.

It is possible that Mallarmé intended to offer humanity a choice of response and interpretation to Le "Livre": the intellectual elite would extract an esoteric meaning from the work, explained to some of them by the "opérateur," and the masses would receive only a vague exoteric sense from the same text. Given the level of intelligence of most of the contemporary public, the poet could not expect any more success. At least the art form would be brought to the

---

118. Jean-Marc Bernard believes that the reverse process is more plausible: a poem must be intellectually re-created by a reader so that he may experience the same emotions as did the poet during the initial composition. Bernard forgets the initial emotionally vague response of a reader prior to his intellectual effort toward a second phase of lyrical emotion, later combined with understanding. See Jean-Marc Bernard, "L'Échec de Mallarmé," *Revue critique des idées et des livres* (25 avril 1913), pp. 151–54.

people.[119] The correct and complete interpretations are inherent in the text. If they are not perceived, the fault lies with the public, not with Mallarmé.[120]

Jacques Scherer believes that Mallarmé would have been totally satisfied if the general public were to understand only these simple aspects of *Le "Livre,"* whether they appear as pure emotion or as falsely interpreted intellectualism.[121] But if emotional responses were sufficient, then poetry would not differ at all from music, and such reactions would be identical with those prompted by organized religions. An ultimate poetic art form needs some intellectual meaning if it is to activate a just and purified universe. It has been seen that, in the 1890s, Mallarmé stated that misunderstanding would occur if a person of average intelligence or with an insufficient literary education were to read a book and think that he had correctly comprehended the meaning.[122] The poet is only fooling his public if he allows this to happen.

Mallarmé desired to attain a vast public, but the required compromises haunted him. He planned a book "full of probable pleasures and which he did not want to be totally devoid of significance for every one; so that, just as the maid entering during the performance of a piano piece by Schumann finds it beautiful because it isn't rebellious to the

119. Suzanne Bernard, pp. 144, 145. An example of reaching the masses with falsely interpreted poetry can be seen in an incident that occurred during Mallarmé's life. The inhabitants of Narbonne, many of whom were peasants, saw in an issue of *La Vogue* the poet's sonnet, "M'introduire dans ton histoire" (To introduce myself into your story), the last line of which is "du seul vespéral de mes chars" (of the only vesperal of my chariots) (*O.c.*, p. 74). For some reason, this verse remained in their minds and became distorted, soon meaning *c'est épatant* (it's great). Eventually the syllables became condensed, and, supposedly even today, these people use the expression *speraldemechar*, instead of *formidable* (terrific). Mondor, *Vie de Mallarmé*, p. 482.

120. Scherer, feuillet 200(A).
121. *Ibid.*, p. 115.
122. Mallarmé, "L'Action restreinte," *O.c.*, p. 372; "La Cour," *O.c.*, p. 414.

harmony of tunes, similarly the passerby draws out a meaning which satisfies him and is worth his three francs fifty. He thinks that he has understood and, according to the Master [Mallarmé], that is only more sinister."[123] A poet demands more from his public than does a composer.

Since the problem of successfully communicating to a contemporary public without certain compromises could not be solved, Mallarmé would have to continue to dream about the ideal future. Despite the present incomplete emotional and intellectual lucidity of the people, there is still hope for them. Their instincts will at least lead them to the Great Work, just as they now have a need to face ideal purity in the form of a concert.[124] Eventually, and in some mysterious way, they will learn to re-create and to understand the interpretations of the text. In this manner, one can consider instinctive intelligence as a prerequisite for reading the ultimate art form. The emotional and intellectual effort expended in understanding the work will consist of a period of indoctrination or education for the public. After this period, le lustre, as pure intellectualism, will be attained, and men will be equal, communicating ideas by thought alone, just as one can now emotionally feel without the use of words. Mallarmé assumed that the vast public of men would possess enough interest to purchase his definitive work. For the poet, the fact that a man will spend money to obtain a work of art is proof of his instinctive intelligence, or at least proof that he has a desire for more knowledge.

Given Mallarmé's faith in this instinctive intelligence of men, his wishes to communicate to them, and his need for others to effect mutual self-discoveries, one can affirm that,

123. Mallarmé, "Igitur—Préface," O.c., pp. 427–28. The preface was written by the poet's son-in-law, Dr. Edmond Bonniot.
124. Mallarmé, "Plaisir sacré," O.c., p. 389; "Solennité," O.c., p. 335.

for him, a general public has the ability to judge an art form's effectiveness in the world. Since every man is the subject of art, he also possesses the right to be judge. Mallarmé recognized this power of the public as early as 1874: "it is for the public, which pays in glory and in money, to decide if it [the work of art] is worth its paper and its words. The public is the master at this point and can demand to see *everything there is*."[125] It is the crowd that accords life to art and to the artist. A work of art will justify its reason for being in the fact that it will be destined for all men and will not remain an unknown masterpiece. According to Mallarmé, "and to prove in reading/ one only proves himself as to others."[126]

In a manner similar to the reciprocal aid in creation between an actor-character and his audience or between a poet and his public, it is now evident that Mallarmé considered his Great Work and its vast public to be reciprocal proofs of one another. Men purchase a work and thereby prove their instinctive intelligence. At the same time, the work is proved to be successful: "to establish that it is worth 1,000 francs (the fact: that the crowd will buy) reciprocal proof."[127]

When Mallarmé desired to reach only his fellow artists as a proper public for poetry, he scorned those who published inexpensive editions intended for purchase by the majority of men. Such a practice debased a superior art form and a literary genius. As his desires for a wider public grew, his actual public remained limited. He began to offer excuses for a lack of success in selling his works: an author should not even bother to try to sell works that perhaps should not be sold and that obviously can not be sold. Even with his

125. Mallarmé, "Le Jury de peinture pour 1874 et M. Manet," *O.c.*, p. 699.
126. Scherer, feuillet 189(A).
127. *Ibid.*, feuillet 114(A).

concerns in Le "Livre" for attaining all of mankind as his public, he was hesitant about lowering the supreme level of art to the material problems of finance. He tried to approach the question of the actual purchase of his work from an aesthetic viewpoint: "a book can therefore contain only a quantity of material—its value—ideal without a number so that it is more or less what it is—to sell it is too expensive and not enough/ from where infinite—ideal—but value (pure. diamond)."[128]

But especially during the later years of his life, Mallarmé had to admit that the proof of success for an artist and his work lay in sales. The public is free to chose whether or not it will purchase an artistic work, since its expenditure of money, that is, of lustrous gold, will indicate the authenticity of a poet's recognition by the world. His lifelong work will not have been in vain.[129]

The question of the proof of a work of art by its purchase was of great concern to Mallarmé throughout the notes of Le "Livre." In what he described as a purely financial operation, he intended to sell the multiple volumes of his work himself during his lifetime. In this way he could be certain that he and his elite "assistants" would not be the only ones to have access to these ideal truths, and that he would not be the sole person to possess and to read the Book.[130] He could eventually die with the knowledge that he and his work had been proven to be successful in the eyes of a general public.

The form of payment for Le "Livre" also concerned him. The 480 members of the elite public at the séances would be the first to judge the Great Work, but rather than actu-

128. Ibid., feuillet 39(A) (suite). See also Mallarmé, "Hérésies artistiques: l'art pour tous," O.c., pp. 259–60; "Etalages," O.c., p. 378.
129. Mallarmé, "La Musique et les lettres," O.c., p. 638; "Confrontation," O.c., pp. 410, 412; Scherer, feuillet 129(A) (suite).
130. Scherer, feuillets 139(B), 113(A), 117(A).

ally pay to listen to Mallarmé, they would guarantee 500 francs each for attending one séance. When the book was printed, the general public, now including the elite, would pay three francs per volume, a purchase price inexpensive enough to be afforded by everyone. If the work were not successful in its sales, Mallarmé would still have recourse to the promised 500 francs by each of his 480 elite public. And since each member of the elite could attend two séances, an individual could presumably promise to pay 1,000 francs if necessary. The poet would at least be assured of having paid for his expenses.[131]

Given the 480,000 volumes hopefully to be sold, the money promised by the elite in case of failure, and the revenue from advertisements included within the newspaper form of the work, Mallarmé would ultimately receive a profit for himself, even after having paid all costs. Although art can not be judged in monetary terms, and although a poet should scorn any financial success as a sign of his mistaken social destiny in contemporary times, money does allow an artist to live and to continue creating great works. In this sense, financial gain has its grandeur and beauty.[132]

In *Le "Livre,"* the poet's financial gain becomes essential to the entire effort of bringing his work to a public. If a volume were to be sold for three francs, Mallarmé usually determined that one franc would be paid to the printer or to the bookstore, and that two francs would be the poet's profit. At other times, he decided that, at two francs per volume, both he and the bookstore would receive one franc each. In a third possibility, a book costing sixty centimes would bring a ten-centimes profit to the poet.[133] It is pos-

131. *Ibid.*, feuillets 62(B), 113(A), 114(A), 117(A), 134(A), 135(A), 139(A), 182, 202(A).
132. Mallarmé, *Correspondance II*, p. 218; "Solitude," *O.c.*, p. 405.
133. Scherer, feuillets 52(B), 53(B), 54(B), 113(A), 143, 182, 167(A), 143(*suite*), 138(*suite*), 166–67*bis*(*suite*).

sible that the money to be gained from the sale would eventually become part of the literary fund that Mallarmé had advocated as a source of revenue for fellow artists, but the poet is clear in his statement that, while selling the work himself during his lifetime, he has a right to earn this money.[134] He is the first reader, the actor, the officiator, the "opérateur"; he is the author.

But an artist is mortal; only his works may continue to live on after his death. It has been suggested that one of the functions of art is to assure immortality for the author, by means of either his own creations, or those of others dedicated to his glory. If a poet becomes eternal through his works, he also attains such a state in the minds of his fellow men. Anatole Mallarmé was to continue to live not only in his father's creative endeavor, but also in the thoughts of the poet, his wife, and daughter. In a similar manner, "it is as much as the sublimity, the accumulated admiration of readers that inflates a great name."[135] Contemporary and future publics prove the success of a poet and his works; a future public will become the guardian of that artist's immortal glory.

The crowd will also be the guardian of the poet's creations, whether they exist in their physical form or in the minds of men. Two negative results have been mentioned as possible outcomes of an ultimate art form's bringing supreme action and a superior original universe to humanity. A circular work may eventually close in order to effect timelessness, and future temporal communication would be impaired. Second, a literary bomb may explode, bringing the Apocalypse to the world and leaving only a void. The future communication of art is dependent upon an active

134. *Ibid.*, feuillet 113(A); Mallarmé, "La Musique et les lettres," *O.c.*, pp. 637–42.
135. Mallarmé, "La Musique et les lettres," *O.c.*, p. 640; *Pour un tombeau d'Anatole*, feuillets 33–35, 46, 57–58, 118, 164–65, 180–81.

role of future publics, the guardians of mystery, who will continue the dissemination of truth from century to century.[136] In one sense, an art form remains eternal only by the continual temporal replaying of its drama by an older generation to a younger one. And if thought is the supreme means of communication, then eternity for art can be attained only in the mind: art will live on in the common memories of mankind.

136. Mallarmé, "Plaisir sacré," *O.c.*, p. 390.

6

The Ideal Relationship Between the Poet and His Public

Although future publics have the power to immortalize a poet, Mallarmé was not certain whether he desired this glorious renown. His relationship with contemporary society has already been seen ideally to be one of isolation, with the knowledge of superiority, or concern and admiration from afar for the downtrodden masses. Such an attitude may have arisen from his actual position in life: a lack of popularity with most men, scorn from many others, later notoriety as a "decadent," and prestige solely among literary men.[1] Glory was difficult to attain in modern times, especially when one composed obscure poetry.

But how should a poet present himself to a future society, or should he present himself at all? An artist in temporary exile awaits the ideal future when he can offer his

1. Henri Mondor, *Vie de Mallarmé* (Paris: Gallimard, 1941), pp. 386, 438–39, 443, 535, 655, 656–57; Paul Valéry, *Ecrits divers sur Stéphane Mallarmé* (Paris: Gallimard, 1950), pp. 10, 26, 73–75.

great work to a supreme public. At that time, should he seek renown and eventual immortality?

Especially early in his life, Mallarmé often stated that he personally desired neither glory nor immortal fame, and, throughout his life, the concept of an anonymous author occupied his thoughts. In his autobiographical letter to Paul Verlaine, he predicted that his published poetry and prose would be only part of his personal and anonymous work. The texts should appear to speak by themselves without the voice of a specific author. In order to remain anonymous, he could either deny his role as author or simply refuse to sign his work. He could then never be held responsible if the work were neither successful nor worthy of praise.[2]

Mallarmé prescribed the same lack of known authorship for all poets: "Literature . . . consists of suppressing the man who remains while writing it. . . ."[3] Like the actor who should disappear behind the impersonal universality of the character whom he is interpreting, the artist should become impersonal to the point of fusion with his work and effacement behind its universal rapport with all men. He thereby becomes merely part of mankind, or humanity's unknown but official representative. With his "lucid and lordly plumed hat on his invisible forehead," the poet-Igitur-Hamlet can be seen as a mirror, an impersonal *type*, in whom all of equal mankind will be reflected, and through whom every man can be reborn.[4]

It has been noted that Mallarmé considered all artists,

2. Stéphane Mallarmé, *Correspondance 1862–1871*, ed. Henri Mondor (Paris: Gallimard, 1959), pp. 225, 258–59, 342; Stéphane Mallarmé, *Correspondance II*, ed. Henri Mondor et Lloyd James Austin (Paris: Gallimard, 1965), pp. 151, 245, 262, 302. Stéphane Mallarmé, *Correspondance III*, ed. Henri Mondor et Lloyd James Austin (Paris: Gallimard, 1969), pp. 166–67, 181–82, 316. Jacques Scherer, *Le "Livre" de Mallarmé: premières recherches sur des documents inédits* (Paris: Gallimard, 1957), feuillets 42(A), 117(A), 201(A).
3. Stéphane Mallarmé, "La Musique et les lettres," *Oeuvres complètes* (Paris: Gallimard, "Bibliothèque de la Pléiade," 1945), p. 657.
4. Mallarmé, "Un Coup de dés," *O.c.*, p. 470.

and especially all poets, to be part of a superior class of geniuses, human and yet in many ways divine. Given this assumption, it was easy for him to envision an additional means of achieving anonymity for any one particular author. One of his motives for neither signing a·work nor revealing himself as the sole author lay in his belief that genius alone would create the ultimate art form. An individual poet is merely one member of a hereditary line of genius poets, all of whom contribute to the composition of an ideal work.[5]

If an artist presents himself as an ideal representative of mankind and as an impersonal and universal being fused to his work, he is egotistically alleging that he equals all of humanity, and that every man must be identifiable in him. Mallarmé set himself up as a Hamlet figure at least partially in order to effect his own purification by means of others. He saw himself as the perfect reflection of man and life, but he was actually creating a private world in his own image. He may have convinced himself that he had become objectively impersonal, but he remained idealistically sub-jective until the end of his life. The "Maître" (Master) of "Un Coup de dés" is every modern man, but he is also the poet, set apart and above all others.[6]

This superior status of the individual poet may include all artists who compose the hereditary line of geniuses and in whom Mallarmé could negate his personal renown. In con-temporary times, these egotistical genius poets know that they belong to a superior race that originated in God and extended throughout the ages to them, including among its ranks Orpheus and Apollo.[7] In an ideal future, a perfected people will recognize these men as gifted mortal gods and kings.

5. Mallarmé, "Le Livre, instrument spirituel," *O.c.*, p. 378; Scherer, feuillet 42(A).
6. Mallarmé, *O.c.*, pp. 462–63, 469.
7. Mallarmé, "Poésies parisiennes," *O.c.*, p. 255; "Le Guignon," *O.c.*, pp. 1410–11; "Symphonie littéraire," *O.c.*, p. 265; "Igitur," *O.c.*, pp. 430, 433, 449.

A poet may be considered to be a member of a supreme race of men because he is chosen to be a glorious artist and, as such, possesses certain powers. In his description in "La Cour" of a future society where poetry will reign supreme, Mallarmé refers to the poet as "the Chosen One" who predicts the future, while becoming identified with it.[8] Negating the concept of total free will, the poet is elected either because he has inherited godlike powers from his artistic ancestors, or because, as a result of his selection, he will assume these abilities. In either case, he, the individual or all poets as a unified group, must be seen as a visionary, a *voyant* who possesses the innate gift of recognizing the total rapports in the universe and of simplifying them into a coherent form to be presented to a general public. The specific word *voyant* was in vogue ever since it had been uttered by Arthur Rimbaud in 1871, and Mallarmé, as of 1873, adopted its use. The concept of a gifted visionary, however, is evident throughout his writings.[9]

How does a poet reconcile the conflicting desires of remaining anonymous and of being heralded as a chosen seer by a future public when he returns from exile with his mysterious work? Mallarmé explains two possible solutions in "La Cour": "Far from pretending to be at one place in the gathering . . . he will appear, showing himself and his back in convenient anonymity. I compare him to an orchestra conductor—without interception, in front of the bursting forth of possible genius—or, he returns at will to the hemicycle in order to attend [the "performance"] in the rows [of seats for the audience]."[10] Even if the poet turns

8. Mallarmé, *O.c.*, p. 414.
9. Emilie Noulet, *L'Oeuvre poétique de Stéphane Mallarmé* (Paris: Librairie E. Droz, 1940), pp. 179–81; Mallarmé, *Correspondance II*, pp. 37, 172–73; "Le Jury de peinture pour 1874 et M. Manet," *O.c.*, p. 696; "Hamlet," *O.c.*, p. 299; "Notes sur le théâtre," *O.c.*, p. 345.
10. Mallarmé, *O.c.*, p. 415.

his back to a public, literally or by not signing his composition, he will present himself as a leader, anonymous perhaps, but apart from other men. At least during the process of communication, the poet can not remain hidden. Just as his glory is revealed in contemporary times to fellow elite artists, this elected position will soon be seen by all. Whether or not the poet, and Mallarmé in particular, desired such fame is debatable.[11]

Eventually the entire public of men will learn the secrets of life and will return to their instinctive and lucid states. At this time anonymity is possible, and the poet, as described above, can become a mere member of an audience from which he had previously emerged. He had undergone the anguish of artistic creation solely in order to engulf himself once again in the people with whom he felt united.[12]

According to Jean-Paul Sartre, an artist begins to question his particularly chosen mission in life when he sees the amorphous mass of a potential public behind his elite readers.[13] This change of attitude aptly describes Mallarmé: in his youth, any mission benefiting mankind was disdained because, in his opinion, most men were not able to form a proper public for art. As his awareness of the masses and of man's latent qualities increased, a future poetic mission became of great concern to him.

Mallarmé often described the life of a poet as that of a scorned martyr who must sacrifice himself for the sake of art. But this martyrdom is not only the pitiful result of an

11. Mallarmé, "Solitude," O.c., p. 405; "Confrontation," O.c., p. 412. There is some evidence that Mallarmé did desire fame, at least among other poets. He advertised to be elected "prince of poets" in 1896, and certain discussions at his Mardis have been identified as having concerned the essential importance of glory. Mondor, pp. 171, 722–23, 727.

12. Mallarmé, "Crayonné au théâtre," O.c., p. 296.

13. Jean-Paul Sartre, Situations, II Qu'est-ce que la littérature? (Paris: Gallimard, 1948), p. 137.

artistic vocation; it is also the sign of a superior hero. Once a work of art is communicated to a public, a poet's future mission is enlarged. If he is a chosen visionary, he will become a chosen martyr as well, sacrificing himself now for the sake of humanity. Even Igitur, who addresses himself solely to an intellectual elite audience, can be seen as a savior, the Messiah who will aid his ancestral race by means of his own death.[14] When a poet offers himself and his work to a general public, he presents himself as a scapegoat, a sacrificial animal to be destroyed by the crowd in view of a reciprocal resurrection for all. But as humble Christs upon the cross, most martyrs either secretly desire to be recognized as such or enjoy fame despite their wishes.

It is easy to accuse Mallarmé of aiding mankind for his own egotistical purposes, because the strain of elitism permeates so much of his work. But very often he does appear to be sincere in defining his future humanitarian role in the world. Like Prometheus, who stole fire, and thereby light, from the gods to bring it to mankind, Mallarmé saw himself as the sower of the seeds of truth, as a messenger from the gods to man, or as a carrier of the ideal art form to the people. Before his effacement into anonymity, he would communicate the multiple genius of men to all of mankind.[15]

As a prophet or magus, he can, however, become a powerful leader. It is evident that, despite his sincere desire for isolation, Mallarmé loved the feeling of being alone on stage as an actor, an orchestra conductor, a priest, or the

---

14. Mallarmé, *O.c.*, pp. 442, 443, 446. See also Mallarmé, *Correspondance 1862–1871*, pp. 242, 247; *Correspondance II*, p. 153; "Le Guignon," *O.c.*, pp. 28–30; "Confrontation," *O.c.*, p. 410.

15. Mallarmé, "Solennité," *O.c.*, pp. 334–35; "Igitur," *O.c.*, p. 449; "La Musique et les lettres," *O.c.*, p. 646; "Sauvegarde," *O.c.*, pp. 418, 419–20; Scherer, feuillets 58(B), 130(A).

"opérateur" of Le "Livre." Ultimately he could become either a dictator or a reigning monarch. The future official religion of art would be seen as the beginning of a joyous epoch that would call for the ministry of the poet. This poet would be Mallarmé, bringing the true word first to the Académie française, the governing body of the ideal state. In this sanctuary, he would occupy the center seat.[16]

For the time being, Mallarmé would have to be content with governing an elite state. If he were to be the supreme ruler, would he become a unique God, even above all other genius poets? Given his superhuman attempts at creating a new universe to offer to humanity, his egotistical belief that he would represent and equal all men, and his function of personally revealing beauty and truth to the masses in the form of a monologue, one can state that Mallarmé intended to surpass all other inspired poets. He did refer to himself at times as a powerful God and creator of life. He is Igitur, the continuator but supreme head of an elite race. He is The Superhuman, the Master, defying Chance by finding the unique Number.[17]

Even from his position at the pinnacle of a divine hierarchy, Mallarmé could continue to regard his fellow poets as possessing godlike qualities. Are these poets simple re-creators of a new universe, or are they actual gods replacing a previous imposter? Although Mallarmé often described these men as divine, he usually implied that they are human geniuses, inspired and predestined, and, therefore, gods merely in the eyes of ordinary men. Even the orchestra leader-conductor-actor who represents the pres-

16. Mallarmé, "Solennité," O.c., p. 336; "Sauvegarde," O.c., p. 417; "De Même," O.c., p. 396; "Plaisir sacré," O.c., p. 390.
17. Mallarmé, Correspondance 1862–1871, pp. 169, 242, 256, 259, 274; Correspondance II, pp. 258, 277, 301; "Igitur," O.c., p. 433, 438, 439; "Un Coup de dés," O.c., pp. 462–63. Mallarmé would be God who fashions man in his own image.

ence of God in a religious ceremony is still only a mortal intermediary.[18]

In 1864 Mallarmé offered a description of a future apotheosis of the poet, personified by Théodore de Banville, who, descended from the gods, sits far above the common crowd in an earthly paradise. In 1892 this same passage, with some modifications, was inserted into another article devoted to de Banville. The poet is in 1864 "the eternal and classical poet, faithful to the goddess, and living in the forgotten glory of heroes and gods"; he walks "as a king through the Edenic enchantment of the golden age"; his ancestors are Orpheus and Apollo. In 1892 the poet is seen as "the invincible, classical Poet obedient to the goddess and living in the forgotten charm of heroes and roses"; he walks "through Edenic enchantment," and his sole ancestor is Orpheus.[19] What Mallarmé calls "the Festival of the Poet" in both texts is described in this way in 1864, with the 1892 variants noted:

> the chosen one is this man with a predestined name, as harmonious as a poem and as charming as a decor. In an apotheosis (Empyrean), he sits on an ivory throne, covered (surrounded) with purple which he alone (—) has the right to wear, and (—) his forehead crowned (shaded) with the gigantic leaves [1864: "feuilles géantes"; 1892: "géantes feuilles"] of a Turbian laurel. Ronsard sings odes (I hear stanzas), and Venus, dressed in azure emanating from her hair, pours ambrosia for him (the Muse, dressed in a smile emanating from her youthful torso, pours out inspiration for him)—however, to his feet role the sobs of a grateful people (at his feet dies a grateful cloud). The grand lyre vibrates in ecstasy in his august (—) hands.[20]

18. Mallarmé, "Catholicisme," *O.c.*, p. 394.
19. Mallarmé, "Symphonie littéraire," *O.c.*, pp. 264–65; "Théodore de Banville," *O.c.*, pp. 520–21.
20. Mallarmé, *O.c.*, pp. 264–65, 520–21. In the 1892 changes noted in parentheses, a dash indicates the deletion only of the one word preceding.

Mallarmé's opinion of poets has not changed, but, at least as they will appear to others in a glorious future, any actual divine qualities have been greatly modified.

Mallarmé contented himself more and more, therefore, with the appellation of poets as re-creators, rather than as creators or gods. As yet the poet has not rediscovered the unique pure language or means of communication. When he does, he will merely have re-created what had always existed in the original universe; his artistic work will be an attempt close to creation, equal in importance to God's work, but not the creation itself.[21] If the poet is a god, his realm is art, and his subjects are fictitious.

It is possible that one of the reasons that Mallarmé increasingly referred to poets as simple re-creators was a sense of fear at overstepping his human limitations and attempting to rival God. He described himself several times as Lucifer and, therefore, as a divine angel who, having tried to usurp the powers of a supreme God, had inevitably fallen into the depths of Hell because of his sins.[22] The solitary, puerile poet-Hamlet of "Un Coup de dés" places himself "in opposition to heaven," thereby exhibiting an excess ("trop") of superhuman arrogance and pride.[23] Such a display of hubris will cause his downfall, and the poet will become responsible for the Apocalypse of poetry, of the universe, and of mankind. Poets must try to check this persistent pride if they desire to witness a glorious future for themselves and for all men.

But this strain of pride is difficult to annul, especially when one truly believes in the superiority of a certain class of men. Whether or not a scorn for the rest of mankind was

---

21. Mallarmé, "Crise de vers," *O.c.*, pp. 364, 367; "Magie," *O.c.*, p. 400.
22. Mallarmé, *Correspondance 1862–1871*, pp. 246, 270, 301; *Correspondance II*, p. 302; *Correspondance III*, p. 84; "M'introduire dans ton histoire," *O.c.*, p. 75.
23. Mallarmé, *O.c.*, pp. 468–69, 470–71.

assuaged, many attitudes first evidenced in "L'Art pour tous" remained with Mallarmé throughout his life. Elitism can be very clearly seen in such articles of the 1890s as "La Musique et les lettres," "La Cour," and "Bucolique." In this last article, for example, the poet complains that communication with a public is useless because he has little contact with these men who, in turn, refuse to listen to him. Even in view of the future, he feels that bringing the ultimate word to humanity is too big a task to undertake. The artist can not concern himself with the general crowd of men.[24]

It has been noted that even when Mallarmé did decide to aid men to rediscover their innate divinity, he often proudly described his new position of leadership as being apart and above other men. Only when he referred to a future fusion of everyone, including the then anonymous poet, into an equal multiple whole, did he fully abandon his elitist attitude. Considering this desire and that of genuinely helping others to rid themselves of contemporary society and of their own modern postures, it is possible to see a strain of social humanitarianism in Mallarmé, to the point of being *engagé* (involved).

As is usual with many aspects relating to the poet, he has been labeled as a totally involved artist, a humanitarian, a socialist, and a man of the people, as well as a man entirely *dégagé* (uninvolved), having had no social destiny whatsoever.[25] Suzanne Bernard approaches the problem in a more objective way; she describes the poet as he saw himself at times, especially toward the end of his life: "It is

24. *Ibid.*, p. 401.
25. Pierre Batistini, "Mallarmé, poète de la foule," *La Revue moderne des arts et de la vie* (1 avril 1949), pp. 16–17; André Lebois, "Stéphane Mallarmé et la politique," *Mercure de France* 121 (1 septembre 1948): 75–78; Philippe Sollers, "Littérature et totalité," *Tel Quel* 24–27 (1966): 94–95; Valéry, pp. 101–3; Robert Vivier, "La Victoire de Mallarmé," *Empreintes* 5 (nov-déc. 1948): 90, 91; Sartre, pp. 170–72.

rather moving to see Mallarmé, the poet of the elite, consider himself in this way as an involved writer."[26]

Mallarmé never used the words *dégagé* or *engagé* in order to describe his role in society. In addition, whenever he did express strong wishes to lead a more socially relevant life, his actual attainment of such an active role should be considered in light of two essential factors previously mentioned: the problem of literary thought and creation as social action or revolution, and the question of all philosophical, religious, and aesthetic queries as impractical and escapist. An additional problem can be found in the paradox between Mallarmé's complex desires and the actual published works that determined his true position in the world.

According to Paul Bénichou, Mallarmé's actual and desired relationship with a general public of men was representative of many artists after 1850. The calm aristocratic scorn preached by these men existed only on the surface. Beneath this exterior lay the regrets of a lost poetic mission that they had never truly renounced. These artists felt separated from the rest of humanity, toward whom they cast a look filled with sad nostalgia.[27]

Especially in his maturity, Mallarmé did exhibit a strong desire to effect this reconciliation between himself and society. If, however, an accord is to be made in the future, an artist has a choice between actual fusion or a ruler-subject relationship. As in a Byzantine mass, the poet-priest can remain at a distance from the crowd.[28] When an artist is unknown and in isolation, he is protecting himself from so-

26. Suzanne Bernard, *Mallarmé et la musique* (Paris: Librairie Nizet, 1959), p. 145.

27. Paul Bénichou, "Mallarmé et le public," *L'Ecrivain et ses travaux* (Paris: Corti, 1967), p. 79.

28. Albert Thibaudet, *La Poésie de Stéphane Mallarmé: étude littéraire* (Paris: Gallimard, 1926), pp. 372–73.

ciety; in a similar manner, anonymity is a defense, a means of preventing a true reconciliation between a known author and his public. Instead of a religious mass, one can see the image of primitive or Japanese theater: to present an impersonal, universal character, the actor wears a mask. He becomes anonymous but maintains a separation between himself and the audience.

In his descriptions of the theater and religious ceremonies, Mallarmé referred to this distance between the actor and the spectators as an impenetrable physical space for those present at the performance, but one able to be crossed by the power of music and, therefore, by an ideal poetic art form.[29] A separation is maintained, but a reconciliation is established. In another similar image: "Always the hero, who treads on fog as much as on our soil, will be seen in a distance that is filled by the vapor of cries, glories, and joy emitted by the instrumentation, thus remote from the beginning."[30] The presence of mist and fog, reminiscent of London and evident particularly in "L'Azur" (Azure), is an excellent means of providing protection or even alienation from other men.[31] Their use implies, once again, a desire to maintain a separation while a vague reconciliation is achieved.

The density of fog can be easily related to the problem of obscurity with its prevention of visibility and, therefore, of lucid comprehension. Mallarmé's life was plagued with charges of obscurity by those who did not understand his suggestive language, confusing syntax, or complex thoughts. Although he often denied these charges, he sometimes delighted in adding the right amount of obscurity, an addition ironically admitted, in order to frustrate the lazy reader and

29. Mallarmé, "Catholicisme," *O.c.*, pp. 393, 394.
30. Mallarmé, "Richard Wagner: rêverie d'un poète français," *O.c.*, p. 544.
31. Mallarmé, *O.c.*, pp. 37–38.

to maintain the high level of an art destined only for an intellectual, ideal, and future public.[32]

It is possible that Mallarmé honestly believed that his works were clearly written and that he naively expected an ideal general public to understand them. He certainly did not expect to find such a large body of men in contemporary times. Reconciliation would have to occur in the indefinite future. It can be suggested, however, that the obscurity of Mallarmé's works was used as a present and future defense: while desiring to relate to all men, the poet was almost ashamed of creating simple and clear works. He feared and defied communication. He needed to retain his distance from others.

One aspect of the problem of obscurity and reconciliation with men can be seen as an ironic paradox. Mallarmé's earlier prose and poetry exhibit much scorn for the people, present the poet as escaping from the world into himself, or into a world of pure intellectualism, and generally do not question the social duty of an artist in society. These works are written in a simple, clear language and style. As he began to study the responsibilities of a poet and of art in the world, to recognize the powers of the masses, and increasingly to desire some communication with a vaster public, his writings, both prose and poetry, become more and more hermetic. Either he had an inordinate amount of faith in people, or he truly preferred to avoid any reconciliation with them.

The parallel and contradictory wishes of communication and separation from society illustrate Mallarmé's actual role in life and attitude toward most subjects: that of vacillation and, therefore, hesitation, rather than any definitive stand

32. Mallarmé, *Correspondance II*, pp. 60, 115; "Le Mystère dans les lettres," *O.c.*, pp. 382, 383–84, 385; "Solitude," *O.c.*, pp. 407, 408–9; Mondor, p. 254; Roger-A. Lhombreaud, "Deux Lettres de Mallarmé à Edmond Gosse," *Revue de littérature comparée* 30 (1951): 358.

or action. The myth of the call to mankind in *Le "Livre"* has been described as presenting the problems of every man's state in life, determinism and free will, and the poet's constant immobility, poised ready to move but afraid to take the initial step. In a similar vein, his proposed play, *Hamlet et le vent*, would have portrayed the sole hero as listening to the wind that tried to speak to him. The young man would not have been able to decide if the wind were simply howling "ou" or attempting to say "oui" (yes).[33] Until he was certain of being called to act, by Fate or perhaps by society, he would continue to hesitate. Like his hero, Mallarmé would vacillate between optimism and pessimism, hope and failure, because he would never see the outcome of any actual deed.

Mallarmé's sudden death makes it impossible to prove that he intended or did not intend to finish and publish *Le "Livre,"* but it can be stated that he did more speaking and writing about an ideal art form and about an artist's future function in society than in performing any definite action. There are three possible reasons behind this hesitation and immobility: he was afraid to begin; he did not know where to begin; or he feared failure either in the composition, the communication, or the public's reaction. He admitted all of these fears.[34] His projects existed only in the conditional mode. In his last testament to his wife and daughter, he wrote of his unfinished work: " 'believe [me] that it would have been very beautiful,' " that is, if he had finished it or if he had acted.[35]

33. Scherer, feuillets 12(A)–15(A), 19(A). An image in "Un Coup de dés" can also describe Mallarmé: "the mystery flutters around the gulf without strewing it or fleeing." Mallarmé, *O.c.*, pp. 466–67; Haskell Block, *Mallarmé and the Symbolist Drama* (Detroit, Mich.: Wayne State University Press, 1963), pp. 45–48.
34. Mallarmé, *Correspondance 1862–1871*, p. 259; Scherer, feuillets 4(A)–5(A), 69(A), 139(A), 181(A), 201(A).
35. Mondor, p. 801; Jean-Pierre Richard, *L'Univers imaginaire de Mallarmé* (Paris: Editions du Seuil, 1961), p. 437.

Inasmuch as everything can be placed within a circle, it is possible to view the interior as a void or as the hollow pit of a whirlpool, where men are struggling to free themselves in order to realize their true beings. Mallarmé's favorite hero, Hamlet, is presented in an image that can easily be applied to the poet and his dreams: within the circle of life, Hamlet is "the lord who can not become." His gestures are mere phantoms. In a similar vein, Mallarmé described Wagner's music and operatic myths as "the Monster-That-can-not-Be!"[36] One could state that the poet's own ideal poetic art form and his goals of reconciliation with society and of communion among men are also fictitious. It has been noted that the word *chimera* has several implications, both good and bad; therefore, in one sense it may be better that such hopes are mere illusions, because true communication or fusion with a public is a monstrous result that Mallarmé feared.

He was also not always certain if such communication would ever be possible. An example of an opportunity for the poet to relate to a crowd of ordinary men is illustrated in the 1887 prose poem, "La Déclaration foraine." The meeting of the poet and his public occurs purely by accident. With a female companion as a visual but silent intermediary, Mallarmé recites the poem "La chevelure vol d'une flamme à l'extrême." The woman does not doubt that the impromptu recitation, inspired by the crowd, was a success in that the poet was able to relate to a general public. Mallarmé is not so certain. For him the poem is one which, unaware of itself, plunges fearfully through the public. The intelligent woman may have understood the multiple meanings suggested in the poem, but the multiple in-

36. Mallarmé, "Hamlet," *O.c.*, p. 300; "Un Coup de dés," *O.c.*, pp. 464–65; "Richard Wagner: rêverie d'un poète français," *O.c.*, p. 541. The swan of "Le Vierge, le vivace et le bel aujourd'hui" is also an immobile phantom. *O.c.*, pp. 67–68.

terpretations of the crowd may have been false or simple emotional responses. His female companion has to agree that the poet's pessimism is possibly warranted.[37]

Jean-Pierre Richard interprets the end of this prose poem as a total success in communicating with a general public. Paul Bénichou sees it as an illustration of a compromise on Mallarmé's part, accepting the partial or false interpretations by a crowd as sufficient. He also mentions, however, that this parody of an ideal spectacle clearly shows how far apart the poet was from his public.[38] It is exactly this distance that adds evidence to a third interpretation: when, in 1887, the poet is finally given the chance to communicate with a general public, he fails because communication exists on separate levels. A true reconciliation between Mallarmé and society can not occur until this misunderstanding is rectified.[39]

At least Mallarmé had actually tried to relate to a public in 1887. By 1895, when he was desperately crying for communication, realizing that he had done nothing useful up until then, a confrontation between the poet and the working class, as described in "Conflit," resulted in an attempt to converse that was merely imagined in the poet's mind. In the same year, in "L'Action restreinte," he admitted that the poet performs his exploits in his dreams so as not to disturb anyone. In "Bucolique," also written in 1895, he stated that an artist should bring his work to the people,

37. Mallarmé, *O.c.*, p. 283.
38. Richard, pp. 347–49; Bénichou, pp. 86–88. Ursula Franklin believes that the recited poem, even if a soliloquy, was a declaration to someone. Although both the crowd and the woman may not have understood it, they at least beheld the celebration of Beauty as presented by the poet before them. The crowd and the solitary poet need each other. Ursula Franklin, "The Prose Poems of Stéphane Mallarmé: An Exegesis," *Dissertation Abstracts International* 32 (1971): 6973A (Michigan State). Microfilm 72–16,424, pp. 226–27.
39. Further evidence of a sense of failure as of 1887 can be found in the three poems "Tout Orgueil fume-t-il du soir," "Surgi de la croupe et du bond," and "Une dentelle s'abolit." Mallarmé, *O.c.*, pp. 73–74.

but only to return immediately with the realization that his efforts were in vain and his art form useless.[40] The 1897 poem "Un Coup de dés" also presents the images of failure. Robert Greer Cohn has interpreted pages 8, 9, and 10 as representing not only the poet's recognition of human fallibility, but also, despite a proud attempt to rival God, of the inevitable apocalypse that could ensue as a result of the poet's downfall, either after a completed mission or as proof of its impossibility.[41]

If the poet could not successfully relate to a public as of 1897, how could he expect to achieve his aim with Le "Livre"? It is easy for a critic to state that Mallarmé failed in most of his ideal goals, since he was never able to complete the great work that would have, supposedly, negated his past inaction. He himself had admitted in 1891 that he would probably not be able to complete the entire ideal Book; he was quoted as having said in 1893 that he, like all poets, was a "predestined failure"; and by 1898 he called his Work a mere combination of dreams and verses.[42]

But in a typical fashion, Mallarmé always countered his pessimism with a persistent strain of optimism about his own future goals and about the future of man and the world. He stated in 1885 and again in 1886 that, even if he could not create an entire Great Work, he would at least complete a fragment. His attempts could stand as an inspiration to future genius poets, all part of that hereditary line, who would continue his work and reveal it as a perfected form to mankind: "This work exists, everyone has attempted it without knowing it; there isn't a genius or a clown who hasn't found a trace of it without knowing it. To

40. Mallarmé, O.c., pp. 358, 370, 401.
41. Ibid., pp. 470–75; Robert Greer Cohn, L'Oeuvre de Mallarmé "Un Coup de dés," trans. René Arnaud (Paris: Librairie Les Lettres, 1951), pp. 293–386.
42. Stéphane Mallarmé, Propos sur la poésie, ed. Henri Mondor (Monaco: Editions du Rocher, 1953), pp. 173, 226; Mondor, p. 665.

point this out and to raise a corner of the veil of what can be such a poem is in its loneliness my pleasure and my torture."[43]

In his last testament, Mallarmé asked his wife and daughter to burn all the notes that he was leaving; they could cause only embarrassment to his family, and they would form no literary heritage. Only he could have done anything constructive with them.[44] Even if one can see Mallarmé's ideal work and goals as existing solely in the conditional mode, the "it would have been very beautiful" also indicates that, in the poet's mind, his projects could still be accomplished. If pages 8–10 of "Un Coup de dés" present images of destruction, then page 11, with its distant Constellation and its faith in the action of human thought, represents hope.[45]

The haunting fear of inability and failure evident in Mallarmé's works of the 1890s was tempered by a belief that the ideal poetic art form and its effective communication to a supreme people lay in the immediate future. For him, no action undertaken to improve mankind and the world, be it physical or intellectual, was in vain.[46] Mallarmé's only action, or semblance of action, can be found in the published works that speak about his ideals and in the rambling notes for Le "Livre." He was still working on these notes when he died; this goal had preoccupied his thoughts and much of his time for thirty-two years. Either he must have had faith in his ability to succeed, or his project to change the world was a monumental exercise in self-deception.

It has been seen that during the development of his thoughts on an ideal universe, Mallarmé also began to for-

43. Mallarmé, "Sur le théâtre," *O.c.*, p. 876.
44. Mondor, p. 801.
45. Mallarmé, *O.c.*, pp. 476–77.
46. Mallarmé, "De Même," *O.c.*, p. 397; "Confrontation," *O.c.*, p. 409.

mulate a theory of history and time where, in the eternal circle of life, the present temporarily exists as a mere interregnum between an equal past and future. Throughout the poet's life, belief in such a theory never wavered, to the extent that his views on art, the poet, and a public in society easily fit within the framework of this encompassing concept.

Despite some concern for present-day social inequities, and despite his feeling of guilt at having been useless in aiding mankind, Mallarmé's dreams and intentions for an active role in society inevitably either depended upon or created an ideal glorious future. He was constantly postponing his action for a more suitable time; the powerful light of the constellation of thought is always in preparation, like the present waiting-room of time. And since the future equals the past, all ideal goals of poetic and human supremacy will actually be nostalgic reflections of a time when the poet was king and when men were divine. Every man will again be the Master who formerly ruled over a unified universe and who will once again rule as the supreme sovereign of an active state.[47]

Although Mallarmé may have sincerely believed that his particular period of time was not yet ready for the revolutionary role of a poet bringing an explosive art form to society, one can also suggest the possibility that his persistent future-nostalgic ideals were naive excuses for present inaction. Based on a fear or a scorn of communicating to all men, and thereby of becoming reconciled to the world from which one is exiled, the pretext of affirming that one will be understood and will perform great deeds only in the future constitutes at least temporary escapism. Seen in this light, Mallarmé did not greatly progress from his early desires of escaping from the real world.

47. Mallarmé, "La Cour," *O.c.*, p. 416; "Un Coup de dés," *O.c.*, pp. 477, 462–63.

In his critique of Mallarmé, Albert Thibaudet presents a hypothetical fragment of future history: after the destruction of humanity, at first only an elite survives, and then a single man. He becomes the inheritor of earthly labor and intelligence, the sum of human culture, because no one else is left. This man, recognizing himself as a lucid hero and then as God, writes a book. It will be the supreme word of truth and beauty, which no one will read. Has life attained the ultimate goal? Thibaudet states that Mallarmé would have answered affirmatively because man exists solely for this work; the book does not appear for mankind.[48] The possibility of a self-sufficient work of art, however, has already been discussed as feasible only if humanity and the world were to be included within that closed circle of art representing ideal aesthetic reality. Even before such a goal could be achieved, the work would have to be communicated to a public; in fact, that public would be needed in order to effect the creation of a perfected art form.

In 1897 Mallarmé wrote in an introduction to *Divagations*, a compendium of his prose works, that these published articles treated a unique subject of his thoughts, his poetic doctrine.[49] In 1898, when asked about his ideal at the age of twenty, he stated that, although only weakly expressed in his writings, this ideal had remained intact; he had been faithful to himself so that his life had retained some meaning.[50] Mallarmé had composed "L'Art pour tous" at the age of twenty. His goal of creating a mysterious language and, by means of an ideal work, of making poetry and the poet supreme had never been abandoned. His belief that most of contemporary men were unworthy of art was never totally negated.

But increasingly after 1862, these ideals were projected

48. Thibaudet, p. 362.
49. Mallarmé, *O.c.*, p. 1538.
50. Mallarmé, "Sur l'idéal à vingt ans," *O.c.*, p. 883.

into a future when mankind would rediscover its true self, either before becoming worthy of receiving the poet's word, or as a result of an aesthetic-spiritual education. With his investigations into other art forms, with his growing awareness of the latent qualities of men, and with his recognition of a personal need for others, Mallarmé began to desire some reconciliation with the ideal successors of those whom he had scorned in 1862. This new communication would not necessarily have to annul the separation described in his early work. The discovery of some form of a relationship between the poet and a public of all men occupied Mallarmé's thoughts throughout most of his life. His ideal and unique work would be in vain unless he could establish a definite role in society for himself and for art.

The complexity of Mallarmé's thoughts, compounded by his own vacillations and hesitations, make a definitive portrait of the man as impossible as a definitive interpretation of any of his works. A specific attitude on his part is soon paradoxically negated by an opposing stand. It is fitting that an examination of Mallarmé close with this concept of paradox, as related to an essential but often underlying aspect of the poet and his works: laughter and irony.

Mallarmé's love and gift for irony has often been mentioned by his contemporaries. Henri Mondor describes the poet as he appeared before his literary disciples: "He made others love in him the same combination of dreams and mockery, of lyricism and gentle satire which he loved so much in Villiers [de l'Isle-Adam]."[51] In his works, the sarcastic smile of exaggeration is sometimes very obvious. His affirmation of the unlimited power of literature and the book, the ultimate saviors of the world, is admittedly overstated. The entire prose aritcle "Solitude" is a biting satire

51. Mondor, p. 586. See also pp. 230–32, 328–29, 755, 785.

on literary disciples, all men of literature, and, especially, journalism. His sarcastic interview, included within "Solitude," with a newspaper reporter about punctuation and desired obscurity is eventually admitted to be an interlude designed as a joke.[52] But, as in all irony, a belief in the partial truth of the sarcastic statement always exists beneath the surface.

If the poet places himself in a position superior to that of ordinary mankind, his satiric attitude may be viewed as that of a man cruelly laughing at those below him. It has been suggested that Mallarmé was confused about mankind's freely chosen or determined role in life. If an individual believed in his free will and defied Fate by attempting to rival a supreme being, then his downfall could be followed by a chorus of Olympian gods, heartlessly laughing at him.[53] But if the artist were able to succeed in his ideal goals, if he were able to become a divine king, or even if he were able to function as a proud mortal ruler, his persistent strain of scorn for others would be translated into laughter, a cruel sign of superiority.[54]

A smile or laugh also implies the irony of desire and truth. A laugh can signify the lucid awareness and understanding achieved by an individual before a work of art. In a similar manner, sarcasm and exaggeration, masking a smile, can be used by an artist against himself as a result of the awareness of his own human limitations and amusement at his perseverance. Mallarmé described art as a combination of dream and laughter. An artist recognizes with a

52. Mallarmé, "La Musique et les lettres," *O.c.*, p. 646; "Sur le chapeau," *O.c.*, pp. 881–82; "Solitude," *O.c.*, pp. 405–9. See especially pp. 407–8.
53. Mallarmé, "L'Azur," *O.c.*, pp. 37–38; "Le Guignon," *O.c.*, pp. 28–30; "Autre Eventail," *O.c.*, p. 58; "Victorieusement fui le suicide beau," *O.c.*, p. 68; "Un Coup de dés," *O.c.*, pp. 466–67, 469, 470, 471.
54. Mallarmé, "Monologue d'un faune," *O.c.*, pp. 1452, 1453; "Improvisation d'un faune," *O.c.*, pp. 1457, 1458; "L'Après-midi d'un faune," *O.c.*, pp. 51, 52; "M'introduire dans ton histoire," *Q.c.*, p. 75; "Catholicisme," *O.c.*, p. 391; "La Cour," *O.c.*, p. 416.

smile that he can not be God because he has not yet rediscovered the supreme language. Even the role of the Master
seriously given to Mallarmé by his followers constituted, for
him, a mere farce.[55] The world of art is a game played with
seriousness by the artist; however, behind this earnest
façade lies the ironic smile of a man who is aware of the
truth that betrays his creation as mere fiction. The poet's
laughter is an admission that he is only a god over a voluntary world of illusion.[56]

If laughter means an awareness of one's human abilities
and weaknesses, then it can be used as a defense, a method
of aiding oneself to cope with the truth. In his study of the
role of irony in Mallarmé's life and works, Jean Royère
states that, as a result of a sense of limitation to ideal goals,
an ironic attitude becomes one of sarcastic resignation, an
antidote to the sublime, and a means of living with
reality.[57] In this sense, the poet's laughter is one not of
superiority, but of stoicism in order to exist.

When used in an obvious way, sarcastic exaggeration will
hopefully be understood by a public, but subtle irony behind a false semblance of seriousness can constitute protection for the artist. Mallarmé employed irony much in the
same manner that he used obscurity: by not revealing everything to a reader, the poet covered up actual meanings,
the truth that he had accepted his human failings, and the
fact that he had realized that his only realm was fiction. An
unworthy public would not understand his suggestive irony,
and the poet could maintain his distance from them. People
interpret all that Mallarmé has written as purely serious

55. Mallarmé, "Villiers de l'Isle-Adam," *O.c.*, pp. 502, 503; "Solitude," *O.c.*, p.
406. The poet also described his last work as a parade, a joyous festival, perhaps,
but also a circus, a farce. Scherer, feuillets 104(A), 105(A), 169(A), 169(A) (*suite*).
56. Laughter is also related to the sound of a flute, a wind instrument played,
for example, by Pan, like Orpheus, a god of wind. See Mallarmé, "Les Dieux antiques," *O.c.*, pp. 1252, 1240.
57. Jean Royère, *Mallarmé* (Paris: Albert Messein, 1931), pp. 141–67.

and honest admissions; he is often laughing at the joke that he is playing on these men.[58] Mallarmé's ideal future public would consist of all of mankind in its original, instinctive, and ultimate form. The poet would bring to them a great work that, on the surface, would first appear as obscure and complexly serious. By means of an emotional and intellectual process, this public would attain a moment of pure lucidity. All men would understand the truths re-created by the poet, and all men would laugh both at their awareness of fictional reality and at their recognition of subtle irony. Just as intellectual comprehension constitutes a common ground for communication between an author and his public, the perception of humor signifies a sense of collaboration and of complicity. Laughter implies superiority; when a public laughs with the poet, it will have attained an equally high level, perhaps of human divinity. Only then may Mallarmé and his vast public be reconciled.

58. Charles Chassé offers some good examples of this mocking irony used by Mallarmé. Because of his complex and often lofty thoughts, critics often try to find elevated meanings in everything that the poet has composed. Poems may seem obscure when they are, perhaps, only obscene and earthy. Chassé includes within this category the two poems "Petit Air II" (*O.c.*, p. 66) and "La Marchande d'herbes aromatiques" (*O.c.*, p. 63), and the "Vers de circonstance" (*O.c.*, pp. 82–186). Charles Chassé, *Les Clefs de Mallarmé* (Paris: Aubier, 1954), pp. 201–9, 210–18. The "keys" to Mallarmé, according to Chassé, are simply to be found in the Littré dictionary. Mallarmé's own observation on his obscure poem "Un Coup de dés" was one of self-mockery and, therefore, gentle mockery of others who would try to dissect the work: " 'Don't you think that this [his poem] is an act of madness?' " Valéry, p. 16.

Bibliography

Adam, Antoine. "Premières étapes d'un itinéraire," *Les Lettres* 3, numéro spécial (1948): 125–34.

Aish, Deborah A. K. "Le Rêve de Stéphane Mallarmé d'après sa correspondance," *PMLA* 56 (September 1941): 874–84.

Ajalbert, Jean. "Mallarmé héros et prophète," *Mercure de France* 281 (1938): 259–89.

Anderson, Richard. "Hindu Myths in Mallarmé: 'Un Coup de dés,' " *Comparative Literature* 19, no. 1 (Winter 1967): 28–35.

Antoine-Orliac. "Apocalypse de Mallarmé," *Les Cahiers du nord, Stèle pour Mallarmé* 2–3, numéro spécial (1948): 187–94.

———. *La Cathédrale symboliste: délivrance du rêve*. 4th ed. Paris: Mercure de France, 1933.

Austin, Lloyd James. "Mallarmé et le mythe d'Orphée," *Cahiers de l'association internationale des études françaises* 22 (1970): 169–80.

———. "Mallarmé et le réel," pp. 12–24, in *Modern Miscellany Presented to Eugène Vinaver by Pupils, Colleagues, and Friends*. Edited by T. E. Lawrenson, F. E. Sutcliffe, and G. F. A. Godoffre. Manchester: Manchester University Press; New York: Barnes and Noble, 1969.

———. "Mallarmé et le rêve du 'Livre,' " *Mercure de France* 1, no. 1 (1 janvier 1953): 81–108.

————. "The Mystery of a Name," *Esprit créateur* 1, no. 3 (Fall 1961): 130–38.

————. " 'Le Principal pilier' Mallarmé, Victor Hugo et Richard Wagner," *Revue d'histoire littéraire de la France* 2 (avril-juin 1951): 154–80.

Ayda, Adile. *Le Drame intérieur de Mallarmé ou l'origine des symboles mallarméens*. Istanbul: Editions "La Turquie Moderne," 1955.

Bacca, Garcia. "La Conception probalistique de l'univers chez Mallarmé," *Empreintes* 5 (novembre-décembre 1948): 73–89.

Bachelard, Gaston. "La Dialectique dynamique de la rêverie mallarméenne," *Le Point* 29–30, numéro consacré à Mallarmé (février-avril 1944): 40–44.

Balakian, Anna. *The Symbolist Movement: A Critical Appraisal*. New York: Random House, 1967.

Barbier, Carl Paul, ed. *Documents Stéphane Mallarmé*. vol. 1. Paris: Librairie Nizet, 1968.

————. *Documents Stéphane Mallarmé*. vol. 2. Paris: Librairie Nizet, 1970.

————. *Documents Stéphane Mallarmé*, vol. 3. Paris: Librairie Nizet, 1971.

Batistini, Pierre. "Mallarmé, poète de la foule," *La Revue moderne des arts et de la vie* (1 avril 1949), pp. 16–17.

Baudelaire, Charles. *Curiosités esthétiques L'Art romantique*. Paris: Garnier Frères, 1962.

Béguin, Albert. *Le Rêve chez les romantiques allemands et dans la poésie française moderne II*. Marseille: Aux Editions des Cahiers du Sud, 1937.

Bénichou, Paul. "Mallarmé et le public," pp. 69–88, *L'Ecrivain et ses travaux*. Paris: Corti, 1967.

Bernard, Jean-Marc. "L'Echec de Mallarmé," *Revue critique des idées et des livres* (25 avril 1913), pp. 144–58.

Bernard, Suzanne. "Le 'Coup de dés' de Mallarmé replacé dans la perspective historique," *Revue d'histoire littéraire de la France* 52, no. 2 (avril-juin 1951): 181–95.

————. *Mallarmé et la musique*. Paris: Librairie Nizet, 1959.

Bird, Edward A. *L'Univers poétique de Stéphane Mallarmé*. Paris: Librairie A. G. Nizet, 1962.

Blanchot, Maurice. "Recherches: ecce liber," *La Nouvelle*

nouvelle revue française 5 (octobre-décembre 1957): 726–40.

————. "Recherches: le livre à venir," *La Nouvelle nouvelle revue française* 5 (octobre-décembre 1957): 917–31.

Block, Haskell M. *Mallarmé and the Symbolist Drama*. Detroit, Mich.: Wayne State University Press, 1963.

————. "Some Concepts of the Literary Elite at the Turn of the Century," *Mosaic* 5, no. 2 (Winter 1971–72): 57–64.

Bolle, Louis. "Mallarmé, Igitur et Hamlet," *Critique* (juillet-décembre 1965), pp. 853–63.

Bonniot, Edmond Dr. "Mallarmé et la vie: avec deux poèmes inédits," *Revue de France* 1, no. 10 (1 janvier 1930): 59–71.

Boulay, Daniel. *L'Obscurité esthétique de Mallarmé et "La Prose pour des Esseintes."* Paris: D. Boulay, 1960.

Bousquet, Joe. "Mallarmé le sorcier," *Les Lettres* 3, numéro spécial (1948): 54–62.

Brogan, D. W. *The French Nation from Napoleon to Pétain 1814–1940*. New York: Harper and Row, 1963.

Brown, Calvin S. "The Musical Analogies in Mallarmé's 'Un Coup de dés,' " *Comparative Literature Studies* 4 (1967): 67–79.

Butor, Michel. "Le Livre comme objet," pp. 104–23, *Répertoire II: études et conférences 1959–1963*. Paris: Les Editions de minuit, 1964.

Carcassonne, E. "Wagner et Mallarmé," *Revue de littérature comparée* 16 (1936): 347–66.

Castoldi, Alberto. "L'Esthétique de l' 'écriture corporelle' dans l'oeuvre de Mallarmé," *Synthèses* 22, nos. 258/259 (décembre 1967-janvier 1968): 45–48.

Cellier, Léon. *Mallarmé et la morte qui parle*. Paris: Presses Universitaires de France, 1959.

Chadwick, Charles. *Mallarmé sa pensée dans sa poésie*. Paris: Librairie José Corti, 1962.

Chaix, Marie-Antoinette. *La Correspondance dans les arts dans la poésie contemporaine*. Paris: F. Alcan, 1920.

Champigny, Robert. "Mallarmé's Relation to Platonism and Romanticism," *Modern Language Review* 51 (1956): 348–58.

————. "The Swan and the Question of Pure Poetry," *Esprit*

créateur 1, no. 3 (Fall 1961): 145–55.

Chantavoine, Henri. "La Littérature inquiète: la poésie obscure: le mallarmisme," *Le Correspondant* 186 (1897): 967–76.

Charpentier, Henry. "Legs de Mallarmé," *Les Cahiers du nord, Stèle pour Mallarmé* 2–3 numéro spécial (1948): 183–86.

Charpier, Jacques. "Un Echec exemplaire," *Les Lettres nouvelles* 5, no. 52 (septembre 1957): 340–42.

Chassé, Charles. "Ce que Mallarmé pensait de la danse," *Les Lettres nouvelles* 4, no. 40 (juillet-août 1956): 118–30.

———. *Les Clefs de Mallarmé*. Paris: Aubier Editions Montaigne, 1954.

———. "Le Thème de Hamlet chez Mallarmé," *Revue des sciences humaines* 77 (janvier-mars 1955): 157–69.

Chastel, André. " 'Le théâtre est d'essence supérieur. . . ,' " *Les Lettres* 3, numéro spécial (1948): 93–105.

Chisholm, A. R. "Mallarmé and the Act of Creation," *Esprit créateur* 1 (1961): 111–16.

———. *Mallarmé's Grand Oeuvre*. Manchester, England: Manchester University Press, 1962.

———. "The Role of Consciousness in the Poetry of Mallarmé and Valéry," *Comparative Literature Studies* 4 (1967): 81–89.

Cohen, J. "L'Obscurité' de Mallarmé," *Revue d'esthétique* 15 (1962): 64–72.

Cohn, Robert Greer. "A Propos du 'Coup de dés,' " *Esprit créateur* 1 (1961): 125–29.

———. *Mallarmé's "Un Coup de dés:" an Exegesis*. New Haven, Conn.: Yale French Studies Publication, 1949.

———. *L'Oeuvre de Mallarmé "Un Coup de dés."* traduit du manuscrit anglais inédit par René Arnaud. 1st ed. Paris: Librairie Les Lettres, 1951.

———. "On Mallarmé's Newly-found Notebook," *Modern Language Notes* 75 (1960): 689–92.

Coléno, Alice. *Les Portes d'ivoire: métaphysique et poésie: Nerval-Baudelaire-Rimbaud-Mallarmé*. Paris: Librairie Plon, 1948.

Cooperman, Hayes. *The Aesthetics of Stéphane Mallarmé*. New York: The Koffern Press, 1933.

Coulon, Marcel. "Les Lettres de Mallarmé à Zola," *Mercure de France* 212 (15 mai 1929): 192–98.

Cours, Jean de. "L'Audition colorée et la sensation du poème," *Mercure de France* 114 (16 avril 1916): 655–57.

Crastre, Victor. "La Parole inouïe," pp. 129–45, *Poésie et mystique*. Neuchâtel: A la Baconnière, 1966.

Davies, Gardner. *Mallarmé et le drame solaire*: essai d'exégèse raisonnée. Paris: Librairie José Corti, 1959.

―――. "Stéphane Mallarmé: Fifty Years of Research." *French Studies* 1–2 (janvier 1947): 1–26.

Delfel, Guy. *L'Esthétique de Stéphane Mallarmé*. Paris: Flammarion, 1951.

Desaise, Roger. "Mallarmé et le sens de l'universel," *Les Cahiers du nord, Stèle pour Mallarmé* 2–3, numéro spécial (1948): 162–78.

Douglas, Kenneth. "A Note on Mallarmé and the Theater," *Yale French Studies* 3 (1949): 108–10.

Duval, Maurice. *La Poésie et le principe de transcendance: essai sur la création poétique*. Paris: Librairie Félix Alcan, 1935.

Escarpit, Robert, ed. *Le Littéraire et le social: éléments pour une sociologie de la littérature*. Paris: Flammarion, 1970.

Evans, Calvin. "Mallarméan Antecedents of the Avant-Garde Theater," *Modern Drama* 5, no. 4 (February 1963): 12–19.

Fare, Michel. "Instigations ou charmes de Mallarmé," *Les Cahiers du nord, Stèle pour Mallarmé* 2–3, numéro spécial (1948): 143–44.

Fernandet, René. "Mallarmé animateur de la rêverie," *Méridien* 5 (janvier-février 1943): 5–11; 6 (mars-avril 1943): 3–9.

Fischer, Ernst. *The Necessity of Art: A Marxist Approach*. Translated by Anna Bostock. Middlesex, England: Penguin Books, Ltd., 1963.

Fongaro, Antoine. "Mallarmé et Victor Hugo," *Revue des sciences humaines* 120 (octobre-décembre 1965): 515–27.

Fontainas, André. "Le Culte de Verlaine et de Mallarmé," *Le Flambeau* 1 (1923): 307–25.

―――. "La Lecture pour Stéphane Mallarmé," *Le Point* 29–30, numéro consacré à Mallarmé (février-avril 1944): 70–73.

Fowlie, Wallace. *Mallarmé*. Chicago: The University of Chicago Press, 1962.

―――. "Mallarmé and the Painters of his Age," *The Southern*

Review 2, n.s. 3 (July 1966): 542–58.

Fraenkel, Ernest. *Les Dessins transconscients de Stéphane Mallarmé: à propos de la typographie de "Un Coup de dés."* Paris: Librairie Nizet, 1960.

———. "La Psychanalyse au service de la science de la littérature," *Cahiers de l'association internationale des études françaises Les Belles Lettres* (juin 1955), pp. 23–49.

Franklin, Ursula. "The Prose Poems of Stéphane Mallarmé: An Exegesis," *Dissertation Abstracts International* 32 (1971): 6973A (Michigan State). Microfilm 72–16,424.

Fretet, Jean Dr. *L'Aliénation poétique: Rimbaud-Mallarmé-Proust.* Paris: J. -B. Janin, 1946.

Gaède, Edouard. "Le Problème du langage chez Mallarmé," *Revue d'histoire littéraire de la France* 68, no. 1 (janvier-février 1968): 45–65.

Gerbod, Paul. *La Vie quotidienne dans les lycées et collèges au XIXᵉ siècle.* Paris: Hachette, 1968.

Ghyka, Matila. "Vision analogue et composition symphonique chez Mallarmé et Marcel Proust," *France libre* 3 (16 mars 1942): 386–90.

Gill, Austin. "Mallarmé fonctionnaire," *Revue d'histoire littéraire de la France* 68, no. 1 (janvier-février 1968): 2–25; 68, no. 2 (mars-avril 1968): 253–84.

Girard, Marcel. "Naturalisme et symbolisme," *Cahiers de l'association internationale des études francaises Les Belles Lettres* 6 (juillet 1954): 97–106.

Glissant, Edouard. "L'Attente du poème," *Les Lettres nouvelles* 5, no. 52 (septembre 1957): 342–44.

Goffin, Robert. "L'Hermétisme freudien de Mallarmé," *Empreintes* 5 (novembre-décembre 1948): 31–41.

———. *Mallarmé vivant.* Paris: Librairie Nizet, 1956.

Herbert, Eugenia W. *The Artist and Social Reform: France and Belgium 1885–1898.* New Haven, Conn.: Yale University Press, 1961.

Huysmans, J. -K. *A Rebours.* Paris: Editions Fasquelle, 1965.

Kahnweiler, Daniel-Henry. "Mallarmé et la peinture," *Les Lettres* 3, numéro spécial (1948): 63–68.

Lavaud, Guy. "La Vraie Leçon de Mallarmé," *Les Cahiers du nord, Stèle pour Mallarmé* 2–3, numéro spécial (1948): 128–38.

Lebois, André. "Mallarmé héros de roman," *Horizons* 9 (9 mai 1948).

——. "Stéphane Mallarmé et la politique," *Mercure de France* 121 (1 septembre 1948): 69–78.

Levinson, André. "Stéphane Mallarmé métaphysicien du ballet," *Revue musicale* 5, nos. 1, 2 (1 novembre 1923): 21–33.

Lhombreaud, Roger-A. "Deux Lettres de Mallarmé à Edmond Gosse," *Revue de littérature comparée* 25 (1951): 355–62.

Loevgren, Sven. *The Genesis of Modernism: Seurat, Gauguin, Van Gogh, and French Symbolism in the 1880's.* Bloomington, Ind.: Indiana University Press, 1971.

Lukács, Georg. *The Historical Novel.* Translated by Hannah and Stanley Mitchell. New York: Humanities Press, 1965.

Mallarmé, Stéphane. *L'Amitié de Stéphane Mallarmé et de Georges Rodenbach.* Lettres et textes inédits 1887–1898 publiés avec une introduction et des notes par François Ruchon. Genève: Pierre Cailler Editeur, 1949.

——. *Correspondance 1862–1871.* Recueillie, classée et annotée par Henri Mondor. Paris: NRF Gallimard, 1959.

——. *Correspondance II 1871–1885.* Recueillie, classée et annotée par Henri Mondor et Lloyd James Austin. Paris: NRF Gallimard, 1965.

——. *Correspondance III 1886–1889.* Recueillie, classée et annotée par Henri Mondor et Lloyd James Austin. Paris: NRF Gallimard, 1969.

——. *Correspondance IV 1890–1891.* Recueillie, classée et annotée par Henri Mondor et Lloyd James Austin. 2 vols. Paris: NRF Gallimard, 1973.

——. *La Dernière Mode.* With an introduction by S. A. Rhodes. New York: Publication of the Institute of French Studies, Inc., 1933.

——.*Divagations* (extraits). Paris: Librairie Saint-Germain-des-Prés, 1969.

——. *Dix-neuf Lettres de Stéphane Mallarmé à Emile Zola.* avec une introduction de Léon Deffoux et un commentaire de Jean Royère. Paris: Jacques Bernard La Centaine, 1929.

——. "Fragments de Mallarmé: interviews, papillon, lettre," *Le Point* 29–30, numéro consacré à Mallarmé (février-avril 1944): 74–75.

——.*Les "gossips" de Mallarmé "Atheneum" 1875–1876.* Textes

inédits présentés et annotés par Henri Mondor et Lloyd James Austin. Paris: NRF Gallimard, 1962.

————. "The Impressionists and Edouard Manet," *The Art Monthly Review* 1, no. 9 (September 30, 1876): 117–22.

————. *Inédits études documents. Empreintes* 5 (novembre-décembre 1948).

————. *Inédits hors-texte études. Les Lettres* 3, numéro spécial (1948).

————. *Mallarmé.* Edited with an introduction and prose translations by Anthony Hartley. Middlesex, England: Penguin Books Ltd., 1965.

————. *Les Noces d'Hérodiade: mystère.* Publié avec une introduction par Gardner Davies. Paris: NRF Gallimard, 1959.

————. *Oeuvres complètes.* "Bibliothèque de la Pléiade." Paris: Editions Gallimard, 1945.

————. *Poésies.* Paris: NRF Gallimard, 1952.

————. *Pour un tombeau d'Anatole.* Introduction de Jean-Pierre Richard. Paris: Editions du Seuil, 1961.

————. *Propos sur la poésie.* Recueillis et présentés par Henri Mondor. Monaco: Editions du Rocher, 1953.

————. *Recueil de "nursery rhymes."* Texte établi et présenté par Carl Paul Barbier. Paris: NRF Gallimard, 1964.

"Mallarmé et la peinture de son temps," *Le Point* 29–30, numéro consacré à Mallarmé (février-avril 1944): 90–98.

Marcou, André. "Mallarmé futur," *Les Cahiers du nord, Stèle pour Mallarmé* 2–3, numéro spécial (1948): 139–42.

Les Mardis: Stéphane Mallarmé and the Artists of His Circle. Lawrence, Kan.: The University of Kansas Museum of Art, Miscellaneous Publications, no. 61, 1966.

Margueritte, Paul. "Le Printemps tourmenté: souvenirs littéraires 1881–1896," *Revue des deux mondes* 51 (15 mai 1919): 241–80.

Mauclair, Camille. *Mallarmé chez lui.* 6th ed. Paris: Editions Bernard Grasset, 1935.

————. *La Religion de la musique.* 10th ed. Paris: Librairie Fischbacher, 1919.

————. *Servitude et grandeur littéraires.* Paris: P. Ollendorff, 1922.

————. *Le Soleil des morts (roman contemporain).* 3d ed. Paris: Paul Ollendorff, Editeur, 1898.

Mauron, Charles. *Introduction to the Psychoanalysis of Mallarmé*. Translated by Archibald Henderson Jr. and Will L. McLendon. Berkeley, Calif.: University of California Press, 1963.

———. *Mallarmé l'obscur*. Paris: Librairie José Corti, 1968.

McLuhan, Marshall. "Joyce, Mallarmé, and the Press," *Sewanee Review* 62, no. 1 (January-March 1954): 38–55.

Mendès, Catulle. *Le Mouvement poétique français de 1867 à 1900: rapport à M. le Ministre de l'Instruction publique*. Paris: Imprimerie Nationale, 1902.

Michaud, Guy. *Mallarmé*. 3d ed. Paris: Hatier Connaissance des lettres, 1953.

———. *Message poétique du symbolisme*. Paris: Librairie Nizet, 1947.

Miquel, Jean. "Le Phénomène futur ou le progrès d'une conscience poétique," *Les Lettres* 3, numéro spécial (1948): 69–83.

Miserez, Nestor. "Aveux et scrupules de Mallarmé," *Les Cahiers du nord*, *Stèle pour Mallarmé* 2–3, numéro spécial (1948): 217–44.

Mockel, Albert. "Stéphane Mallarmé un héros," (1899), pp. 177–207, *Esthétique du symbolisme*. Bruxelles: Palais des Académies, 1962.

Monda, Maurice et Montel, François. *Bibliographie des poètes maudits I Stéphane Mallarmé*. Paris: Librairie Henri Leclerc et Librairie de la Bibliothèque Nationale et de la Bibliothèque de l'Arsenal, 1927.

Mondor, Henri. *Autres Précisions sur Mallarmé et inédits*. Paris: NRF Gallimard, 1961.

———. *Histoire d'un faune*. Paris: NRF Gallimard, 1948.

———. "Mallarmé, Debussy et 'L'Après-midi d'un faune,'" *Les Cahiers du nord*, *Stèle pour Mallarmé* 2–3, numéro spécial (1948): 117–22.

———. *Mallarmé lycéen*. 4th ed. Paris: NRF Gallimard, 1954.

———. *Mallarmé plus intime*. 14th ed. Paris: NRF Gallimard, 1944.

———. *Vie de Mallarmé*. Edition complète en un volume. 34th ed. Paris: NRF Gallimard, 1941.

Muhlfeld, Lucien. *Le Monde où l'on imprime*. Paris: Perrin et Cie Librairie Académique Didier, 1897.

Munro, Thomas. " 'L'Après-midi d'un faune' et les relations entre les arts," *Revue d'esthétique* 3 (juillet-septembre 1952): 225–43.

Nelli, René. " 'Igitur' ou l'argument ontologique retourné," *Les Lettres* 3, numéro spécial (1948): 147–54.

Nordau, Max. *Vus du dehors: essai de critique scientifique et philosophique sur quelques auteurs français contemporains.* Traduit d'allemand par Auguste Dietrich. Paris: Félix Alcan, Editeur, 1903.

Noulet, Emilie. *Etudes littéraires.* Mexico: Talleres grafico, 1944.

———. *L'Oeuvre poétique de Stéphane Mallarmé.* Paris: Librairie E. Droz, 1940.

———. *Suites: Mallarmé Rimbaud Valéry.* Paris: A. G. Nizet, 1964.

———. *Le Ton poétique; Mallarmé, Verlaine, Corbière, Rimbaud, Valéry, Saint-John Perse.* Paris: J. Corti, 1971.

———. *Vingt Poèmes de Stéphane Mallarmé.* Genève: Librairie Droz, 1967.

Park, Ynhui. *L'Idée chez Mallarmé.* Paris: Centre de Documentation Universitaire, 1966.

Patri, Aimé. "Mallarmé et la musique du silence," *Revue musicale* 26, numéro spécial 210 (février 1952): 101–11.

Paxton, Norman. *The Development of Mallarmé's Prose Style* with the original texts of twenty articles. Genève: Librairie Droz, 1968.

Poulet, Georges. "Mallarmé," pp. 298–355, *Etudes sur le temps humain II: la distance intérieure.* Paris: Plon. 1952.

Rabbin, Marcelle, " 'Le Pitre châtié' ou la société comme cirque," *French Review* 45, no. 5 (April 1972): 980–87.

Raybaud, A. "Mallarmé, inventeur de la théâtralité?" *Synthèses* 22, nos. 258/259 (décembre 1967-janvier 1968): 99–106.

Raymond, Marcel. *De Baudelaire au surréalisme.* Edition nouvelle revue et remaniée. Paris: Librairie José Corti, 1966.

Régnier, Henri de. *Figures et caractères.* 4th ed. Paris: Mercure de France, 1911.

———. "Hamlet et Mallarmé," *Mercure de France* 17 (1896): 289–92.

———. *Nos Rencontres.* Paris: Mercure de France, 1931.

———. *Proses datées.* 8th ed. Paris: Mercure de France, 1925.

Renéville, Roland de. *L'Univers de la parole.* Paris: NRF Gallimard, 1944.

Retté, Adolphe. *Le Symbolisme: anecdotes et souvenirs.* Paris: Léon Vanier, Editeur, 1903.

Richard, Jean-Pierre. *L'Univers imaginaire de Mallarmé.* Paris: Editions du Seuil, 1961.

Rietmann, Ch. E. *Vision et mouvement chez Stéphane Mallarmé.* Paris: Les Presses modernes, 1932.

Roulet, Claude. *Elucidation du poème de Stéphane Mallarmé "Un Coup de dés jamais n'abolira le hasard."* Neuchâtel: Aux Idées et Calendes, 1943.

Rouveyre, André. "Le Pèlérinage des amis de Mallarmé," *Mercure de France* 212 (15 juin 1929): 654–56.

Royère, Jean. "De l'hermétisme en poésie," *Les Cahiers du nord, Stèle pour Mallarmé* 2–3, numéro spécial (1948): 179–82.

————. *Frontons.* 1st series. Paris: Marcel Sheur, éditeur. Collection "Masques et idées," 1932.

————. *Mallarmé.* Paris: Albert Messein, Editeur Collection de la Phalange, 1931.

————. *La Poésie de Mallarmé.* Paris: Emile-Paul Frères, éditeurs, 1919.

St. Aubyn, Frederic Chase. *Stéphane Mallarmé.* New York: Twayne Publishers, Inc., 1969.

Sartre, Jean-Paul, *Situations, II Qu'est-ce que la littérature?* Paris: NRF Gallimard, 1948.

Scherer, Jacques. *L'Expression littéraire dans l'oeuvre de Mallarmé.* Paris: Librairie A. G. Nizet, 1947.

————.*Le "Livre" de Mallarmé: premières recherches sur des documents inédits.* 6th ed. Paris: NRF Gallimard, 1957.

Schmidt, Albert-Marie. "Mallarmé fondateur de religion," *Les Lettres* 3, numéro spécial (1948), 106–13.

Sollers, Philippe. "Littérature et totalité," *Tel Quel* 24–27 (1966): 81–95. Also in *Logiques.* Paris: Editions du Seuil, 1968.

Soula, Camille. "Définitions," *Le Point* 29–30, numéro consacré à Mallarmé (février-avril 1944): 81–88.

Souriau, M. *Le Mystère de Mallarmé*: conférence prononcée à l'Université Populaire de Lille le 30 janvier 1955. Lille: Revue des sciences humaines, 1955.

Thibaudet, Albert. *La Poésie de Stéphane Mallarmé: étude littéraire.* new ed. Paris: NRF Gallimard, 1926.

————. "Réflexions sur la littérature: la rareté et le dehors," *La Nouvelle Revue française* (1 août 1927), pp. 235–43.

Valéry, Paul. *Ecrits divers sur Stéphane Mallarmé.* Paris: NRF

Gallimard, 1950.

Verdin, Simonne. "L'Action restreinte," *Synthèses* 22, no. 258/259 (décembre 1967-janvier 1968): 113–118.

Vivier, Robert. "La Victoire de Mallarmé," *Empreintes* 5 (novembre-décembre 1948): 90–93.

Wagner, Richard. *Wagner on Music and Drama. A compendium of Richard Wagner's prose works.* Translated by H. Ashton Ellis. New York: E. P. Dutton and Co., Inc., 1964.

Welch, Liliane, "Mallarmé and the Experience of Art," *The Journal of Aesthetics and Art Criticism* 30, no. 3 (Spring 1972): 369–75.

Welleck, René and Warren, Austin. *Theory of Literature.* 3d ed. New York: Harcourt, Brace, and World, Inc., 1956.

Williams, Thomas. *Mallarmé and the Language of Mysticism.* Athens, Ga.: The University of Georgia Press, 1970.

Woolley, Grange. *Richard Wagner et le symbolisme français: les rapports principaux entre le wagnérisme et l'évolution de l'idée symboliste.* Paris: Les Presses Universitaires de France, 1931.

————.*Stéphane Mallarmé 1842–1898: A Commemorative Presentation including translations from his prose and verse with commentaries.* Madison, N.J.: Drew University, 1942.

Wyzewa, Théodor de. *Nos Maîtres. Etudes et portraits littéraires.* Paris: Librairie Académique Didier Perrin et Cie, Librairie Editeurs, 1895.

Zola, Emile. *Lourdes.* Paris: Fasquelle Editeurs, 1954.

Zuckerkandl, Frédéric, "L"Absent' chez Mallarmé," *Synthèses* 285 (mars 1970): 20–25.

Zweig, Paul. *The Heresy of Self Love.* New York: Basic Books, Inc., 1968.

Index